WITHDR

D1070612

David Martin is Professor of Sociology
at the London School of Economics and
Political Science. He is author of *Dilemma*
of Contemporary Religion (1978), *A General*
Theory of Secularization (1978) and *The*
Breaking of the Image (1980).
Peter Mullen is Vicar of Tockwith and
Bilton with Bickerton in Yorkshire. He
is a regular contributor to national
newspapers, radio and television,
and author of *Working with Morality* (1983)
and *Rural Rites: Tales of a Country Parson*
(1984).

Contributors

Henry Asige Ajega
Nell Challingsworth
Brian Davies OP
Douglas Davies
Rex Davis
John Drury
James D. G. Dunn
Paul S. Fiddes
John Gunstone
Walter Hollenweger
Martin Israel
David Martin
Peter Mullen
Ronald Noakes
John Richards
Andrew Walker
Julian Ward
Cyril Williams

STRANGE GIFTS?

STRANGE GIFTS?

A Guide to Charismatic Renewal

Edited by
DAVID MARTIN
and
PETER MULLEN

BASIL BLACKWELL

© Basil Blackwell Publisher 1984

First published 1984

Basil Blackwell Publisher Ltd
108 Cowley Road, Oxford OX4 1JF, UK

Basil Blackwell Inc.
432 Park Avenue South, Suite 1505,
New York, NY 10016, USA

British Library Cataloguing in Publication Data

Strange gifts?
  1. Pentecostalism
  I. Martin, David, *1929*- II. Mullen, Peter
  270.8′ 28   BR1644
  ISBN 0-631-13357-7
  ISBN 0-631-13592-8 Pbk

Library of Congress Cataloging in Publication Data

Strange gifts?
  Includes index.
    1. Pentecostalism—Addresses, essays, lectures.
  I. Martin, David A. II. Mullen, Peter.
  BR1644.S77 1984   270.8′ 28   84-8861
  ISBN 0-631-13357-7
  ISBN 0-631-13592-8 (pbk.)

Typeset by System 4 Associates, Gerrards Cross, Buckinghamshire
Printed in Great Britain by
Redwood Burn Ltd, Trowbridge

Contents

The Contributors

HENRY ASIGE AJEGA is the general secretary of the African Israel Church in Kenya.

NELL CHALLINGSWORTH was educated near Melbourne, and is a professional teacher of dancing, who has had experience of many forms and varieties of the art, social, therapeutic and liturgical. She has lectured on the subject all over the world. Her book, *Dancing Down the Years* (1979) was a best seller. She has also published *Liturgical Dance Movement* (1981).

BRIAN DAVIES OP is Vice-Regent of Studies and lecturer in philosophy at Blackfriars (the study house for the English Dominicans). He is also tutor in theology at St Benet's Hall, Oxford and part-time lecturer in the theology department at Bristol University. He is the author of *An Introduction to the Philosophy of Religion* (1982).

DOUGLAS DAVIES has studied both theology and anthropology and he is now teaching in the theology department of Nottingham University and serving as a non-stipendiary priest in a suburban parish. His research interests include Mormonism and Sikhism as well as pastoral theology. His book *Salvation and Meaning in Religious Studies* will be published shortly.

REX DAVIS is Subdean of Lincoln and Warden of Edward King House. He has worked with the Australian Council of Churches and the World Council of Churches, and he has done pastoral work in England, Australia and the USA. His book *Locusts and Wild Honey* (1978) is a study of the Charismatic Renewal and the eucumenical movement.

JOHN DRURY is Dean of King's College, Cambridge and co-editor of *Theology*.

JAMES D. G. DUNN is Professor of Divinity at the University of Durham He has written much on Pentecostalism and the Charismatic Renewal and his books include *Baptism in the Holy Spirit* (1970), *Jesus and the Spirit* (1975), *Unity and Diversity in the NT* (1977) and *Christology in the Making* (1980). He is now working on a commentary on Romans for the Word Biblical Commentary.

PAUL FIDDES is a Baptist Minister and he has been Tutor in Christian Doctrine at Regent's Park College, Oxford since 1975.

JOHN GUNSTONE is an Anglican parish priest and honorary canon of Manchester Cathedral. Since 1975 he has been full-time secretary of the Greater Manchester County Ecumenical Council. He is the author of a number of books on liturgy and charismatic renewal, including *Pentecostal Anglicans* (1982), which was written after serving on the General Synod working party which produced *The Charismatic Movement and the Church of England* (1980).

WALTER HOLLENWEGER is a minister of the Reformed Church of Switzerland and was until 1971 Secretary for Evangelism at the World Council of Churches in Geneva, with special emphasis on Eastern Europe and Latin America. He has particular interest in communicating the Christian message to people of many different cultures. His books include *The Pentecostals* (1972, 1976) and *Conflict in Corinth: Memoirs of an Old Man* (1982).

MARTIN ISRAEL is an honorary senior lecturer in pathology at the Royal College of Surgeons. He is also priest-in-charge of Holy Trinity Church, Prince Consort Road, S.W.7. He devotes much of his time to the ministry of counselling and healing, and has written a number of books on these subjects.

DAVID MARTIN is Professor of Sociology at the London School of Economics and since 1975 has been President of the International Conference of the Sociology of Religion. His books include *The Dilemmas of Contemporary Religion* (1978), *The Breaking of the Image* (1980) and he co-edited *No Alternative: The Prayer Book Controversy* (1981).

PETER MULLEN is vicar of Tockwith, Bilton and Bickerton near York. He has written on theology and religion for *The Times*, the *Guardian* and *The Spectator* and he has published articles and reviews in *Theology*,

Modern Churchman and *Faith and Freedom*. He has also written and presented programmes for TV. BBC Radio 4 broadcast his dramatic chorus *St Mark* in 1979. He was co-editor of *No Alternative: The Prayer Book Controversy* (1981). His most recent books are *Working with Morality* (1983) and *Rural Rites: Tales of a Country Parson* (1984).

RONALD NOAKES has been a medical missionary to seamen and chaplain to the RAF. He is now vicar of Whixley, north Yorkshire.

JOHN RICHARDS is an Anglican clergyman and Director of Renewal Servicing, at Addlestone, Weybridge, Surrey. From 1977-80 he was an associate director of the Fountain Trust. He has considerable experience of the Church's work in the spheres of healing and deliverance, and his books include *But Deliver us from Evil: an Introduction to the Demonic Dimension in Pastoral Care* (1974) and *Exorcism: Deliverance and Healing* (1976).

ANDREW WALKER is Director of the London Centre for Ecumenical Studies and a lecturer at the West London Institute of Higher Education. He was consultant on Pentecostalism to the World Council of Churches and he contributes regularly to *The Sociological Review*, the *Guardian* and to radio and television.

JULIAN WARD has turned his back on his early career as an aeronautical engineer and five years of research in aerodynamics to study at the Missionary Training College, Glasgow and the London Bible College. He has served as the pastor of churches in London and Guildford. In 1974 he became lecturer in theology and philosophy at Elim Bible College, Capel, Surrey, where is now the Director of Studies.

CYRIL WILLIAMS is a Congregational Minister who held pastorates in Wales and London before taking up university work at Cardiff, Ottawa and Aberystwyth. He is now Professor of Religious Studies at St. David's University College, Lampeter. He has written extensively in Welsh and English and his most recent book is *Tongues of the Spirit* (1981).

Two or three of our company were much affected and believed she spoke by the Spirit of God. But this was in no wise clear to me. The motion might be either hysterical or artificial.

(from the journal of John Wesley for 28th January 1739 —
on encountering a Camisard prophetess)

Introduction

DAVID MARTIN and PETER MULLEN

In order to understand the movement variously described as 'Charismatic Revival' or 'Charismatic Renewal' it is necessary to observe it from many angles. Therefore *Strange Gifts?* contains essays which illuminate as many aspects of the movement as possible — theological, historical, philosophical, sociological and aesthetic. The practice of charismatic religion is an emotionally charged affair and so any discussion of it is bound to raise emotive issues. There are so many books written from, as it were, within the camp that we saw no need to add another. What is needed is a collection of essays from both sympathisers and critics and this is what we have provided.

Charismatics are sometimes called 'Fundamentalists' and, while that is a pejorative term in some circles, no member of the movement would object to the word as a description of the way in which charismatics try to root their beliefs and practices in the earliest discipline of the church. James Dunn's article is a discussion of the types of Christian communities which existed in New Testament times. He describes how this first period was a time of 'evolving organisation' and how, according to the Pauline ideal, it was a community based on 'the shared experience of the Spirit'. But Professor Dunn concludes, 'There is no single model of Christian community which emerges from the New Testament as *the* New Testament Church.' Paul Fiddes combines historical and theological enquiry when he asks 'whether the movement has made any contribution to the Christian doctrine of the Holy Spirit'. He also observes that the movement has often seemed to draw attention to the humble and accepting love which is characteristic of God himself, but he remarks, 'It would be a tragic irony if the same movement should now find in the experience of the Spirit a witness to dominating power rather than loving persuasion.'

W. J. Hollenweger examines the influence of the Spirit in all areas of life and by doing so he breaks out of the 'narrowness of western pneumatologies since St Augustine and the Reformation'. He makes the important point that 'every single person, and not merely every Christian, has the Spirit of God.' David Martin wants to know how we tell the difference between 'the things held to be by the action of the Holy Ghost' and those other things which are based on 'the exercise or exhibition of social power'. How much is 'the charismatic buzz of the kiss of peace' a way of going beyond 'the limits of manners and ritual restraint' and how much is it 'an organised invasion of other selves'?

Even those without much experience of the Charismatic movement have heard of the practice of 'speaking in tongues'. C. G. Williams examines this phenomenon and remarks, 'If St Paul . . . valued it as a divine gift and a method of prayer, those who would dismiss it as "gibberish" need to think twice.' What sort of people are attracted to the Charismatic Movement? John Gunstone, a sympathiser, gives us 'an impressionistic view of Charismatic Renewal' in which he describes and assesses the influence of healing, prayer groups and styles of worship on the traditional Church of England. He says that the phrase 'Charismatic Movement' is 'just another name for the Church of Jesus Christ'. Peter Mullen believes that many of the doctrines specifically associated with the movement are incoherent and self-contradictory; so the personal and pastoral casualties that it produces should be seen not as occasional and unvoidable 'abuses' or 'excesses' but as evils which are caused by the movement's deeply rooted inconsistencies.

Rex Davis evaluates the contribution made by the movement to the whole life of the church, and particularly to its worship. He concludes, 'I am pretty convinced that a lot of the better things happening in the worship of local congregations owe more than people admit to the Charismatic Renewal.' Nell Challingsworth, a professional teacher of dance, describes the influence of liturgical movement and dancing. She says, 'even one or two dances in the smallest chapel can express the overwhelming joy of liturgical dance movement.'

Martin Israel's essay on the Holy Spirit admits that 'many congrega-tions have ben split asunder by the force of an ill-digested Charismatic Renewal.' But he also says that 'when the movement shows a constructive understanding of psychic sensitivity, a proper respect for the critical function of the intellect and a deep concern for raging social issues, it will have fulfilled its central concept of renewal.' Douglas Davies examines the relation between the spirit of revival and the spirit of the age. He says, 'If my suggestion about the post-industrial clientele of charismatic religion is correct, then the churches must be all the more concerned because it is likely that the majority of congregation members, as currently composed, belong to this broad group.'

John Richards expands the movement's teaching about divine healing. He says the healing movement within the Charismatic Revival must strive to be both 'sacramental and charismatic'. Ronald Noakes places the movement in its historical context and sees it as the latest efflorescence of revivalism and as following the trend set by Dr Billy Graham and also by the Oxford Group of Moral Rearmers of the 1930s. Andrew Walker's essay highlights the perspective of the Orthodox church on Charismatic Renewal: 'For Orthodox Christians living in the west, the charismatics are in many ways natural allies standing as they do for the fundamentals of the gospel and against modernism in theology.'

W. J. Hollenweger's second contribution concerns the place of the Charismatic Revival in the Third World. He says, 'We should not imitate the songs, the stories, the treatment of the sick, the exorcism and the glossolalia of Third World charismatics. I only want to free these phenomena from their aura of exoticism or absurdity and point out the opportunities for sound liturgical and missionary communication.' Julian Ward writes from his position of Director of Studies at the Elim Bible College. Hence it would be accurate to describe him as a traditional charismatic — a member of the Pentecostal Church. He sees Pentecostalists and other charismatics as prophets to 'a lukewarm Christendom, and to a secular society'. Andrew Walker's other essay throws light on the rather sensational charismatic sect known as the Restoration House Churches. Henry Asige Ajega's contribution is a striking account of typical events in the African Israel Church Nineveh which 'was formed on the principles of the Charismatic Movement'. Brian Davies offers a critique of the practice of speaking in tongues from a development of Wittgenstein's famous 'private language' argument. John Drury supplies the Epilogue in which he says that religion must be something 'that anyone can do — though it will take all his committed powers, summoned by fear and reverence for goodness, to do it.

Anything less will not be good news, just sensational news with the promise of an appallingly nasty after-taste.'

Models of Christian Community in the New Testament

JAMES D. G. DUNN

The New Testament preserves several different models of Christian community. Some were what actually happened; others an ideal held before first century believers. In some cases we have enough information to provide a reasonably clear picture (particularly with Paul). In other cases we must be content with hints and allusions.

Discipleship: Following Jesus

Jesus called men (and women) to follow him. Among the various characteristics of the life of discipleship we may mention particularly the following.

First, it was *eschatological*. Jesus called for discipleship in view of the coming kingdom (Mark 1:15; etc.). In one sense discipleship was a celebration of the kingdom, of the priority and power of God already manifested in and through Jesus' ministry — particularly insofar as that discipleship was characterised by Jesus' table-fellowship (Mark 2:15f.; Luke 15:1f.), since there is a strong implication that Jesus saw his table-fellowship as an anticipation of the messianic banquet (Mark 2:17, 19; Luke 6:21; 2:30; Mark 14:25; cf. Isa. 25:6; 65:13). In another sense discipleship was a preparation for the kingdom yet to come in its fullness — not least in so far as those who followed Jesus shared in his summons to Israel to make ready for the coming kingdom (see particularly Mark 6:7-12/Luke 9:1-6).

Secondly, it was *discipleship* — a matter of individuals following Jesus either literally (Mark 1:17; 2:14; 10:21; Luke 9:57-62) or while they remained where they were (Mark 5:19; Luke 19:8f.). We can speak quite properly of '*circles* of discipleship' round Jesus. Closest to Jesus were 'the beloved disciple' of the fourth gospel (if he is in fact a historical individual rather than a symbol of discipleship), and the inner three (Peter, James and John); then the twelve (Mark 3:14); then those who went about with him, (including the women mentioned in Luke 8:2f.); then those who were evidently close to Jesus but did not leave home, such as Martha and Mary; then 'whoever does the will of God' (Mark 3:34f.) and 'the poor' (Luke 6:20; Matt. 25:31-46). It should not be inferred that the various circles were distinct from each other. On the contrary, they seem to have merged into each other or overlapped, (Mary was 'closer' to Jesus than some of the twelve).

Thirdly, it was *open*. It is not possible to draw a clear line round one of these circles of discipleship and mark an inside and an outside. In contrast to the Baptist, Jesus evidently did not practise baptism, neither as a rite of preparation for the kingdom nor as a rite of entry into discipleship (John 4:2). In contrast to the Pharisees he laid no requirements of ritual purity on those who ate with him (Mark 7:1-23). In contrast to the covenanters of Qumran he welcomed to his table those who were least acceptable on religious grounds (Luke 14:12-24).[1] There was no ritual barrier for the would-be disciple to surmount; no ritual exclusiveness to mark off the disciple from others. Jesus' discipleship was open to whoever was open to him — be they Pharisee or prostitute or tax collector (Matt. 11:19; Mark 12:28-34; Luke 7:36).

Fourthly, it focused on *Jesus*. There is no suggestion of communities existing apart from Jesus; everything depended on Jesus himself. Indeed it is misleading to speak of 'community' at all when describing discipleship of Jesus. Apart from what is implied in Luke 8:3 and John 12:6 there seems to have been no real internal structure of responsibility, far less any hierarchy of authority. Jesus alone was prophet and teacher (see especially Matt. 23:8); he was the only authority figure. Some enjoyed a more intimate relationship with him than others (as we have already seen); but any attempt to claim special authority or status was severely rebuked (Mark 10:35-44). The fact that twelve were chosen presumably implies that their discipleship represented eschatological Israel, the coming kingdom (cf. Matt. 19:28), but there is no indication that they had some special role *within* the circles of disciples, as e.g. 'priests' to the others' 'laity'.

This model of discipleship depends too much on the exceptional circumstances of Jesus' earthly ministry to provide a pattern for Christian community today. But it should not be put aside as irrelevant. If 'discipleship of Jesus' still has any meaning for the 1980s (and it certainly has), then the character of that discipleship, particularly of celebration and mission, of openness and service, should be a constant challenge to any ecclesiastical structure which does not positively promote such discipleship. The church exists to enable the same quality of discipleship as that to which Jesus called his first followers.

The Mother Church: Loyally Conservative

The only first century church which we can view over a lengthy period is the church in Jerusalem. Although Luke's account in Acts (our principal source) is from a particular perspective, we can gain a clear enough view of the Jerusalem church at several points between 30 and 70 AD. What we see is a community in transition, especially as regards its organisation. The principal factors in its development were threefold: the initial outpouring of the Spirit; reaction to the Hellenists and the Gentile mission; and the pressure of Jewish (religious) nationalism which steadily increased throughout this period.

Initially its chief feature was *enthusiasm*. The quotation from Joel 2:28f. characterises it as a community of prophets (Acts 2:17f.). The prophetic Spirit was not confined to a few, and a principal mark of divine acceptance, as the new movement subsequently spread, was the sharing of the same experience (Acts 8:15-17; 10:44-7; 19:6). Such experiences of immediate inspiration evidently were highly prized (Acts 4:8, 31; 6:3; 11:24). Likewise important shifts in policy were prompted and justified by visions (Acts 9:10; 10:3-6, 10-16; 22:17f.). In the beginning at least there was also a spontaneity about their coming together in each others' homes, whether for a meal or for teaching (Acts 2:42-6; 5:42) — a continuation presumably, in part at least, of the earlier life-style of discipleship, but now at the prompting of the Spirit.

The period was marked by an *evolving organisation*. Initially the twelve seem to have provided the focus, symbolising the self-consciousness of the new movement as eschatological Judaism (Acts 1:6, 20-6; 6:2; Matt. 19:28; 1 Cor. 15:5), with the inner circle of three apparently most prominent (Acts 2-5; 12:2). The seven who were elected in the wake of Hellenist unrest over the administration of the common fund were probably the most prominent or most active of the Hellenists, as the subsequent ministries of Stephen and Philip seem to indicate (Acts 6-8). They were not particularly 'subordinate' to the twelve, despite Acts 6:3, and to designate them 'deacons' is misleadingly anachronistic and presupposes a more developed organisation than was most probably the case. Subsequently, the two main developments were the emergence of James, brother of Jesus, as the leader first of the 'pillar apostles', and then on his own (Gal. 2:9, 12; Acts 12:17; 15:13-21; 21:17); and the appearance of a system of eldership round James (Acts 11:20; 21:18). Converted priests and Pharisees do not seem to have been accorded any particular status within the church (Acts 6:7; 15:5), nor do we read of prophets (like Agabus) or teachers exercising a role of leadership, as they seem to have done at Antioch (Acts 13:1-3).

Perhaps most striking of all, particularly as the Gentile mission developed, was the degree to which the Jerusalem church identified with and remained loyal to the Judaism in the midst of which it dwelt. The leadership system of James and the elders was probably patterned on the Jewish synagogue (ruler of the synagogue and elders of the local community). Throughout the period the temple remained central in their worship, despite Stephen's attack on it (e.g. Acts 2:46; 5:42; 21:26; 22:17; cf. Matt. 5:23f.). And strong devotion to the law continued to characterise their life despite Paul (Acts 11:2f.; 21:20; Gal. 2:12; cf. Matt. 23:2, 23; 24:20). Very few Hellenists or practitioners of a law-free life-style would remain long in Jerusalem after Stephen's martyrdom. Their practice of baptism and belief in Jesus as Messiah and risen from the dead would mark them off as a sect *within* Judaism (like the Pharisees or Essenes) but not distinguish them *from* Judaism.

In all this the mother church is probably less of a model and more an example of how a church will tend to conform to its dominant environment. The *ad hoc* evolution of organisation in the high period of enthusiasm gave way to a more stable and regular system patterned on the closest parallel structure already well established. Under growing pressure from the powerful political currents of religious nationalism, the church was not able to hold the full range of the expanding Christian spectrum within itself. It became only one part, one end of the spectrum of Christian faith and life-style, a prime example of how difficult a church emerging from and living within a strong older religious tradition will find it to be anything other than conservative in its faith and life-style.

The Pauline Ideal: Charismatic Community

Paul's concept of community is determined by his understanding of the church as 'the body of Christ' (see particularly 1 Cor. 12; Rom. 12 and Eph. 4). These passages are not descriptions of the historical reality of the Pauline churches, or not entirely so, but we can certainly say that they express the ideal which Paul held out before his churches and the principles he encouraged his converts to apply in their coming together and common life. To appreciate the force of Paul's concept of church we must note the following points.

The basis of community is the *shared experience of the Spirit*. 'The *koinonia* of the Spirit' (2 Cor. 13:13-14; Phil. 2:1) means primarily 'participation in the Spirit', the common experience of the Spirit which was the other side of the coin from their common faith in Christ (e.g. Rom. 8:9; 2 Cor. 1:21f.; Gal. 3:2-5); note the strong appeal to experience in Phil. 2:1f. It was this shared experience which drew them together and out of which their oneness grew: 1 Cor. 12:13 — one Spirit, therefore one body; Eph. 4:3f. — the unity of the Spirit is something given, the oneness of their starting point as believers, not something they create, but something they can maintain. In short, for Paul the unity of the Christian community is not primarily something structural, but rather the unifying power of a shared experience of grace inspiring a common gratitude and purpose.

The *locus* of community is the *local church*. In the earlier letters of Paul there are probably no instances of *ekklesia* meaning 'the universal church': it always seems to denote the Christians living or gathered in one place — hence the plural in Rom. 16:16. 1 Cor. 7:17; 16:1, 19, etc., and its use in reference to home-churches in Rom. 16:5; 1 Cor. 16:19 and Col. 4:15 (in Ephesians it is different). So too 'the body' in Rom. 12 and 1 Cor. 12 is not the universal church, but the church in Rome and the church in Corinth. It is particularly clear from the way Paul develops the metaphor in 1 Cor. 12 that the body referred to was the Corinthian body of believers: 12:27 — 'you (Corinthians) are Christ's body'. It is not clear how the home-churches in a particular place functioned in relation to 'the church' in that place; the descriptions in 1 Cor. 10-14 refer presumably to gatherings of the whole church of Corinth. The fact that smaller groups within the church in Rome are also called churches should not be ignored (Rom. 16:5).

The ongoing life of the local community is *charismatic* in character. As the shared experience of the Spirit is the beginning of community, so it is the continuing manifestations of the Spirit or gifts of the Spirit which constitute the life and growth of the community as the body of Christ. The 'functions' of the body are precisely the charismata of the Spirit (Rom. 12:4) — charisma for Paul denoting any word or act which embodies or manifests grace (*charis*), and is a means of grace to another. Charismata (or charisms) thus understood are the living movements of the body (1 Cor. 12:14-26; Eph. 4:16). Without them the body is dead. Christian community exists only in the living interplay of charismatic ministry, in the actual being and doing for others in word and deed.

It follows that to be a member of the body of Christ is by definition to be charismatic. There are no dead organs in the body of Christ: each has some function — 'to each' is given some charisma or other (1 Cor. 7:7; 12:7, 11). To share in the Spirit means also being open for the Spirit to prompt some word or deed which will minister grace to the rest. At no time did Paul conceive of two kinds of Christian — those who have the Spirit and those who do not, those who are charismatic and those who are not, those who minister to others and those who are ministered to. For example, although there were regular prophets (see below), any believer might be moved to prophesy, and indeed all believers should seek and be open to this most valuable of charismata (1 Cor. 12:10; 14:1, 5, 26, 39; 1 Thess. 5. 19f.). There was certainly no concept of a monoministry or of a priestly office confined to a particular individual or group within the body.

The *unity* of the church is a function of its *diversity*. The members of the body have different functions, different ministries (Rom. 12:4; 1 Cor. 12:4ff.) — otherwise the body would not be a body (1 Cor. 12:17, 19). Without the diversity of charismata there can be no unity, for without the Spirit's activity in and through each there is no unity and no body. The unity depends on the diversity functioning as such, and can be injured as much by one member taking too much to himself as by one member failing to respond to the Spirit's prompting (1 Cor. 12: 14-26; Rom. 12:3). The sharing in one loaf (as part of the common meal — only the cup is 'after supper', 1 Cor. 11:25) is (or should have been) an expression of the oneness of the grace that knits the many together, not by eliminating their diversity or despite their diversity but in their diversity and through their diversity (1 Cor. 10:17).

Within the diversity of ministries shared by all, some evidently had more *regular* ministries. They 'had' a particular charisma, not in the sense that it was theirs to use or not as they chose, but in the sense that the Spirit regularly moved in and through them to express some word or act which would benefit the community — for only if the Spirit was behind and in any word or act would it be a charisma, and only if it was exercised in dependence on grace and divine strength would it be a means of grace to others (Rom. 12:6; cf. 1 Pet. 4:11). First and foremost, and unique, was the role of apostle (1 Cor. 12:28). As the founder of the church he had brought the gospel that converted and the traditions about Jesus' teaching and ministry (1 Cor. 7:10; 9:14; 11:23-5; 15:1-3; etc.). Second in importance were the prophets and teachers (1 Cor. 12:28), the one responsible for being open to new revelation (1 Cor. 14:6, 26, 30), the other responsible for passing on and interpreting the traditions of the faith (Gal. 6:6). There were also a wide variety of other regular and overlapping ministries in the Pauline churches — including preaching, a wide range of services, administration and/or some kinds of leadership (Rom. 12:7-8; 16:1, 3, 9, 21; 1 Cor. 12:28; 16:15-18; etc.). Among them we see the first use of the titles 'bishops/overseers' (plural) and 'deacons' (Phil. 1:1), but what their functions were at Philippi is not clear. As yet none of these were clearly defined, far less established offices. We should also note that in Ephesians Paul's concept of the local church as a charismatic community is universalized (either by Paul or by a close disciple), and the ministries of apostles, prophets, evangelists, pastors and teachers are presented as ministries of the whole church (Eph. 4:11-16).

The *authority* of these various ministries lay primarily in the act of ministry itself. It was not something given by another person, even the church's apostle(s). Only the risen Christ appointed apostles (1 Cor. 9:1; 15:7; Gal. 1:1, 15f.). And though Paul expected respect for himself and his emissaries from his churches (e.g. 1 Cor. 11:17, 34; 16:1; 2 Thess. 3:6-12), everything he says strongly implies that he did not appoint prophets or teachers or individuals to particular ministries. There were those who, like Stephanas, acted (at the prompting of the Spirit) to meet some need for the benefit of the church (1 Cor. 16:15 — literally 'appointed themselves to' their ministry). There were those who 'worked hard' at particular ministries (1 Cor. 16:16; 1 Thess. 5:12). That was the expression of their spiritual maturity and the community should recognise it (1 Cor. 16:16; 1 Thess. 5:13; cf. Gal. 6:1-2). But where a community was lacking leadership in various areas (over grave moral issues, in the disorder of their gatherings for meals and for worship — 1 Cor. 5-6, 10-14) Paul did not vest authority in one individual or group. The authority of prophets and teachers was evidently limited to the sphere of their ministries; likewise, it would appear, the authority of Stephanas (just as the apostle's authority was limited to his sphere of ministry — 2 Cor. 10:13-16, see the New English Bible). Paul evidently hoped that when the church came together the Spirit would give to some member of the community, the words of wisdom appropriate to the situation (1 Cor. 6:5; cf. 12:8, 28; 14:26).

The *responsibility of the community* itself should not be undervalued. It is clear from Paul's concept of the body of Christ that each member individually and all members together have a responsibility for the welfare of the whole (1 Cor. 12:24-6). So we are not surprised when Paul exhorts all the members of different communities to teach, admonish, judge and comfort (Rom. 15:14; 1 Cor. 5:4f.; 2 Cor. 2:7; Col. 3:16; 1 Thess. 5:14), and when he encourages all to seek the most beneficial charisma (prophecy). Still more important, the community as a whole had the responsibility of testing all words and acts claiming the inspiration and authority of the Spirit (1 Cor. 2:12, 15; 1 Thess. 5:20f), even those of Paul himself (cf. 1 Cor. 7:25, 40; 14:37). It was part of the congregation's responsibility to give assent, to say 'Amen' to the inspired utterances (1 Cor. 14:16), to recognise the authority of the Spirit in those ministries undertaken at his compulsion (1 Cor. 16:18; 1 Thess. 5:12f.) but also to evaluate and if necessary reject any word or deed, however inspired it might seem to be, which was counterfeit or did not benefit the community (1 Cor. 2:15; 12:3; 1 Thess. 5:21f.). In other words the gift was not complete until it had been evaluated and received (1 Cor. 12:10; 14:27-9; 1 Thess. 5:19-22 NEB).

The Pauline concept of church differs from the discipleship of Jesus' ministry in that it was a concept of charismatic *community*, characterised by mutual interdependence, where each member, though experiencing the Spirit for himself, must depend on his fellow members for a whole range of ministries. So too it differs from the pattern which evolved at Jerusalem in that it was essentially a concept of *charismatic* community, 'of free fellowship, developing through the living interplay of spiritual gifts and ministries, without benefit of official authority or responsible "elders" '.[2] Its challenge is exciting, but the defects are obvious too. First, the model of the body focuses exclusively on the mutual internal relationships of the community. Paul himself was obviously committed to evangelism. But the other most relevant passage seems to envisage outreach happening only as a sort of by-product of the community's worship (1 Cor. 14:23-5) — though we may assume that the 'boundaries' of the church were still very fluid, with 'uninstructed and unbelievers' continually passing over them (both in and out); note also 1 Cor. 10:27. Secondly, within Paul's eschatological perspective — looking for the imminent coming again of Christ (1 Thess. 4:13-18; 1 Cor. 7:29-31), and seeing the apostles as the last act on stage before the final curtain (1 Cor. 4:9) — his churches did not require a structure that would endure. Charismatic community was a one generation ideal — nor is it finally clear whether his vision actually worked for any length of time in any particular church. On the other hand, Paul's concentration on the building up of the church was fully appropriate in that evangelistic situation, and underlines the importance of a spiritually sensitive suppportive community for new converts. Perhaps we need to revive the one genera- tion perspective lest we bestow on our successors the sort of entrenched structures and traditions which have proved so inhibiting for the present generation.

The Pastoral Epistles: Early Catholicism

The latest letters in the Pauline corpus (1 Tim., 2 Tim., Titus) reflect a significantly different concept of church and community — so different that the question of authorship is virtually irrelevant here. If written by Paul or at his behest they show that Paul himself had abandoned his ideal of charismatic community and, looking towards the next generation of Christianity, had accepted the need for a more carefully structured community, with authority more clearly defined. My own judgment however is that the Pastorals reflect a second generation situation (c.70-100 AD) when the organisational pattern of the Jewish churches (eldership; see above; also Jas. 5:14f.) had begun to merge with the evolving structure of the Pauline churches (overseers and deacons — cf. Did. 15:1-2) — hence the near synonymity of 'elders' and 'overseers' in the Pastorals. Either way the model given in the Pastorals is quite distinct from that presented in the earlier, undisputed Paulines.

Elders appear for the first and only time in the Pauline corpus (1 Tim. 5:1f., 17, 19; Titus 1:5). 'Overseers' (bishops — 1 Tim. 3:1-7; Titus 1:7ff.) and 'deacons' (1 Tim. 3:8-13) appear as descriptions of established offices (1 Tim. 3:1 — 'office of overseer'). The presentation of 1 Tim. 3 suggests that deacons were subordinate to overseers, though we cannot tell from this chapter what their respective functions were.

Timothy and Titus are not simply emissaries from Paul visiting one of his churches as his spokesman, as in earlier days (1 Cor. 4:17; 2 Cor. 7:13f. etc.). Rather they are envisaged as having an authority which even Paul never exercised — an authority over the community much like that of a monarchical bishop. Theirs is the responsibility to keep the faith pure (1 Tim. 1:3f.; 4:6ff., 11-16 etc.), to order the life and relationships of the community (1 Tim. 5:1-16; 6:2, 17; Titus 2:1-10, 15), to exercise discipline and mete out justice, not least in the case of the elders (1 Tim. 5:19ff.), to lay on hands (1 Tim. 5:22) and to appoint elders (Titus 1:5). A concept approaching that of 'apostolic succession' is beginning to emerge — Paul to Timothy, to 'faithful men', to 'others', though whether the succession is yet conceived in formal terms, from office to office, is not clear (2 Tim. 2:2).

The Pauline concept of charisma has been narrowed and regulated.

It seems to be understood more as a single gift given once and for all in the course of ordination, a gift which Timothy now possesses within himself and which equips him for his different responsibilities. From being an event (word or act) or series of events which carry their authority in themselves and must be evaluated by others, charisma has become the power and authority of office (1 Tim. 4:14; 2 Tim. 1:6). The only general congregational activity mentioned is prayer (1 Tim. 2:8).

In the Pastorals therefore we see Christian communities developing an increasingly hierarchical structure and authority so as to ensure their continuance into future generations. The Pauline vision of the body, of a community of mutually interdependent ministries, has been left behind. So too has the important Pauline tension between prophet and teacher, between (new) revelation and (old) tradition. There is no question that the Pastorals' model can endure (it did!); the question rather is whether it has lost something vital in the earlier Pauline vision, not least the vision itself.

The Lukan Alternative: Enthusiasm and Catholicism

The striking feature about the Acts of the Apostles is that it seems to be working with two models of Christian community and trying to hold them together. How much is straight history and how much history viewed from a one-sided perspective, or history with a pattern impressed upon it, is always a problem in interpreting Acts. But some Lukan emphases and some significant silences give us sufficient clues.

Luke not only presents the beginnings of Christianity as enthusiastic in character, but he also seems deliberately to heighten the enthusiastic features. For Luke the Spirit is most clearly seen in extraordinary and obviously supernatural phenomena, something tangible, unmistakable, whether inspired speech or manifest physical impact (Acts 2:3f., 17f., 33; 8:16-19; 10:44-6; 11:15f.; 19:2, 6). He seems to put great weight on the ecstatic visions which guided the development of the young church (Acts 9:10; 10:3-6, 10-16; 16:9f.; 18:9; 22:17f., 26:19f.), and he shows none of Paul's reservations over the abuse which could and did arise from claims to authoritative revelation based on visions (cf. 2 Cor. 12:1ff.; Col. 2:18). He seems deliberately to heighten the importance of miracles (particularly Acts 8:13; 19:11), and calls them regularly 'wonders and signs', whereas that phrase is used more often elsewhere in a more negative sense denoting something to be wary of (Mark 13:22/Matt. 24:24; John 4:48; 2 Cor. 12:12; 2 Thess. 2:9). He seems to imply that all inspired utterance can be taken at face value as the work of the Spirit, making no attempt to distinguish prophecy from glossolalia (Acts 2:4, 16-18; 10:46; 19:6; contrast 1 Cor. 14), and attributing contradictory directives to the Spirit without comment (Acts 20:22; 21:4).

On the other hand Luke presents a Christianity which shows more features of early catholicism than we would expect on the basis of historical analysis. The expectation of the imminent parousia, which was still strong in Paul's time and which must have been if anything stronger at the beginning (Jesus' resurrection as the 'first-fruits' = the beginning of the final resurrection — Rom. 1:4; 1 Cor. 15:20-3; 'Our Lord, come' — 1 Cor. 16:22), is only hinted at. Eschatology in Acts (10:42; 17:31; 24:25) is much more like 'the doctrine of the last things' than the imminent expectation of Paul (and Jesus) — a second generation perspective. He passes over in silence the continuing tensions and significant differences within the early church between Paul and Jerusalem (Gal. 2:11ff.; 2 Cor. 10-13; Phil. 3), showing Jerusalem to be much more the authoritative centre of the whole mission (including the Gentile mission) than Paul would have accepted (particularly 2 Cor. 10:13-16, NEB), presenting a much narrower picture of apostleship (= the twelve) than Paul would have accepted (especially 1 Cor. 15:7; Rom. 16:7; 1 Cor. 9:5f.; Gal. 2:9), and depicting Paul as actually appointing elders in his churches from the beginning (Acts 14:23; cf. 20:17). It is difficult to avoid the conclusion that Luke is stamping his portrayal of early Christianity with a greater degree of homogeneity in self-understanding and uniformity of organisation than was historically the case.

The boldness and challenge of Luke's presentation deserves more attention than it has been given. He attempts to present a church or churches in which enthusiasm and regular order coexist in harmonious interaction. But he also depicts an enthusiasm which does not go hand in hand with expectation of an imminent second coming, and which is therefore not dependent on and so not destroyed by the delay of the parousia. How difficult it is to hold these two together, enthusiasm and early catholicism, is evidenced by the fact that Acts has provided inspiration and authority for both enthusiasts and catholics, without each usually being aware of the support afforded to the other by the same document.

The Johannine Alternative: Pietism

The gospel and epistles of John seem to share with Acts a similarly altered eschatological perspective (cf. John 21). The future eschatological hope is by no means lacking (e.g. John 5:27-9; 14:3f.), but few would dispute that the emphasis is on realised eschatology (see especially John 3:8; 5:24; 11:25f.; 1 John 3:14). The difference from Acts is that whereas Acts shows a church whose organisation can withstand the delay of the parousia, John seems to understand Christianity as much more an individual affair, the immediacy of the disciple's relationship with Christ through the Spirit who constitutes Christ's continuing presence in the believer (John 14:15-20; 1 John 3:24).

The individualism of the fourth gospel is one of the most striking features of this remarkable document. The sense of mutual inter-dependence in belonging to Christ, so strong in Paul, is lacking in John: each sheep hears the shepherd's voice for himself (John 10:3f., 16); each branch is rooted directly in the vine (John 15:4-7); each seems to eat and drink for himself (John 6:53-8; 7:37f.); the unity of believers is patterned on the unity of Father and Son and depends on the individual's union with Christ (John 17:20-3). There are similar statements in 1 John (e.g. 3:24; 4:13; 5:10-12).

The disciples closest to Jesus do not form any kind of hierarchy, nor are they given any particular office. They are never called 'apostles' and only once 'the twelve' (John 6:67) and presumably include (some of) the women who feature so prominently in this gospel (chapters 4, 11, 20); they are simply 'the disciples', and John thus probably intends them to represent all (including future) disciples in their common responsibility of mutual love and mission (John 14-16; 20:22). In particular 'the beloved disciple' is probably used by John to symbolise the individual believer in the immediacy and closeness of his relationship with Jesus (13:23-5; 20:2-8). The picture does not change in the Johannine epistles. We may note especially 1 John 2:27, where the anointing (of the Spirit) obviates the necessity of teachers — the Spirit indwelling each believer is teacher enough. A specifically pastoral role however is given to Peter in the epilogue to the gospel (John 21:15-17).

There is a very strong sense of 'us' and 'them' in the Johannine writings. The Johannine Christians have passed from darkness to light, from death to life (John 3:19-21; 5:24; 8:12). In 1 John in particular the distinction between believer and unbeliever is clear-cut (1 John 2:4, 23; 3:6, 9f., 14f.; 4:5f.). The frequent call for love is for love of the brethren (John 13:34f.; 1 John 3:10-18, 23f.; 4:20f.). Those who 'went out' demonstrated thereby that they were never 'in' (1 John 2:19).

This understanding of Christian community has been appropriately likened to conventicle Christianity, to the pietistic Christianity of 'conferences for the deepening of the spiritual life', where, though she/he seeks to worship in Spirit and truth (John 4:24) in company with others, it is the immediacy and growth of her/his own spiritual life which the individual counts as of greatest importance. The greater the love of the brethren, the greater apparently the divorce from the world and the lack of involvement with the world. This too is New Testament Christianity. And the influence of the Johannine writings on countless generations of Christian spirituality shows how important it has been — and continues to be — in a world dominated by materialistic concerns and values.

The Matthean Church: the Law-abiding Brotherhood

Matthew is generally thought to have been written about AD 80, at a time when (in the aftermath of AD 70) rabbinic Judaism was beginning to formulate its distinctive character, and when Jewish Christians (in Syria?) found themselves having to say to their fellow Jews, 'We know and keep the law better than you because we follow Jesus' (see e.g. Matt. 5:17-20; 23:3, 23). There are four passages which shed light on the concept and practice of Christian community reflected in Matthew.

Matt. 7:15-23. Matthew's church seems to have suffered somewhat from the ministry of wandering prophets — a charismatic ministry which, in Matthew's view at least, was wedded to antinomianism (7.22f.; cf.

24:11, 24). Matthew does not reject such ministry (cf. 10:7f., 41; 17:20), but seeks to ensure that it is more closely integrated with a continuing loyalty to the law — not so very different from Paul's emphasis in Gal. 5:13f., but with greater stress on keeping the Jewish law.

Matt. 16:13-20. Peter is clearly the apostle most highly regarded within this community, principally because he was for them the church founder *par excellence* (16:18), both as the one whose preaching called the mother church of Jerusalem into existence (Acts 2), and presumably as *the* apostle to the circumcised in general (Gal. 2:7f.) as of many Jewish Christian churches in particular (including Matthew's). But also because, in Matthew's presentation, Peter is the typical disciple, representing both the insight and authority of faith (16:17, 19; cf. 18:18; 21:21f.) and the weakness of 'little faith' discipleship (14:28-31; cf. 17:20).

Matt. 18:1-20. This 'community rule' seems to envisage no special leaders who can be distinguished from the ordinary church members. The passage speaks only of 'these little ones' — obviously the membership as a whole, since in order to enter the kingdom of heaven each must become such a one (18:1-6, 10). The 'rule' lays responsibility on every one to find the lost sheep, to win back the erring brother, to 'bind and loose' (18:12-20).

Matt. 23:8-10. This passage contains a solemn and quite explicit warning to the Matthean church against conferring any rank or title or special status on any individual member — God alone is 'Father' and Jesus alone is 'Teacher' and 'Master'. The greatness to which they are all called by Jesus is not that of executive power and authority but that of humble service (20:25-7; 23:11f.).

The Matthean community is perhaps best described as a brotherhood (Matt. 5:22-4, 47; 7:3-5; 18:15, 21, 35; 23:8) grouped round the elder brother, Jesus (Matt. 12:49f.; 18:20; 25:40; 28:10), striving to develop a form of outgoing life and all-member ministry amid Jewish hostility, and conscious of the opposite dangers both of a hierarchical structure which might inhibit the manifold ministry of the brotherhood and of a charismatic prophetism which divorces miracle and revelation too sharply from a proper loyalty to the law. In other words, we see reflected in Matthew what seems to be an attempt to develop or maintain a form of Pauline 'churchmanship' within, and more appropriate to, a rabbinic Jewish context.

Fragmentary Reflections Elsewhere

1 Peter shares the Pauline concept of charismatic ministry (1 Peter 4:10f.). The concept of a priestly ministry is referred to the church as a whole (2:5, 9); and the title 'pastor and overseer' is used only of Jesus (2:25). The only prophets (including Christian prophets?) mentioned are spoken of in the past tense (1:10-12). A clearly defined circle of elders is addressed in 5:1-5, although 'elder' here may simply mean 'older' (5:5). If the community referred to here belongs within the spectrum sketched out above, it could be characterised as a church (probably within the Pauline mission) which has already begun to integrate charismatic community with a system of eldership.

Hebrews mentions 'leaders' who are clearly distinct from the rest of God's people (13:7, 17, 24). A ministry of teaching is spoken of in 5:11-6:8, but as with 'the spiritual ones' in Paul (1 Cor. 2:12-3:4; Gal. 6:1), it is a status of spiritual maturity and experience rather than of office which is envisaged. No other ministries are referred to individual members, and elsewhere responsibility for service and exhortation is laid on the whole membership (Heb. 6:10; 10:25; 12:15). The most striking feature is the writer's focusing of all priestly ministry in Jesus in an exclusive and exhaustive way (2:17; 3:1; 4:14f.; 5:1; etc.) so that there is no room or role left for any priestly intermediary within the Christian community. Such a priesthood belonged to the past, the era of shadow, but Christ has brought the reality thus foreshadowed to every believer (chapters 7-10), so that each can now 'draw near' the very presence of God for himself without depending on other believers or any human intermediary (4:16; 6:19f.; 10:19-22). In short, if 1 Peter falls somewhere between Paul and the Pastorals in ecclesiology, Hebrews seems to share more of John's individualistic pietism.

In *Revelation* the ecclesiology envisaged is too obscurely reflected to give a clear picture. Apostles belong to the founding era (21:14). All believers are priests (1:6; 5:10; 20:6). The elders in the heavenly throne room presumably represent the church as a whole (4:4, 10; 5:8; etc.). Likewise the 'angels' of the churches in chapters 2-3 are most probably heavenly counterparts of the churches in question. Most prominent are prophets (e.g. 10:7; 11:18; 16:6) and witnesses (2:13; 11:3; 17:6), who are envisaged as particular individuals in 2:13, 20 and 22:9. Whether these were clearly distinct ministries within any community, let alone formed a hierarchy within the churches, is not at all clear to us. But in so far as a generalisation can be ventured, it would seem that the church of Revelation is one which lives through and out of prophecy.

Conclusion

There is clearly no single model of Christian community which emerges from the New Testament as *the* New Testament church. We see different churches in different situations (inevitably?) reflecting something of the dominant characteristics of their environment — the church at Corinth mirrors the libertarian abuses of Corinthian society, just as the church in Jerusalem and the church of Matthew mirror the law-centredness of Jewish society. We see already, in both Jerusalem and the Pauline churches, evidence of the now familiar historical sequence — the transition from first generation community, enthusiastic, loosely structured, innovative, to a second generation community with a developing hierarchical structure and a growing consciousness of tradition and the need to preserve rather than to innovate. We see already what has become the most regular way of escape from a too rigid institutionalisation, in the pietism of John and probably Hebrews. All these are what we might call *sociological truths*, the facts of life and social relationships both within the church and between the churches and their environment — truths we cannot ignore and must always live with.

But we also see *theological principles* which must always provide the motivating starting point from which we move out to challenge merely sociological pressures, the yardstick by which we measure the quality of our community, the vision by which we live and which we refuse to conform to the pattern of this world. Here the challenge of Jesus' call to discipleship and Paul's vision of charismatic community should particularly be mentioned, as being those models of community which show the least influence of these same sociological pressures. Of the various elements in these two models worthy of consideration not least is their eschatological character. That is to say, part of what gave them their challenging quality was their focus on the present and unconcern to organise for the future. May it be that the model of Christian community which emerges from the New Testament with most force today is the one-generation model: the church which organises for the future may simply be ensuring that the future will be so burdened with the past that it cannot bring to reality Christian community in the present.

Notes

1 J. Jeremias, *New Testament Theology: The Proclamation of Jesus* (SCM Press, London, 1971), p. 175.
2 H. von Campenhausen, *Ecclesiastical Authority and Spiritual Power in the Church of the First Three Centuries* (A. & C. Black, London, 1969), pp. 70f.

The Theology of
the Charismatic Movement

PAUL S. FIDDES

Anyone who attempts to give an account of the theology of the
Movement for Charismatic Renewal soon finds that the object of his
enquiry is curiously elusive. In the first place, the Christian theologian
naturally wants to protest that 'we are all charismatics', and that no
single group can lay claim to being alone endowed with the charisms
of the Holy Spirit. If the Church is not charismatic then it is not the
Church.[1] But realism compels us to recognise that there is a distinctive
movement, with its own particular patterns of experience and conviction about the work of the Holy Spirit, which has had a profound effect
upon the life of the Christian Church in all its denominations during the
past 25 years. In this sense of the word 'charismatic', I have to declare
myself at the outset as an observer rather than a participant, despite the
often levelled criticism that participation is an essential qualification for
understanding.

But, given the distinct identity of such a movement, I suggest that
we have to press on beyond anxious enquiries about whether it stands
in continuity with biblical and church tradition about the Holy Spirit,
to ask the important theological question as to whether it has made
any *contribution* to the Christian doctrine of the Holy Spirit. We ought
to be interested in asking whether this recent movement of thought
and experience has added any dimension to our understanding of God
as Spirit, and whether it has correspondingly thrown light upon the
notion of the human spirit. Our resources for answering these queries
are not only the explicit affirmations made by members of the movement
— Catholic and Protestant — but also what is implicitly disclosed by
the phenomenon of the movement itself.

There is a second preliminary problem which leads on from this. By its nature, the Movement for Charismatic Renewal has been less concerned with theology than with experience. The experience is treated as primary, and theological interpretation as secondary. In this relegation of theology to a subordinate, reflective role the Charismatic Movement has some interesting parallels with the Liberation theologians; indeed, in some places the two are interfused in a common search for freedom in every sense.[2] Further, some of the most substantial theological thinking about the charismatic experience seems to have been done by those who are fringe participants or even commentators on the movement, rather than by those who are most deeply involved within it.[3] On the other hand, there is an ocean of 'testimony' material, often tenuously connected to New Testament texts.

The theological reflection that has taken place has centred upon the concept of 'baptism in (or with) the Spirit', and we shall also take this as our point of focus. This idea includes two dimensions which have encompassed the emphases of the movement at least until recent times, namely renewal and spiritual gifts, often expressed as a new awareness of the 'presence' and the 'power' of God. The term 'baptism in the Spirit' points first to an experience of renewal of relationship with God, a new sense of encounter with the holy being of God subsequent to Christian initiation through conversion and baptism. Second, it points to a new realisation of the gifts (charisms) which the Spirit gives to the Church for the strengthening of its fellowship and for its mission to the world.

While theological discussion has usually concentrated upon the legitimacy of the idea of a new stage in the process of Christian initiation, we ought to pursue our theological investigation further and ask why this idea has taken the particular form of expression it has, namely a stressing of the activity of the Holy Spirit. What is the significance of assigning so firmly this renewal of our experience of God to the Spirit? The movement itself has sometimes been rather disappointing in its affirmations here; as one notable Catholic participant has noted, the danger is less likely to be that of falling into a Spirit-cult than a Jesus-cult.[4] In rightly insisting that the experience of the Spirit of God is inseparable (in New Testament terms) from the activity of the exalted and risen Christ, Spirit and Jesus have frequently been invoked in an interchangeable way, so that the mention of 'Spirit' sometimes seems to be redundant.

The Report commissioned by the General Synod of the Church of England on the effect of the Charismatic Movement within Anglicanism (1981) comments that some members of the movement seem to be Trinitarian only by accident,[5] and it calls for more serious theological thinking about the Triunity of God in the light of the charismatic experience. We should enquire about the significance, then, of attributing renewal to the Spirit of God rather than to 'God the Father' or 'God the Son'. To reply that the New Testament describes the Spirit as bearing witness to the Father and the Son is simply to repeat the categories by which the earlier church tried to understand its own experience; we must go on to ask what the meaning of such expressions is for ourselves in trying to understand the transcendence and immanence of God.

A third preliminary problem we must register is a shift in the direction of the Movement for Charismatic Renewal since 1980, at least among the Protestant churches. In the period 1970-80 when the charismatic experience was integrated into the mainstream life of the Christian denominations, there was a strong theological link made between 'charism' and spiritual renewal. But the new decade has been marked by a linking of charism much more with questions of authority. Charismatic spiritual leadership has often become a new kind of authority which in places has led to sectarianism. While we might well find some sociological reasons for the attractiveness of authoritarian small groups today, our theological concern is to elucidate what kind of view of the Holy Spirit is implied by this new emphasis. In particular, we must explore the emergence of a theology of 'submission' to the Spirit. Our present discussion then will begin by examining the theology of renewal itself, and then go on to consider its application in charisms and a life-style of 'submission'.

The Theology of Renewal

The term 'baptism in the Spirit' indicates in the first place a conviction about spiritual renewal, and theological debate about a renewing 'baptism' has centred upon two questions. Is there a foundation in scripture and church tradition for a decisive renewing event following conversion-baptism? If there is, is the term 'baptism' a proper one to describe it?

Exegesis of scripture within the movement has found a consistent sequence
of spiritual experience in the narratives of the gospels and the Acts of
the Apostles which is thought to support the idea of a critical new stage
or new turning point in the process of Christian initiation. This sequence
is traced in the experience of the earliest disciples, and an analogy is
discerned in the developing consciousness of Jesus himself, who is often
regarded as the archetypal 'charismatic' to whose likeness we are to be
conformed.

Exegetes within the movement have drawn attention to some or all
of the following sequences.[6] According to the accounts in the synoptic
gospels, there is at least a slight gap between the baptism of Jesus in
water and the descent of the Holy Spirit upon him. In Luke's narrative,
for instance, Jesus is depicted as being in prayer after his baptism when
the Spirit comes (Luke 3:21; cf. Matt. 3:16; Mark 1:10). A New
Testament scholar critical of the charismatic emphasis, J. D. G. Dunn,
nevertheless also finds this sequence significant as evidence that the earliest
church did not simply identify baptism in water and in spirit.[7] More
extensively, there is a gap between the baptism in water of Jesus' own
disciples by John, and their being filled by the Spirit at Pentecost, which
Luke at least considers to be the fulfilment of the promise that they
would be baptised in the Spirit (Luke 3:16; Acts 1:5; cf. Matt. 3:11;
Mark 1:8). A more fundamental christological parallel is the gap between
the birth of Jesus through the power of the Spirit according to Matthew and Luke, and his being filled with the Spirit at his baptism. A
final sequence is found in the life of the early church, when Luke narrates
two incidents where converts who have been baptised in water only
subsequently receive the Spirit (Acts 8:16-17; 19:2-6; cf. 18:25).

Members of the Charismatic Movement have appealed to these
examples to justify a pattern of experience which they believe should
be characteristic of all Christians, namely a point of renewal of spiritual
experience some time after conversion-baptism. Among most thoughtful
people within the movement it is stressed that this critical point is a
'breakthrough' to consciousness of what is already present in the believer.
This is variously described as a 'manifestation' or 'release' or 'upsurge'
of the Spirit, but essentially it is 'a breaking through to conscious
awareness of the Spirit already received and present through Christian
initiation'.[8]

The christological parallel is urged as important here. As Christ was generated through the power of the Spirit so the believer is regenerate through the Spirit, and as the Spirit was present in Jesus before his baptism but 'the fullness of the Spirit only gradually became effective in him',[9] so the Spirit is present in the believer before the 'breakthrough' to the surface of experience. In this way the advocates of charismatic renewal distance themselves from the classical Pentecostal idea of the 'second blessing'. Renewal is not a second baptism, but a manifestation of the original baptism of regeneration. Classical Pentecostalism had also sometimes drawn the parallel of the believer's experience with the birth and baptism of Jesus, but had expounded the sequence rather differently, as between the work of the Spirit incorporating the believer into Christ and the gift of the Spirit's own indwelling presence. Neo-Pentecostalism rejects this notion that in regeneration the Spirit only gives us Christ and in the second blessing also gives us himself. It has also increasingly come to reject the more subtle distinction between the Spirit's being 'with' and then 'in' the believer.[10]

The charismatic theology of a 'breakthrough' of the Spirit is very widespread among both Roman Catholic and Protestant members of the Renewal Movement, often using that particular catchword. The Catholic approach is consistently sacramental, envisaging a breakthrough of the Spirit already received in water-baptism. This sequence finds some support in the tradition of separating baptism of infants from the confirmation of conscious believers, but as a matter of fact the Catholic charismatic theologians often regard the renewal as a breakthrough of the grace of God given in both baptism and confirmation. One theologian speaks of a 'renewal of confirmation',[11] perhaps recognising that confirmation as well as paedo-baptism might involve little conscious commitment by the candidate himself. What is basic is the notion of completing the objective prevenient act of the gracious Spirit of God with a subjective appropriation of grace by the believer. An influential document of the Catholic Charismatic Movement[12] distinguishes between the 'theological' and 'experiential' senses of the term 'baptism in the Spirit', the second being a 'conscious awareness' of the first.

Protestant approaches to understanding the breakthrough have been more varied, sometimes stressing conscious conversion as the point of the original gift of the Spirit, with water baptism as a sign of this, whether undertaken by an infant or an adult believer. Thus the objective-subjective sequence has not been as clear cut as in most Catholic thinking. The simple objective-subjective sequence also breaks down where a sacramental approach to Christian initiation is taken by those churches who practise baptism of (adult) believers, so that the original gift of the Spirit is located in a sacramental event which already fuses the objective grace of God with subjective faith. For all these diversities, however, there is at present an ecumenical consensus about the meaning of salvation which has made possible the widespread acceptance of a 'breakthrough' idea. Among theologians of all Christian denominations, salvation is understood as a process rather than a single point, with its beginning in the mysterious and hidden work of the Spirit deep beneath the surface of the human spirit, and having its ending only in the eschatological hope of the new creation. Wherever the sacrament of water baptism, and wherever objective and subjective dimensions of grace are placed along this continuum, there seems to be room for the idea of a 'breakthrough' to surface awareness of a previously hidden work of the Spirit.

Yet if we place Charismatic Renewal in this context, we must not overlook the distinctive pattern of the charismatic experience. It is characteristic of the Renewal Movement that there should be a critical turning point in the process of Christian maturity, not just a continuous emergence of new levels of insight and devotion. Here the new Pentecostalism has a family resemblance to the older Pentecostalism that is hard to deny. The newer movement does, it is true, have room for a gradual coming of renewal and is more flexible in its description of the shape of this experience — 'there is no law of experience'. [13] But it does still identify a critical new stage, however fluid the borderline of this stage might be, and however many further developments in the spiritual life follow it. The very language of 'the breakthrough' implies this. [14] The newer Pentecostalism is also different from the older in that it does not insist upon the gift of 'tongues' as evidence of the break-through of the Spirit. However, most theologians of the movement consider that the exercise of tongues is an appropriate sign of the crisis experience, as this non-verbal, non-conceptual form of free utterance is understood as a suitable way in which the believer can surrender his mind and emotions to God, 'letting go' of himself and experiencing 'release' from his inhibitions. [15]

Those who identify a significant point of 'breakthrough' in awareness of the Spirit (or the power of Christ), now go on to consider whether it should be called a 'baptism'. Many theologians of the Charismatic Movement recognise that in New Testament terms the moment of conversion to Christ and water baptism must be called a 'baptism in the Spirit'; it is, for instance, the point of entrance into the Messianic age of the Spirit. But they are anxious to designate the point of renewal also as a baptism, while affirming that it is not a 'second baptism'. They are well aware of their sympathetic critics' suggestion that it would be less confusing to reserve the term 'baptism in the Spirit' for conversion-baptism, and to call the renewing experience a 'filling' with the Spirit, but in general they prefer to retain the expression 'baptism in the Spirit'. Their argument has at least three strands.

First, they argue that the breakthrough is a completing of the original act of initiation, and so initiating language is most suitable. It is an aspect of that initiation, though separated in time from the sacramental rite, making manifest what is inherent within it. It is one baptism. R. Laurentin, a Catholic theologian, has tried to make this more precise in sacramental terms by speaking of the *res* or ultimate effect aimed at in the *sacramentum* as being something existential.[16] Secondly, they point out that the term 'baptism' is a metaphor which might be applied to various events. In the New Testament it is only one image among others for denoting the activity of the Spirit, taking its place among such synonyms as 'sending', 'pouring out', 'filling', 'giving', 'falling upon', 'coming' and 'being received'. Thus, while it might in some contexts have the delimited meaning of initiation, in others it can simply mean being overwhelmed by the Spirit or immersed in the Spirit.[17] They suggest then that there is no reason why it should not be applied to the situation of renewal, as they believe that Luke at least used it in Acts 1:5. In a third strand of the argument, these considerations are supported by an appeal to the diversity of scripture, and by a warning about trying to force the New Testament into a single pattern of belief about the meaning of baptism. This is an eloquent appeal to the diversity of experience and conviction in the early church of which New Testament scholars are acutely aware today.

Of course, critics of the Charismatic Movement reply that it does itself precisely rely upon too schematic a reading of the New Testament material, in finding a pattern of renewal at all. Of the four sequences outlined at the beginning of this section, they suggest that the first three can be understood as having a historical particularity within the ministry of Jesus and the birth of the early church, as formative events in the history of salvation which do not have to be exactly reduplicated. In the case of the incidents in the book of Acts, their very diversity should warn us against making a theology of Christian initiation out of narrative. In the case of Cornelius, for example, the 'baptism in the Spirit' precedes water baptism (10:44ff.). These events witness to the remarkable freedom of action of the Spirit, and they betray the theological intention of Luke as he presents the Spirit's taking an initiating role in the widening of the mission of the early Church. In each incident, the way the Spirit comes prompts the Church to widen its understanding of the scope of the gospel. [18] Most critics of the Charismatic Movement have conceded that Luke's stories do not treat baptism with water and with Spirit as coincidental, though differing conclusions can be drawn from this which do not necessarily support a strict pattern of initiation and renewal. In the narratives about the Samaritans, Cornelius and the Ephesian believers there is some sense of surprise or oddness expressed that water baptism and filling with the Spirit do not coincide; this un-expected dislocation allows Luke to make his theological points about mission, but we might also conclude that it assumes that water and spirit baptism ought normally to belong together. [19]

Such a reading of Acts would bring Luke closer to the Pauline theology that baptism in the Spirit is the beginning of salvation. It would incline us further to understand Paul as identifying water baptism with spirit baptism as the normative point of this beginning. [20] In opposition to this latter exegesis, J. D. G. Dunn finds that Paul and Luke distinguish baptism in water from baptism in the Spirit; but he declares that he diverges from the charismatic approach in so far as he finds the New Testament equating spirit baptism with conversion. [21] As a matter of fact, however, we have seen that many charismatic theologians would hold water and spirit baptism together with conversion at the beginning of salvation. The point is that with their theology of a 'breakthrough' they want at the same time to hold them apart as well, adding that the original initiation in the Spirit needs to be brought to conscious awareness in a deliberate subsequent experience. Once again we see the theological importance of the sequence of 'breakthrough' for the charismatic theologians. But is there really any theological foundation for this emergence of an earlier baptism into the light of day?

Some theologians within the Charismatic Movement appear themselves to doubt the theological validity of a pattern of 'breakthrough'. There are some reservations voiced which go beyond the variations we have already noted above, and which seem to undermine in the end any strict sequence of initiation and renewal. On the one hand, there is the opinion of Thomas Smail (an Anglican) that a 'breakthrough' of the Spirit separated in time from conversion baptism is a provisional and not an ideal situation. [22] He maintains that a whole Christian initiation would integrate God's granting of rebirth through the Spirit with an experiential 'unfolding' of its implications in the consciousness of the believer, moulding him into the true humanity of Christ. The regenerating presence of the Spirit and the 'drawing out' of this gift into experience have become dislocated into separate moments of time, partly due to defects in the Church's theology of initiation. Smail readily admits that consequently the sequence of the birth and baptism of Jesus can supply no temporal pattern for the experience of the believer, though he wants to hold strongly to the analogy in theological terms. This approach stands in contrast, for example, to the view of H. Mühlen that a space of time is absolutely necessary before the 'breakthrough to charismatic prophetic activity', since time was needed for Jesus to grow in his insight and awareness of God and this equally applies to us now. [23] Smail accepts, however, that in our actual situation there will need to be a 'breakthrough' later than conversion-baptism.

A rather different challenge is made to a strict 'breakthrough' pattern by F. A. Sullivan (a Roman Catholic theologian). [24] The fact of the Spirit's becoming a matter of new conscious experience cannot, in his view, be explained simply as a subjective change in the recipient. The Spirit must be becoming objectively present to the believer in a new way. New effects of grace must mean theologically a new kind of divine presence, not just an unfolding of what is already given. Sullivan appeals to the terminology of Aquinas for the idea of a new 'sending' of the Spirit, 'inhabiting' the believer in a new way in order to 'innovate' an increase of grace and virtue. Since the Spirit of God cannot literally be sent, in the sense of moving from one place to another, there is no theological difficulty in the notion that the Spirit who already indwells the believer becomes present in a new way. Thus Sullivan follows Aquinas in speaking of the knowledge of God in the soul 'breaking out into a more ardent love', while denying that this is a breaking out of some 'total gift of the Spirit' given in initiation. He readily admits that this means that the 'baptism in the Spirit' is not a once-in-a-lifetime event, and that God can give us new powerful gifts of his Spirit to move us into ever new states of grace.

Both these modifications of the 'breakthrough' pattern have a commendable theological concern to bring together the objective activity of God and the subjective faith of the believer. They are also examples of the flexible approach which is possible within the theology of renewal developed by the Charismatic Movement. Indeed, as we have seen, the theology of renewal can fit quite well into contemporary ideas of salvation as a continuous process and a realisation of the diversity of the New Testament witness to faith. However, the malleable quality of the theological idea of a 'breakthrough' only serves to make clear that it is really a way of interpreting an experience. The primary datum is a certain experience of spiritual renewal which has had a healthy impact upon the lives of many people, and behind which lies a whole complex of factors including temperament and culture. The idea of a 'breakthrough' integrates this particular mode of experience into mainstream Christian thinking about salvation, but the idea does not itself contribute any new dimension to the theology of Christian initiation.

However, the reflections of the Charismatic Movement upon the extended process of salvation, and its concern to blend objective and subjective elements in human experience of God, ought to have an effect upon the level of expectation which the Church brings to its rites of initiation. The witness of the movement ought to encourage us to expect a new sense of the presence and the power of God to be communicated at the moments of confirmation or the baptism of believers. They must be taken seriously as occasions of heightened spiritual awareness and giving of grace. The Charismatic Movement points to the need for the mysterious and hidden work of the Spirit to be focused in a particular objective event, while it has presented no conclusive theological argument for that event's being other than the usual entry of believers into the community of faith through confirmation or believers' baptism.

Moreover, the theologians of the Charismatic Movement have argued impressively that there is no reason why these events should not be called 'baptism in the Spirit', whatever process of salvation has already preceded them in time.

If, as it seems, the Charismatic Movement has not contributed anything substantial to the theology of Christian initiation, has it made a contribution to the Doctrine of God? One motivation behind the development of an idea of 'breakthrough' has been the trinitarian concern not to drive a wedge between the Person of Jesus Christ and the power of the Spirit. It is widely agreed that one cannot be incorporated into Christ without being indwelt by the Spirit, or without existing in the realm of the Spirit — to employ two different biblical spatial metaphors. This conviction might be framed in the traditional form of saying that the risen Christ is the bestower of the Spirit. That is one way of elucidating the Johannine statement that the Spirit bears witness to Christ, and the Pauline near-identification (though not total identification) of the risen Lord with the Spirit: as Christ sends the Spirit, the charisms witness to his Lordship. Conversely, however, one might understand the witness of the Spirit to Christ in terms of the activity of the Spirit in the earthly Jesus; the same Spirit of God who worked in Jesus of Nazareth, bringing to birth in him truly human qualities, is at work now in human lives conforming us to the pattern of true humanity which he made visible in Christ. So the Spirit witnesses to Christ in so far as the Spirit can be recognised by his effects in Christ's life as set out in the gospels. While the charismatic theologians retain the first manner of expression about the Spirit's testimony to Christ, they also lay considerable stress upon the second, presenting Jesus as the archetypal charismatic. [25] As we have seen, the analogy between the growth of Christ into prophetic consciousness and the growth of our awareness of the Spirit is important for the theology of the Renewal Movement. Again, however, this charismatic theology is drawing attention to an important theme of christology without making a distinctive contribution.

But the theology of 'breakthrough' indicates something else about our experience of God which does seem to open up new horizons of thought. We notice that there is something rather ambiguous about the idea of 'breakthrough to consciousness', for it seems to cover two rather different kinds of 'breaking through'. On the one hand, there is the emergence of what *was* implicit and beneath the surface into clear articulation; there is opportunity for the exercise of conscious faith in a conceptual and even rational way. A Catholic might make a personal commitment to what was given to him objectively in the sacrament of baptism. The Protestant member of the Charismatic Movement often speaks of a 'fuller commitment' in language not unlike other holiness movements of the past — though without the theology of perfectionism or full holiness that characterised them. That is one kind of breakthrough — from below to the clarity of the above. But there is another kind — a breaking through from above to below the surface of consciousness. There is a becoming 'aware' of what cannot be adequately conceptualised, a noticing of the depths of being that we often call intuitive or emotive. It is as if we break through with the Spirit into the subconscious of the human spirit.

Many of the charisms reported by the Charismatic Movement operate in the area that we usually describe as a matter of sympathy or mood or empathy. They are concerned more with non-verbal communication than with concepts or arguments. The charisms of 'tongues', 'prophecy', 'discernment' and 'healing' all evoke dimensions of the human personality which are often hidden or overlooked, opening up areas of personal inter-action and providing means of expression at a level that lies 'too deep for words'. The theologians of the Charismatic Movement rarely reflect upon this themselves; for the most part the phenomenon has to be explored by observing the experience and behaviour of those involved in it. There is present what John V. Taylor has identified as the 'Dionysiac element' in experience of God; he suggests that the 'upsurging of the unconscious' is 'very often the medium in which (the Holy Spirit) works; for this is the sphere from which our sudden recognitions and "annunciations" seem to arise.'[26] While Taylor himself develops a whole theology of the Spirit along these lines, he also recognises in the Charismatic Movement a renaissance of awareness of this 'wild-wind' quality of the Spirit; he suggests that the Movement challenges us to include within the life of faith 'the hidden irrational areas of reality' where the Creator Spirit is 'a mighty rushing wind sweeping along all the subterranean corridors below consciousness.'[27]

The theologians of Charismatic Renewal themselves are rather wary about such language. They do recognise the element of the subconscious in the phenomenon of tongues in particular, while stressing that the actual act of speaking in tongues is not an uncontrollable 'ecstatic' seizure but a gift which the speaker can exercise at his voluntary choice. It is a 'kind of prayer of the subconscious' (Tugwell)[28] or 'meditation and the relaxation of tension . . . not limited to intellectual forms' (Hollenweger).[29] Again, the function of the Spirit as the 'go-between God', building relationships between persons is well recognised among charismatic theologians; they frequently appeal to the Augustinian concept of the Spirit as the bond of love between the lover and the beloved within the Trinitarian being of God. But there is infrequent explicit recognition from the Charismatic Movement itself that this linking of relationships between people happens at subconscious and intuitive levels as well as consciously. However, the practice of the members of the movement in being concerned for mutual sympathy and 'sharing', together with a high estimate of gifts of 'discernment' and 'insight' is eloquent testimony to the reality of the phenomenon.

One Roman Catholic writer, E. D. O'Connor,[30] has attempted to relate the charismatic experience to the mystical tradition of 'unitive life'. He speaks of the Spirit's operating at levels of the human personality deeper than acts of will, as 'the grace of quiet'. This grace is characterised, he believes, by its unifying of mind and body, and he claims those who have had the charismatic experience have, like past mystics, obtained a more immediate awareness of the unity of their own being. An example is their experience of 'breath', which is known as a physical and a spiritual element at the same time. At the heart of this experience is love, which is the commandment proper to unitive life, binding man to God, to his neighbour and to himself. At the same time, love can be intuitive, not requiring 'the intervention of objective and conceptualised thought in order to express itself'.

With some exceptions, then, the Charismatic Movement witnesses more implicitly than explicitly to an awareness of God and the self which transcends rational categories. Its concern for 'Spirit' in this area is nevertheless a challenge to religious language. Its use of the biblical images of Spirit in its songs and prayers (wind, water, beating wings, oil and fire) points to a need for a more playful kind of theological language, evocative rather than strictly analogical. Theology has tended to concentrate upon analogies for God of a kind which claim a high degree of reference (pre-eminently, 'Father' and 'Son'), though their symbolic character is of course admitted. The Charismatic Movement points to the need also for symbols which are more evocative and impressionistic, opening up hidden areas of being often neglected. In this sense the Spirit 'witnesses' to the reality of the Father and the Son.

There is, of course, a general trend towards subjectivity in our society today in reaction against the scientific and rationalist basis of civilisation since the Enlightenment, a trend of which the Charismatic Movement can be considered sociologically a part. It has been dubbed a form of 'Christian existentialism' [31] and has sometimes been justly criticised for its extreme subjectivity and over-emphasis upon feeling at the expense of thought and affirmation of credal truths. Ironically, this may be due to a lack of explicit recognition and theological study of the way that experience and charisms happen at non-conceptual levels. If perhaps the Charismatic Movement had been more self-conscious of this aspect of itself, it might have made a more considerable contribution to the doctrine of God. But my impression is that its awareness of 'sub-surface' levels of experience has tended recently in a different direction, towards a theology of submission to God, as we shall see in the next section.

Charisms and Submission

The theology of renewal is bound up closely with two other concepts — charism and submission — and all that we have discovered about the sequence of 'breakthrough' and the intuitive areas of that breakthrough is highly relevant here.

We observed that the experience of a point of renewal was primary, and the theological account of it secondary. Among the various reasons why renewal is felt to be a distinct point is the experience of some people that there was a time when they began to exercise spiritual gifts (NT 'charismata'). The exercise of these charisms is fundamental to both Protestant and Catholic accounts of renewal, but there is a greater tendency for Catholics to make the charismatic element the central theological point. Despite Catholic references to a moment of *metanoia* which is often related to the historic tradition of a 'baptism of tears', it is Protestant accounts that tend to emphasise a new relationship with

God as central, perhaps indicating their line of descent from holiness movements of the past. The rediscovery of the ministry of the whole people of God has been an important recent feature of Catholic life, and the paragraph on charisms in the Constitution on the Church of Vatican II has given considerable impetus to the acceptance of the Charismatic Movement in the Catholic Church. This paragraph revised the traditionally held view that charisms are extraordinary signs of holiness, and proposed instead that the Spirit '. . . distributes special graces among the faithful of every rank. By these gifts he makes them fit and ready to undertake various tasks and offices for the renewal and building up of the Church.'[32] In accord with this, H. Mühlen[33] defines the 'breakthrough' of the Spirit as a 'baptism of witnesses', i.e. enabling the believer to proclaim the gospel in word and service. Catholic writers are inclined to understand the vital charism of prophecy as general proclamation of the word, while Protestant writers often limit it to particular discernment into the hidden factors of a situation or personal life.

There is a great deal of agreement among all charismatic theologians about the nature of spiritual gifts. They are agreed first about their diversity. They conclude that the three main lists of charismata in the New Testament (in Romans 12, 1 Cor. 12 and Ephesians 4) can hardly be exhaustive since they differ from each other, and that new gifts will be manifested to fit new situations. Moreover, they affirm that the less spectacular gifts such as administration, hospitality, teaching and generous giving are no less charismata than the unusual gifts of tongues, healing and prophecy, though the latter have attracted more attention outside the Charismatic Movement. All members of the church have gifts, and these differ. Secondly, there is general agreement that the charismata are given for the sake of the whole fellowship to build up the body of Christ, not for the private satisfaction of the individual exercising the gift. These emphases have had a healthy effect upon the life of the church, releasing personal resources previously hidden.

Thirdly, there is a general consensus that the charismata are signs of the work of the Spirit, though these are not understood as wonder-working proofs. Rather, there is felt to be a need for objective happenings to balance the subjectivity of an experience of renewal,[34] or the charismata are understood as objective form by which God is 'present among us and in our midst, accessible to sense experience as the Spirit of Jesus

Christ'.[35] This affirmation leads to a fourth agreed characteristic of the charismata which is of considerable theological significance, namely that they are to be understood in a dynamic way as actions of the Spirit. It is generally accepted that 'charisma' in the New Testament means 'an expression (or manifestation) of grace', which can be nothing other than the gracious activity of God himself. Since Paul uses 'charisma' as a virtual equivalent for *pneumatikon*, it seems that the latter term should similarly be understood as 'an expression of Spirit' (cf. 1 Cor. 12:7). Thus we arrive at a total meaning of 'charisma' as an *act* of God's gracious Spirit, creating a gift for service. According to the Pauline view, charismata are not faculties or abilities of the believer, but energies of the Spirit.

The theologians of the Charismatic Movement have appreciated this New Testament insight (along with other New Testament scholars),[36] but when this is combined with a concern for the exercise of the more intuitive and 'non-rational' gifts such as tongues, prophecy and healing, it leads to rather diverse conclusions. First of all there is the issue of the relationship between so-called 'natural' and 'spiritual' gifts. One line of thinking insists that 'grace perfects nature' (in Aquinas' phrase), so that 'in every case the gift of grace will presuppose, build upon and perfect the natural capacities that are already present.'[37] Precisely because the charisma is an action of the Spirit, there is a place in the natural world or the natural faculties where the action happens. This applies equally, perhaps especially, to those charismata which fall outside normal rational and conceptual areas. They also have a natural basis, in the sub-surface areas of the personality, where there are inter-personal or psychosomatic interactions lying at a level which is hidden from normal perception. They stretch our understanding of what nature is. This kind of approach is characteristic of (but not exclusive to)[38] Roman Catholic writing on the subject, though curiously there is a reluctance to appeal to the analogy of the sacraments[39] where there is also a concurrence between divine action and created elements. Perhaps this is because Catholic theologians are anxious to keep the charismata of the whole people of God distinct from the sacrament of ordination.

On the other hand, there is another line of thinking (more usually a Protestant one)[40] which insists upon the sovereign otherness of God and his actions from human capacities, so that a firm line is drawn between 'natural gifts' and 'spiritual gifts'. The more unusual gifts are not, of course, considered exclusively as the 'spiritual' ones: all the charismata, whatever their appearance, are understood as supernatural interventions of a different order from natural faculties. In christological terms, the first approach stresses the nature of the Church as an extension of the incarnation, while the second stresses the 'not yet' of a hope for the eschatological manifestation of the Lordship of Christ.

Perhaps a more satisfactory account would draw something from both these approaches, where the rooting of the charismata in a natural base would not mean that they were permanent possessions of the believer, but that there remained a sovereign elusiveness about their coming. [41] It would be a matter of God's will whether a natural event or faculty took on an extra depth or further dimension of grace, i.e. whether it became a charisma. Such a mediating position has ambiguities: while the Spirit's activities are not considered to be a permanent part of the believer's faculties, residing predictably with him, there would seem to be a more continuous exercise of gifts than a merely sporadic outbreak. The gift strictly exists only when it is being exercised, but the implication is that it could be exercised in a constant manner, due to the underlying nature. However, such ambiguity is perhaps appropriate to the mystery of the work of the Spirit.

The idea of the Spirit's activity raises a further related issue, that of submission and authority. There is among many charismatic groups a strong mood of submission — first submission to the Spirit of God and then to certain people within the Christian community, notably members to leaders (often 'elders'), women to men in matters of leadership, wives to husbands, and children to parents. A kind of hierarchy of submission is envisaged, which is claimed to make for spiritual health. The Charismatic Movement seems in fact to have shifted into a new phase at present, where this concern for authority within the community can overshadow the previous concern for renewal. We can agree that a theology of 'submission' to God can highlight in a positive way the creature-creator relationship, contrary to the human tendency to deify ourselves. In order for man as a created being to transcend himself and his limits, he needs to trust in the One who transcends him. But there are dangers in thinking of that attitude of trust and obedience as 'submission' and I suggest that these dangers become definite distortions

when submission becomes a hierarchy of submission within the Christian
community. A stress upon submission can lead to anti-intellectualism,
political passivity and authoritarianism within the church and the family.

If we enquire why this mood of submission has become dominant,
we shall find ourselves tracing once more the familiar theological themes
of 'breakthrough', hidden areas of the consciousness and charismatic
actions of the Spirit.

First, because some of the high-profile gifts (tongues, prophecy,
healing) operate in areas of the personality which are more intuitive than
rational, there is a tendency to consider the believer as a merely passive
recipient of an overwhelming spiritual power to which he must submit. Because he apparently has little rational control over them, he may
understand the Spirit as an invasive force. In fact, much of the writing
about tongues and prophecy proposes that there is spiritual profit in
the believer's abandoning himself to God, in his being willing to 'be
a fool', in letting himself go and renouncing his pride of self-possession.[42]
This mood of abandonment to God's Spirit needs to be balanced (as
it sometimes is) by a theology of nature which understands the actions
of the Spirit taking their base in natural capacities and faculties, so that
there is a synergism between human freedom and divine grace.

Some theologians of the Charismatic Movement have reflected upon
the relationship between the divine Spirit and the human spirit in this
way, drawing upon the experience of charismata happening at subliminal
levels. There is an experimental area, as it were, in which the theological
concept of a third way between autonomy and heteronomy (what Tillich
termed 'theonomy') can be worked out. R. Laurentin, for example,
maintains that 'to the extent that a man abandons himself to the action
of the Spirit, everything in man proceeds both from the Spirit and from
man's free choice . . . The Holy Spirit does not eliminate our spirit,
but becomes one with it.'[43] Laurentin also makes the trinitarian point
that the believer must be the sole subject of the cry 'Abba' and not
a mere instrument of the Spirit, since the whole concept of the Spirit
is a mode of the being of God which does not *have* the characteristic
of sonship, but witnesses to it. However, it is clearly easy to lose this
sense of the Spirit's awakening man's liberty from within and to fall
into the habit of mind of mere submission. The very expression
'breakthrough' of the Spirit' tends to foster the notion of a coercive act.

A second reason for the dominance of the mood of submission is the widespread belief that certain people must be submitted to because they possess certain gifts of the Spirit; they are acknowledged as representatives of the Spirit, and submission to them is thereby submission to the Spirit who gives the gifts. This viewpoint comes from making too simplistic an identification between the actions of the Spirit and the actions of the believer; whilst the Spirit acts simultaneously in and with the human will, this does not mean they are identical. Some of the theologians of the Charismatic Movement have tried to rectify this attitude. H. Mühlen explains that 'God never acts wholly immediately and directly on us and through us', because natural life is not dissolved by grace; the human spirit and the divine Spirit remain distinct, and natural impulses must not be simply confused with the impulses of the Spirit. Because God acts indirectly, 'charismatic impulses are never coercive', for 'no one can know with absolute certainty, excluding all doubt, whether the Holy Spirit is active in him.'[44] Thus the church community has the right, indeed the duty, to test what is claimed to be a charisma (for example, a word of prophecy): it is not self-validating. Since the charismata are not faculties possessed by people but actions of the Spirit within human faculties, the exercise of spiritual gifts can confer no inherent authority upon the one who exercises them. The whole church must discern whether a natural impulse has been made into a charisma by the Spirit, or whether it remains simply natural.

But behind these considerations about the nature of charismata, there lies a deeper question. How does the Spirit of God act towards man at all? The third factor behind a hierarchy of submission is the popular concept of a God who dominates his creation as an absolute monarch, and so sanctions a whole chain of command beneath him. But this image ignores the biblical picture of a God who calls man into a partnership of friendship with himself, and who shares man's tensions and frustrations in order to bring him to full manhood. If we speak of submitting to God, the cross and the incarnation tell us that God also submits to the conditions of his world, and freely experiences suffering and limitation. We must speak of a God who, in humble love, desires relationship with his creation, and who is satisfied in his own being through the contribution which creation makes to the outworking of his purpose.[45]

In fact, much of the theological thinking of the Charismatic Movement hints at this kind of view of God, rather than a God of coercive power. Affirmations about the unobtrusive and anonymous nature of the Spirit, and the moving of the Spirit into near-identity with the human spirit point to a love of God which gives itself away and embraces weakness. H. Wheeler Robinson many years ago expounded what he called 'the kenosis of the Spirit' — the humility of the Spirit of God in accepting lowly human life as a medium of his presence and activity, first in the incarnation and then in the Church. [46]

It has often seemed that the Charismatic Movement was drawing attention to this kind of accepting and humble love which is most characteristic of God's nature, and which we should repeat ourselves. It would be a tragic irony if the same Movement should now find in the experience of the Spirit a witness to dominating power rather than loving persuasion.

Notes

1 cf. P. Potter, 'Charismatic Renewal and the World Council of Churches', in *The Church is Charismatic*, ed. A. Bittlinger (WCC, Geneva, 1981), pp. 73-87.

2 See L. J. Cardinal Suenens and D. H. Camara, *Charismatic Renewal and Social Action: A Dialogue* ('Malines Document III', 1979), reprinted in *Presence, Power and Praise: Documents on the Charismatic Renewal*, ed. K. McDonnell (Liturgical Press, Collegeville, Minn., 1980), vol.III, pp. 291-357; also W. Hollenweger, *Pentecost between Black and White: Five Case Studies on Pentecost and Politics* (Christian Journals Ltd, Belfast, 1974). But for a critical statement about lack of social involvement by the Charismatic Movement, see the document of the Council of the Latin American Episcopate, *Renewal in the Spirit* (1977), in *Presence, Power and Praise*, vol. II, p. 363f.

3 For a historical and documented account of this trend, see E. D. O'Connor CSC, 'The Literature of the Catholic, Charismatic Renewal 1967-1975', in *Charismatic Renewal*, ed. E. D. O'Connor CSC (SPCK, London, 1978), pp. 149-51. Notable examples among Protestant writings are the studies by J. D. G. Dunn, *Baptism in the Holy Spirit* (SCM, London, 1970), and *Jesus and the Spirit* (SCM, London, 1975).

4 K. McDonnell, 'The Experience of the Holy Spirit in the Catholic Charismatic Renewal', in *Conflicts about the Holy Spirit (Concilium)*, ed. H. Küng and J. Moltmann (The Seabury Press, New York, 1979), p. 97.

5 *The Charismatic Movement in the Church of England* (CIO Publishing, London, 1981), p. 38 cf. p. 48.

6 e.g. M. C. Harper, *The Baptism of Fire* (Fountain Trust, London, 1968), pp. 6-7, 15; T. A. Smail, *Reflected Glory: The Spirit in Christ and Christians* (Hodder and Stoughton, London, 1975), pp. 75-89, 134-52; R. Laurentin, *Catholic Pentecostalism* (Darton, Longman and Todd, London, 1977), pp. 33ff.; H. Mühlen, *A Charismatic Theology: Initiation in the Spirit* (Burns & Oates, London, 1978), pp. 92-105.

7 Dunn, *Baptism in the Holy Spirit*, pp. 33-7.

8 McDonnell, 'The Experience of the Holy Spirit', p. 97.

9 Mühlen, *A Charismatic Theology*, p. 102.

10 This distinction is based on John 14:17. See the critique in F. D. Bruner, *A Theology of the Holy Spirit* (Hodder and Stoughton, London, 1970), pp. 69-70.

11 Mühlen, *A Charismatic Theology*, p. 94.

12 *Theological and Pastoral Orientations on the Charismatic Renewal* ('Malines Document I', 1974), repr. in *Presence, Power and Praise*, vol.I, pp. 13-69.

13 Smail, *Reflected Glory*, p. 150, cf. pp. 40-2.

14 e.g. D. L. Gelpi SJ, *Charism and Sacrament* (SPCK, London, 1977), pp. 150-2 urges a 'life long transformation in the Spirit' but still identifies a 'decisive charismatic breakthrough' or an 'initial charismatic breakthrough'.

15 e.g. S. Tugwell OP, *Did You Receive the Spirit?* (Darton, Longman and Todd, London, 1972), pp. 69-72; F. A. Sullivan SJ, *Charisms and Charismatic Renewal* (Gill and Macmillan, Dublin, 1982), pp. 141-3.

16 Laurentin, *Catholic Pentecostalism*, pp. 45-7.

17 See Smail, *Reflected Glory*, p. 139; Sullivan, *Charisms and Charismatic Renewal*, pp. 65-6.

18 Dunn, *Jesus and the Spirit*, pp. 136-69, 153-6.

19 cf. G. R. Beasley-Murray, *Baptism in the New Testament* (Macmillan, London, 1963), pp. 108-20.

20 A central text here is 1 Corinthians 12:13. Earlier exegesis within the Charismatic Renewal Movement denied that the baptism in the Spirit mentioned in this context was either initiation into the body of Christ or water baptism, translating the preposition *eis* (into) as 'with reference to', e.g. Harper, *The Baptism of Fire*, pp. 11-12. More recent writing has modified this position, as I indicate. Smail, *Reflected Glory*, p. 142, offers an intermediate approach, dividing the parallelism in the verse between initiation (baptism) and experiential participation ('drinking').

21 Dunn, *Baptism in the Holy Spirit*, pp. 226-7.

22 Smail, *Reflected Glory*, pp. 85-8.

23 Mühlen, *A Charismatic Theology*, p. 95.

24 Sullivan, *Charisms and Charismatic Renewal*, pp. 69-75. His approach has been influential among others more actively involved in the renewal movement, though they have not always recognised how much this modifies a concept of 'breakthrough'; cf. Gelpi, *Charism and Sacrament*, pp. 148-9, L. J. Cardinal Suenens, *A New Pentecost?* (Darton, Longman and Todd, London, 1975), pp. 81-6.

25 e.g. Smail, *Reflected Glory*, pp. 61-74, appealing to the older Pentecostal theology of Edward Irving.

26 J. V. Taylor, *The Go-Between God: The Holy Spirit and the Christian Mission* (SCM, London, 1972), p. 51.

27 ibid., p. 221.

28 Tugwell, *Did You Receive the Spirit?* p. 71; cf. 'The Speech-Giving Spirit', in *New Heaven? New Earth?* by S. Tugwell and others (Darton, Longman and Todd, London, 1976) where Tugwell describes tongues as 'Words that have a strangely deep power, and that are at one with the "words" of birds and beasts' (p. 147).

29 W. Hollenweger, *The Pentecostals* (SCM, London, 1972), p. 344.

30 E. D. O'Connor CSC, 'The Holy Spirit, Christian Love and Mysticism', in *Charismatic Renewal*, ed. O'Connor, pp. 133-44.

31 *The Charismatic Movement in the Church of England*, pp. 41-2.

32 *Vatican Council II: The Conciliar and Post Conciliar Documents*, ed. A. Flannery OP (Dominican

Publications, Dublin, 1975), p. 363. The drafting of this paragraph, which was written four years before the generally accepted beginning of the Catholic Charismatic Renewal in 1967, was influenced by Cardinal Suenens. See Suenens, *A New Pentecost?*, pp. 30-2.

33 Mühlen, *A Charismatic Theology*, p. 95.

34 Tugwell, *Did You Receive the Spirit?*, pp. 89-90.

35 Mühlen, *A Charismatic Theology*, p. 59.

36 See Sullivan, *Charisms and Charismatic Renewal*, pp. 29-32; cf. E. Schweizer, *Church Order in the New Testament* (SCM, London, 1961), p. 180; Dunn, *Jesus and the Spirit*, pp. 253-6.

37 Sullivan, *Charisms and Charismatic Renewal*, p. 13; similarly, Laurentin, *Catholic Pentecostalism*, p. 130.

38 For a similar emphasis among Protestant writings, see Hollenweger, *The Pentecostals*, pp. 370-3, A. Bittlinger, *Gifts and Graces* (Hodder and Stoughton, London, 1967), pp. 70-2.

39 A notable exception is Gelpi, *Charism and Sacrament*, affirming that 'Every graced transmutation of experience is endowed with some degree of primordial sacramentality' (p. 107). P. Hocken, 'The Significance and Potential of Pentecostalism', in *New Heaven? New Earth?*, pp. 32-5, urges the need for more reflection on the idea of sacramental efficacy as a means of integrating outward sign and inner reality within charismatic experience.

40 e.g. see the popular account by M. Harper, *As at the Beginning* (Hodder and Stoughton, London, 1965), p. 105f. But J. D. G. Dunn judges that this was also the view of St Paul; see Dunn, *Jesus and the Spirit*, pp. 255-6.

41 cf. Smail, *Reflected Glory*, pp. 124-6.

42 Tugwell, *Did You Receive the Spirit?*, p. 63.

43 Laurentin, *Catholic Pentecostalism*, pp. 158, 157.

44 Mühlen, *A Charismatic Theology*, pp. 175, 179.

45 cf. J. Moltmann, *The Church in the Power of the Spirit*, English translation (SCM, London, 1975), pp. 72-4.

46 H. Wheeler Robinson, *The Christian Experience of the Holy Spirit* (Nisbet, London, 1928), pp. 83, 87.

All Creatures Great and Small: towards a Pneumatology of Life

W. J. HOLLENWEGER

This essay examines western (including charismatic and Pentecostal), Eastern Orthodox, non-white indigenous and Old Testament pneumatologies, and therefore attempts to extend the narrowness of western pneumatologies since Augustine and the Reformation. It reopens the debate on the *filioque* and investigates what these non-western pneumatologies can contribute first to a better understanding of the Charismatic Movements and the non-white indigenous churches and secondly to the questions which are asked today by physicists and biologists on the relationships between matter and energy, between life and 'eternal life'. Finally it suggests some practical consequences for evangelism and mission by starting with the belief that every single person (and not merely every Christian) has the Spirit of God. The notions in this paper are exploratory and provisional and arise from the needs and challenges which face today's Christians, especially in the Charismatic and Pentecostal Movements.

It is generally believed that Pentecostal and Charismatic Movements are particularly strong in their doctrine of the Spirit. This is in my view a serious over-statement if we study their beliefs in depth.

The Aporia of Western Pneumatologies

The two models of pneumatology which we find in the Pentecostal and Charismatic Movements are variations of western pneumatologies. The first is the classical pentecostal doctrine which teaches that after conversion and baptism in water, a further and quite different religious 'crisis experience' is necessary for all believers. This is known by Pentecostals and neo-Pentecostals as 'baptism in (or of) the Spirit'. It is usually, but not always, characterised by the initial physical sign of speaking in tongues. More cautious charismatic groups in the Roman Catholic and Lutheran churches call it 'renewal of baptism', indicating that this second religious experience does not add something substantially new to baptism in water but renews and brings to life what is potentially there through that baptism. In both cases they follow the pattern of Acts 2, Acts 8 and Acts 19 (i.e. the pneumatology of Luke). In all the instances recorded and interpreted by Luke, a further religious experience was necessary in order to bring the disciples in Jerusalem, Samaria and Ephesus up to the standards of fully mature Christians.

The second model of pneumatology, which one finds mainly amongst the theologians of charismatic prayer groups within the mainline churches, rejects any understanding of the Spirit which could be interpreted as different from their own denominational pneumatology. They are inclined to say, 'Since we have become charismatics we understand our own (Catholic, Reformed, Anglican, Lutheran) tradition better; there is no need for a critical review of the pneumatological position of our church; there is, however, a need to prove that we are very faithful adherents of our denomination; charismatic spirituality does not change any of our tunes, but it changes the rhythm and sometimes the key; it does not change our churches, but it lights them up; it does not change our ministry, but it makes it more credible; it does not change our ecumenical commitment, but it makes it more alive.'

I doubt whether this is true or useful. If charismatic spirituality does not change our traditional denominationalism, what is the use of it? Both these models maintain a Christ-centred theology and stand firmly within the western theological tradition. No Pentecostal and no charismatic believer would state that the Spirit differed in any way whatsoever from the Spirit of Christ, the *Christus praesens*. They follow strictly the tradition of the *filioque*, without of course arguing their case with the vocabulary of this late patristic and early medieval controversy. The modern relevance of this controversy to our topic has recently been shown in some significant consultations between Roman Catholic, Protestant and Eastern Orthodox theologians organised by the World Council of

Churches. Their reports are available in *Spirit of God, Spirit of Christ*, edited by Lukas Vischer.[1] The *filioque* has been a serious bone of contention for a long time between the eastern and the western churches. In the western form of the Nicene-Constantinopolitan Creed the term 'and the Son' (therefore *filioque*) was inserted by western theologians in the sentence 'the Spirit proceeds from the Father and the Son', thus defining the work and function of the Spirit as inseparable from the work and function of Christ.

There is no need to examine the details of this controversy here. For our purposes it is enough to summarise the motives for this insertion in the words of the World Council of Churches:

> It can be argued that the *filioque* underlines the fact that the Holy Spirit is none other than the Spirit of Jesus Christ; that this understanding of the Spirit is fundamental to the New Testament witness; and that the *filioque* is a necessary bulwark against the dangers of christologically uncontrolled 'charismatic enthusiasm', dangers against which the churches today need to be on guard.[2]

This statement reflects the opinion of Augustine, John Calvin, Martin Luther and the majority of western theologians (both Protestant and Roman Catholic), including Karl Barth (see *Church Dogmatics* I/1, paragraph 12). In the *filioque* they see a safeguard against free-floating spiritualism. Pentecostals and charismatics follow the western tradition, at least in their writings. This cannot be over-emphasised in the light of all the accusations to the contrary, and it is born out by the hundred or more official documents by and on the Charismatic Movement published by Kilian McDonnell in his *Presence, Power Praise*.[3] The documentation for the Pentecostal churches is contained in my work, *The Pentecostals*.[4]

Eastern Pneumatologies

The eastern theologians have always protested against this overwhelming consensus of the western tradition, mainly because in their opinion a Spirit 'which proceeds from the Father *and the Son*' compromises the unity of the Godhead. I do not want to pursue this argument here but concentrate on the present-day criticism of Old Catholic and Orthodox theologians on the *filioque*. The Old Catholic theologian Herwig Aldenhoven, who belongs to a church which rejects the *filioque*, concludes that the *filioque* is in part responsible for the 'authoritarian view of the Church and ministry', and the professionalisation of the Spirit, which prevails in the west.

If the churches through their ministry are considered to be the normative interpreters of Christ and the sole custodians of the Spirit of Christ, no spirit, be it even the Holy Spirit, can contradict this Church. Taken to its logical conclusion the *filioque* is perhaps more a doctrine about the administration of the Holy Spirit by the Church than a doctrine about the Spirit; in the case of the Roman Catholic Church that leads to a doctrine of the Petrine ministry. Western christocentrism culminates in the dogma of the Pope as Vicar of Christ', states the Orthodox theologian Boris Bobrinsky in the reports by the World Council of Churches.[5] Herwig Aldenhoven holds a similar view: 'Only when recourse to the institutional church is made the main defensive measure against sectarian fanaticism — and here the Bible too assumes the role of an institution — can the *filioque* be used as a theological argument.'[6]

There have always been other traditions in the west, but they have been 'lost' or suppressed in the course of history. I am not thinking so much of theologians like Karlstadt and Schwenkfeld as of the Zurich reformer Huldrych Zwingli and his disciples in the Church of England. Zwingli preferred the eastern to the western tradition. For him the Spirit is not confined to the Church or to the preaching of the gospel. He expects to find pagans in heaven. Maybe it is this (perhaps unconscious) memory of the Zurich reformer (who played a significant part in the early stages of the preparation of the *Book of Common Prayer*) which made the Anglican Church very cautious in her defence of the *filioque*.

So to sum up, the western tradition has restricted its doctrine of the Holy Spirit to the realisation of a Christ-centred theology and the doctrine of salvation. The *creator spiritus*, the life-giving *ruach Yahweh* is a perplexing 'lost' entity for the west. In other words, the pneumatology of Pentecostal and Charismatic Movements shares the deficiencies of the pneumatologies of western tradition.

The question must therefore be asked: what is the precise function of a Holy Spirit who is the prisoner of the Church and its interpretation of the Bible. Is the Spirit superfluous if he only glorifies, increases and carries out the work of Christ? Is the 'risen Christ' not perfectly able to fulfil these functions without the Holy Spirit?

Old Testament Pneumatologies

This is not the whole story. The Word of God, the basis for the doctrine of the Holy Spirit, is of course contained in the Old Testament as well as in the New Testament. In the early Hebrew writings the Spirit is the giver of all life, not just of Christian or religious life. All life is sustained by the breath of God (*ruach Yahweh*). If God withdraws his Spirit, life disappears. No wonder that this Spirit is a woman. *Ruach* is feminine in Hebrew. Furthermore *ruach* is not strictly confined to activities which are morally acceptable to us. Not only good, righteous and religious life, but the whole of life is sustained by her, just as a mother nurtures not only her nice and well-behaved children, but all of them. In fact this Spirit fulfils some of the functions which mother goddesses fulfil in other religions. Man and woman, leviathan and lion, are alive by the Spirit of God: 'Thou sendest forth thy Spirit, they are created . . . Thou hidest thy face, they are troubled. Thou takest away their breath (spirit) they die, and return to their dust.' (Ps. 104:29-30, and see Gen. 2:7). If God calls his Spirit back, then 'all flesh perishes and man shall turn again unto dust' (Job 34:14). That is why Job knew: 'The Spirit of God hath made me, and the breath of the Almighty hath given me life' (Job 33:4).

This Spirit of God is responsible for phenomena and behaviour which we would in modern anthropological language associate with the *force vitale*, such as leadership in peace and war (Judg. 3:10; 6:34), an ecstatic experience like tearing off one's clothes (1 Sam. 11:6; 19:20ff.). The Spirit is responsible for extraordinary strength (Judg. 14:6, 19; 15:14) and in one case a deceiving spirit was employed by God (1 Kgs. 22:19ff.). It may be that this understanding of the Spirit is connected with the view which we find in the book of Job, namely that Satan has access to God, or in modern psychological language, that Satan himself is 'the other side' of God. The Spirit of God does not operate only in God's chosen people. Cyrus, who did not know God, is called 'the anointed' (Isa. 45:1): he is 'a christ'. And even the ass of Balaam is worthy of divine inspiration when the prophet is disobedient, although 'the Spirit' is not expressly mentioned in this context (Num. 22-24).

The same reasons which prompted western theologians to be cautious of a 'free-floating' Spirit made early Israelite prophets cautious in relation to the Spirit. Their criteria were ethical and not primarily related to the *force vitale*. Only when the ecstatic experience of Spirit possession became a thing of the past, could a prophet like the third Isaiah prophecy, 'The Spirit of God rests upon me . . .' (Isa. 61:1f.) As long as the so-called 'Judges' (or perhaps better 'saviours' or 'messiahs') and the *Ish ha-Elohim*, the wonder working 'men of God' were roaming the country proving their Spirit possession by all kinds of extraordinary acts, Hosea, Amos, Jeremiah and Isaiah did not want to be identified with them. Likewise the reformers of the sixteenth century (and many western theologians following them) formulated a pneumatology which was almost identical to their christology, so to give them a weapon in their fight against the enthusiasts of their time.

Non-White Indigenous Pneumatologies

This Old Testament attitude to the Spirit of God is not unlike that held by the 'non-white indigenous churches' of the Third World, which selectively take over religious, political, social and medical traditions of their non-Christian past. As all serious observers know, this is not done indiscriminately. However, their criteria are mostly not ours. With a few exceptions westerners refused to make a thorough investigation and engage in theological debate on these issues by referring to whatever seemed implausible or outside the bounds of their experience as 'superstition', or, in some particularly crude and unhappy instances, 'the devil's work'. No wonder these churches ignore western theology, when it denies the very reasons for their conversion to Christianity, such as healings, dreams and visions. Any missionary knows that many, if not most, converts give as the reason for their conversion a dream, a vision, a healing or another similar experience: people very seldom become Christians merely from hearing the gospel preached.

After their conversion to Christianity, sometimes shamans, herbal doctors or priests introduce into the church some of the skills and insights of their non-Christian past. This has happened both in western missionary churches and in indigenous churches. They also continue to have visions and dreams of their ancestors, including non-Christian ancestors. Western theologians have usually opposed and rejected nearly all these practices, which are nevertheless gaining ground in all Third World churches. After all, we in Europe have also introduced many important features of our non-Christian (Roman, Hellenistic, Germanic or Celtic) past into our liturgy and our theology. One has only to mention Aristotle as an important example of the past and Karl Marx as an example of the present. We would be hard-pressed if we had to argue scripturally for our funeral rites, our remembrance days, the graves of war-lords in our cathedrals, our marriage ceremonies, our ecclesiastical vestments, our theological thought categories, our style of preaching. They are understood to belong to the good and creative things of our own non-Christian past, that is if we do not identify them with Christianity. (Whether these carry-overs always belong truly to the realm of the life-giving Spirit of God is of course another question.) In any case, they show us that we have as a matter of course always accepted the Spirit as present outside and before the coming of the church and the preaching of the gospel.

This process of accepting non-Christian features into the Christian Church and theology has of course to be done with discrimination. Nevertheless, the adoption of thought patterns, liturgical formulations and religious rites from paganism was a continuous process in Israelite religion and in New Testament and European Christianity. What is wrong if Third World churches introduce features of their own non-European cultural and religious past into their form of Christianity? The answer to this question seems to me obvious. We have not yet developed the theological tools for understanding this process. We were not able to attribute the good and life-giving elements in paganism to the Holy Spirit, therefore our theology came into conflict with the experiences of Christians from other cultures.

The difficulty of this position became clear to me when a well-known charismatic leader and professor of systematic theology gave a Bible study at a World Council consultation. His text was 1 Kings 22:19 f. What did he do? Did he accept that the pneumatology of this text (a 'deceiving spirit' employed by God) contradicted his Presbyterian or charismatic understanding of God's Spirit as entirely holy? No, he simply stated that this text had to be interpreted within the context of the whole of scripture. So far so good. One would have expected him to argue his case within the pneumatologies of early Hebrew traditions, the Yahwist, the Elohist, the Deuteronomist, the prophets. But no, to interpret this passage within the context of the whole Bible meant for him to replace this Old Testament pneumatology with the pneumatology of the evangelist Luke. He simply talked about Acts 2, thus perpetuating the well-known game that if we do not like a certain statement in scripture we look for a more suitable passage which is more in line with our understanding, and simply ignore or dismiss the other passages. A modern critical exegete might (perhaps!) be allowed to do this. He might explain away such a passage by appealing to the cultural or religious crudeness of this passage which is no longer acceptable to Christians. But for a charismatic leader who believes in the inspiration of the whole Bible, this is a difficult position to take!

Matter and Spirit

I now want to indicate some areas with which a modern pneumatology would have to deal and I start with Einstein's famous formula which established a relationship between energy and matter. By linking trinitarian theology to this kind of question, however, I depart from the hitherto accepted language about God as exclusively a 'person' or 'three persons in one'.

In its simplest form Einstein's formula reads like this: $E = mc^2$. E stands for energy, m for matter and c for the speed of light. This formula states that matter can be understood as a form of energy and vice versa. It is therefore possible to transform matter into energy, which has of course been achieved for certain forms of matter, and means that matter contains (or better, is equal to) enormous quantities of 'frozen energy'. The formula also deals a death-blow to all world-views which see matter (respectively, energy) as constant in the whole universe. In fact the formula poses serious problems for our understanding of matter. Add to this the later discoveries of the principle of uncertainty and the quantum theory and we realise that the more we discover about the world in which we live the more enigmatic it becomes. Things are not as simple, predictable and linear as we once thought. I do not propose to discuss this issue in detail here, but I have raised it with a number of scientists. For instance I asked a mathematician, rector of a well-known technical university in Germany, how one would nowadays define matter. He looked at me in horror. 'I wish you hadn't asked me that,' he said. In fact we do not know what matter really is. If it is not a definable constant, what is it?

The practical side of this enigma has been known by physicists for some time. John Hasted, Professor of Experimental Physics at the University of London, has examined the changes which occur in objects of stone and metal in the presence of certain adolescent boys. He discovered that the molecular structure of these objects was changed in a way that would normally only be possible under very high temperatures. But he had not measured any high temperatures. The objects had only been exposed to the presence of, and sometimes to a light touch by, these adolescent boys. What are these forces which change and twist stone and metal under strict laboratory conditions, forces which so far are not detectable with the instruments available to us?[7] A corollary to this question would be: what are the forces which heal people of very serious illnesses just by laying on of hands, inside and outside Christianity?

Finally, I have discovered similar discussions amongst the biologists. If we start from the principle of evolution (in spite of all its flaws and shortcomings) then we have to ask the obvious question: what is the next mutation or creative step in the development of the human race? Can we know what evolution of life means? What does chance mean in this context? I do not want to spoil these questions by simply declaring that here we have proof of God's existence, or at least of the creative work of the Holy Spirit. That would be a naïve argument and would add nothing to our knowledge of God and the world. My intention is to show that it is also the theologian's task to understand the world. The scientists in question complained that the theologians they have consulted have shrugged off these questions by saying, 'This has nothing to do with theology. Theology is about religion, that is to say, it is about God and human relationships. We have nothing to contribute to the world of science.'

Have theologians really nothing to contribute? Surely modern scientific enquiry is establishing that the world, matter and energy, the organic and inorganic universe, is much more complex, enigmatic and unpredictable than we have so far imagined. What does it mean that the more questions we answer the more questions we have to ask? Could the Spirit of Life be one way of expressing the question of the relationship between matter and energy, or, theologically speaking, one way of approaching the question of creation? The Spirit of Life is responsible for the life of leviathan and lion, man and woman, good and evil. In short a pneumatology of life brings into focus the question: what holds our universe together? A thinking Christian can express his pneumatology of life in these terms: if God recalls his Spirit, all life ceases; if God lets his Spirit act, life goes on and develops through creations and mutations.

The Spirit, Giver of Life

I rather think it is time to acknowledge that the Spirit is the giver of all life in all cultures and religions and perhaps even the agent which holds our universe together. One might object that because I do not see the Spirit exclusively as a 'person', this is a form of panentheism, and that I am therefore departing from the accepted formula *tres personae, una substantia*. That is true, because I realise that the categories of patristic trinitarian theology, whilst fitting their cultural context admirably, are unable to tackle today's crucial questions. Moreover heresy hunting is sometimes a way of avoiding important issues and defending a sterile status quo. There is a kind of correct orthodoxy which is not based on purity but on sterility and impotence.

However, the charge of panentheism is only justified if that is all that I have to say, restricting myself to the Old Testament pneumatology. This is not my intention, although in this essay I had to emphasise what I consider has been neglected in the past. It seems clear that a pneumatology of life must be firmly based on a new form of trinitarian doctrine which is linked up with the other tenets and traditions of Christian belief, thus demonstrating why the trinitarian doctrine is necessary in order to understand the Spirit both as a 'free-floating' Spirit and an aspect of the Spirit of Christ. The 'free-floating' Spirit only seems 'free-floating' in our experience and perception: from a trinitarian point of view, the Spirit is 'one' with the Father and the Son and cannot therefore be held responsible for whatever we fancy. On the other hand, to be one with the Father and the Son does not mean that the Spirit cannot do things which are outside our understanding of the Bible and Christian tradition. But it has to be made clear how these experiences and insights (in our own and in other cultures) can be understood as expressions of the Spirit of Life. Then not every fancy and every religious exuberance will be acceptable. But the criterion will no longer be whether they are common to us or even thinkable. The Spirit is greater than anything we can envisage. Western theologians will at this stage introduce christological categories but why do they constantly disregard those elements in Christ's ministry which do not fit their categories, such as his healings, his exorcism, his oral style of theology? Ah, they say, these things are just the trappings of revelation, they are only the cultural and historical vehicle of God's revelation. I wonder what the basis is for such a statement?

Perhaps the best way to state the trinitarian relationship can be formulated like this: the question of the relationship between what I have called *force vitale* and the appearance of God's revelation in a man, Jesus of Nazareth, is central to the Christian tradition. Theologically speaking it is the question of the relationship between creation and salvation. Where this question is dismissed as irrelevant, a central concern of Christianity has been abandoned.

The answers to this question can be given in different thought-patterns, in different models and on the basis of different experiences. The ecumenical unity of the Christian church is not based on a common statement but on a common question. That, it seems to me, has always been the role of the great ecumenical creeds, except that we misunderstand them nowadays as answers. To formulate the unity of the Church in a question and not in an answer is necessary because our European and American answers are heavily tainted and conditioned by our cultures, including our non-Christian cultures.

Finally one might ask: but what about the New Testament pneumatologies? Is not the New Testament clear about the Spirit being almost identical with the Spirit of Christ? In general that is true. But there are exceptions, for instance in Acts 2:17 where the Spirit is expected to be poured out on all flesh, not just on Christian or religious flesh. Furthermore, is it not possible to understand New Testament pneumatologies as specific but necessarily exclusive interpretations of Old Testament pneumatologies?

As Hellenistic spirits had overwhelming power in New Testament times, Christians were certain that their Spirit emanated from the living Christ. That is a pastorally legitimate position. In a situation where people have all kinds of useful and not so useful religious experiences, the primary task of a theologian is to distinguish not so much between the demons and the Spirit of God, as between manifestations of the Spirit which are 'for the common good' (1 Cor. 12:7) and those which are not. That is also our task. We might learn from Paul how to handle such a situation. He confirmed the Corinthians in their belief that they had spiritual gifts. He wrote to them: 'I thank my God always on your behalf, for the grace of God which is given you by Jesus Christ; that in every thing you are enriched by him, in all utterance, and in all knowledge; . . . so that you come behind in no gift (charism) . . .' (1 Cor. 1:4-7). This he wrote to a church which was morally, theologically and socially very defiant and which he had to criticise on many issues.

If Paul recognised the Spirit in these people with whom he disagreed on central issues, might we not also acknowledge the Spirit at work outside our plausibility structures, our ethical codes and our priority systems? Once that is granted we might still go on criticising certain issues. But to deny that certain people have the Spirit would demand much more backing — even if we follow Paul's pneumatology. Sometimes I have the impression that we have been so busy map-reading that we forget to step out and see what the Spirit has already done. We have therefore not developed the theological tools which could help us to understand why the Spirit of God is present where the gospel has not been preached and where the Church is not present. Nevertheless, the premonition that the Spirit is there already could encourage us to go and have a look.

So where do we go from here? What I have said is not exhaustive and I am sure that others will issue cautions. That is necessary and healthy so long as the central question, relating to the inadequacy of our pneumatology and our inability to understand what the Spirit does in other cultures, is not missed.

Practical Consequences

If we are prepared to include in our understanding of the Spirit, the Spirit as giver of life, then this will have important implications for mission and evangelism. If the Spirit is in all people, we can invite whoever is willing to co-operate with us 'for the common good'. They can co-operate in our churches whether they are baptised nor not, whether they sign our credal statements or not, because we know that the Spirit is poured out on all flesh. If we consult the New Testament we will discover that Jesus also evangelised along these lines. Jesus asked his disciples to help him (Mark 3:9) before they were really converted (in the case of Peter this is explicitly stated, Luke 22:32). Any missionary and any good evangelist knows that he must first receive before he can give. He needs food, shelter, information about their language, culture and religion, from those whom he wants to evangelise.

It is my experience that many so-called unchurched people are prepared to offer their gifts, their charisms if we ask them to share what they have. Is the denial of charisms in non-Christians or unchurched people one of the reasons for the uneasy relationship between churches and artists, actors, writers and musicians? Many of them want to follow Christ in their vocation, with their gifts. As these do not fit our criteria, their gifts are ignored in the same way as we ignore the gifts of the indigenous Christians of the Third World. If we can recognise the Spirit in unusual places and in unexpected people, in all creatures great and small, we might win new friends.

Notes

1 Lukas Vischer, ed., *Spirit of God, Spirit of Christ: Ecumenical Reflections on the 'filioque' Controversy* (Geneva/London, 1981).

2 ibid., p. 17.

3 Kilian McDonnell, *Presence, Power, Praise: Documents on the Charismatic Renewal*, 3 vols. (Liturgical Press, Collegeville, Minn., 1980).

4 W. J. Hollenweger, *The Pentecostals* (SCM, London, 1972; 2nd edn. 1976).

5 Vischer, *Spirit of God, Spirit of Christ*, p. 136.

6 ibid., p. 130f.

7 The detailed description of the experiments is contained in the highly technical publication by John Hasted, *The Metal-Benders* (London, 1981).

The Political Oeconomy of
the Holy Ghost

DAVID MARTIN

What follows is a reflection on the relationship between things held
to be by the action of the Holy Ghost and the exercise or exhibition
of social power. Such a reflection is primarily sociological, since the focus
of attention is on the way an invocation of the Spirit may be used to
legitimate authority in the Church or make acceptable some demonstra-
tion of charismatic influence. The processes whereby men claim legitimacy
and secure acceptability are of central concern to sociology. Nevertheless,
from time to time I shall have to desert the role of sociologist and invoke
theological, psychological and moral criteria in order to make evaluative
judgements. If I say that a particular deployment of the Holy Ghost
to buttress power is in my view illegitimate, I am using criteria beyond
the scope of sociology. My initial comments will focus on hieratic
authority, and I go on later to look at the charismatic power of the
Spirit in less established groups.

The Many Names and Forms of the Spirit

Let me begin by sketching a framework for thinking about the Holy
Ghost, more especially for thinking about how he is held to operate
today. To speak of the Holy Ghost is, I take it, to re-identify what
the ancient Hebrews called *Ruach*. *Ruach* is the breath or wind of the
Spirit which came upon Old Testament prophets, driving them to give
utterance, and sometimes causing them to shake and quake physically.
Even in the Old Testament this 'rushing mighty wind' could seize whole

groups with an irresistible contagion. It could dissolve the companies of the 'prophets' into collective ecstasy. Not everybody approved of these manifestations, and when King Saul was carried away by an ecstatic wind he encountered the sardonic query 'Is Saul also among the prophets?'

King Saul provides more than one illustration of the ambiguity attending the activities of the 'Spirit'. Not only did he dance in the company of the prophets but his soul was darkened by an evil spirit. He called up the Witch of Endor, who allowed him illicit communication with the 'spirit-world'. And he was at the same time the one whom the spirit prompted Samuel to anoint with the holy chrism, the oil which made him the Lord's anointed, and gave him kingly authority and a certain immunity. Saul then exemplifies a wide range of spiritual operation, and shows us why it is important, as the New Testament says, to 'discern the spirits, whether they be of God'. Nowadays certain transmutations (or if you like secularisations) have occurred, which mean that we use different languages to refer to 'spiritual' phenomena. The 'election' of the Lord's anointed, signified and achieved by the chrism, is now a political election which asserts *vox populi, vox Dei*; the exorcism of minds infected or possessed by evil spirits is usually a matter for pscyhology; and communication beyond the scope of normal science is the province of parapsychology, even though specialised spirit mediums also offer their services.

However, these carefully controlled adoptions of the elect, these seizures, both benign and maleficent, and these occult (or hidden) communications, do not exhaust the range of spiritual operation. The Spirit works on an even wider scale. He is the Creator Spirit, who brooded over the face of the primal chaos and breathed into man so that he became animated. The animation of humankind is the emergence of the living soul. Since man is made in the image of the Creator, the Spirit is also the source of human inspiration, and by extension of human genius. The word inspiration means 'to be breathed into', and genius implies a tutelary spirit, or a daemon, hence such terms as evil genius and daemonic. Once again, the dark side of the spirit appears, and we have it yet again in the ambiguous genii who emerge from captivity in a bottle. Who knows where the genie may take us?

Of course, we are already noticing both the religious context of such

Romantic notions as 'genius' and the way the religious language may
be extended into vaguer realms, some of them doubtfully Christian,
even secular. Mahler in his eighth symphony combined both by invoking
the Spirit in the *Veni Creator Spiritus* and by using Goethe's Faust.
Certainly spiritual phenomena are not trapped in the ecclesiastical zoo,
but can be viewed as general characteristics of the human world, whether
we consider a shaman or a Beethoven. Shelley wrote 'The Necessity
of Atheism' but in 'Adonais' he apostrophised the soul of the dead Keats,
returned to the bosom of the world-spirit.

> The breath whose might I have invoked in song
> Descends on me...

So we may say in summary that the Spirit has to do with power, might
and efficacity, and our conception of him slides imperceptibly through
the theological gamut towards less specific formulations where he loses
the capital 'S' and may become plural: spirits. What is dogmatically
defined in the so-called Athanasian Creed, may break loose in some new
Age of the Spirit, such as was proclaimed by Bianco da Siena and the
Abbot Joachim. Spirit may merge with everything that has life and breath,
or slide into Platonic or pantheistic notions of an energy which moulds
chaotic substance into pattern and form. We are, therefore, dealing with
the power of energy, with endowment and with animation. A more
awkward field for sociology is difficult to imagine, since we are trespassing
on the springs of creativity, its manifold powers and its ambiguous,
equivocal energies.

   Once the orthodox doctrine of the Spirit is examined more closely,
the focus of concern is hardly less daunting. One of the sevenfold gifts
attributed to the Holy Ghost is the power of social integration:

> Dissolve litis vincula
> Adstringe pacis foedera

The Paraclete is to dissolve the chains of enmity and preserve the bond
of peace. He is therefore that Spirit of Unity, invoked by churches and
by sects, as the power that binds. His freedom is a certain kind of bonding,
which includes the social bond. The Roman Church invokes Him as the

source of apostolic unity, and so does the Reverend Moon's 'Holy Spirit Association for the Unification of World Christianity'.

Creation, life, prophecy, inspiration, animation, endowment, energy, power, grace and unction: these seem too multiform and metaphysical for social analysis. Yet the exercise and channelling of power is a major sociological concern, and so, too, is the maintenance of the bond of unity. But such notions have to be earthed in an analysis of the way settled channels of spiritual power are made legitimate, and in ideas concerning the energies and claims which maintain social integration. How is spiritual power deployed and checked by legitimate authority and how is the social bonding of faith serviced and maintained? More than that we have an interest in the way the Spirit can be used to leap over local boundaries and either create wider, more ecumenical loyalties, or else foment new schisms. He breaks across boundaries and cuts bonds as much as He maintains internal unity and social integration. The warmth of the Spirit, symbolised in fire, leads to heat and then to fission, or else it inaugurates a boundaryless social world of spirit-filled beings, Brethren of a Free Spirit of of a New Age, united only by spiritual affinity. Thus, the Spirit not only blows 'from out the boundless deep' but can animate the soul with Faustian energies and a hubristic spirit which is eventually 'out of bounds'. He sustains bonds; He cuts them; He leaps, so far as may be, out of social bondage altogether.

Legitimated power, canalised energy, integrated bonds, together with schismatic convulsions, characterise churches and sects, while the apprehension of a free-floating spiritual affinity by signs and by signals is one of the principal social modalities of our contemporary world. I would like to concentrate my discussion of spiritual powers on the way churches and sects handle the notion of approved channels, and then finally to look at the way the churches have partly succumbed to sectarian understandings of special powers or 'gifts' or else to the apprehension of vague spiritual affinities through the giving and receiving of signs.

The Spirit and the Churches

When we look at the Spirit as understood and manifested in ecclesiastical bodies, we are trying to understand how 'spirit' is placed at the command of designated functionaries or corporate authorities. (An account of how the spirit is channelled by those set aside in orders or by those in synods who give orders, does not, of course, touch in any way on the validity of ecclesiastical claims.)

The priest invoking the spirit, is not, of course, a shaman inviting spirit possession. You do not expect an Episcopal or Roman priest half way through the consecration, to emit a loud shriek and writhe convulsively on the altar steps. Such things may occur, of course, particularly in today's climate of free-floating liturgy, and Saint Joseph of Cupertino is alleged to have emitted awesome shrieks before levitating far above the congregation. What normally occurs is an invocation carried out by those who have received a 'valid' ordination, within the designated genealogy exemplified by the 'apostolic succession'. All these successions, ordinations and valid celebrations illustrate the canalisation of the spirit in legitimate forms, and, moreover, in forms which express the unity and integrity of ecclesiastical bodies over time.

Sacramental theory is a focusing of spiritual power, *hic* et *nunc*, here rather than there, at the command, or if you prefer, at the sacred word, of the priest. For some people, including the traditional Catholic anthropologist Mary Douglas, this is institutionalised magic: the sacred word, once spoken, alters a substance, and makes real the divine presence. Others may see the whole ritual performance as a transforming symbolism, reified by Aristotelian terminology of accidence and substance, and debased into recondite hocus-pocus,[1] at the service of the priestly caste. But, in any case, it is certainly a claim to power, by virtue of a designated priestly character and of a channel of legitimate ordination and succession. According to such claims, if I attend a holy meal of saki and rice in a Japanese Holiness Church, I am at best present at a shadow sacrament, one which is defective as to intention, outside the true succession, and lacking in the precise form which guarantees the sacramental substance and 'real presence'. To the Japanese pastor, of course, we are exhibiting a right spirit by sharing the meal. The spirit of unity and truth is manifested in us, by us and through us, in our common actions.

The claim to potency and efficacy is also made with respect to the collective action of the religious body, though the location of the power varies. It may rest in episcopal collegiality, in the Holy Synod, in General Councils or in papal pronouncements in which the Pope speaks vicariously for Christ. All these are instances of the way churches canalise the authoritative, definitive, last word. *Il Papa*, and/or the College of Bishops have the last and final word, by the power of the spirit vested in them. We are, therefore, concerned with a central theme of R. K. Fenn in his book *Liturgies and Trials*, which is authoritative speech.[2] The Spirit is called on to guarantee this special speech, just as he is called on in some liturgies, especially those of the Eastern Church, to 'realise' the sacramental sign (or even to bring the dead 'material' to life and to resurrection).[3] To rephrase the matter, whether we deal with the enunciation of collective doctrine or the institution of the sacrament, our concern is with realisation: making real, realising the truth. 'Institution' is both the original 'act' ('our Saviour Christ's most holy institution') and the settled, continuous social condition. It is difficult to imagine a more inclusive claim to potency and spiritual power.

This power not only inspires awe, but is a terror towards heretics and dissidents. Heresy means 'choice' and when choice is exercised it has to be (if I may use the correct ecclesiastical word) inhibited. Ecclesiastical discipline is the inhibition of choice by reference to the standard formula, 'It seemed good to the Holy Ghost and to us.'

If I may give a personal illustration of how this may be wielded in practice, even today, a bishop attempted to reprimand and presumably also to 'inhibit' me by saying 'You have set yourself up against the mind of the Church and the Holy Spirit.' I remained extremely uninhibited, but the technique which he used is as standard as one may think it is outrageous. It asserts that the Holy Spirit has been bottled up in an episcopal or synodal flask, and guaranteed by an *appellation controlée*.

The Spirit can also be deployed by ecclesiastical authorities to ease them out of traditions in which they no longer believe, or which they regard as 'distorting'. Just left with the power of the father (whether it be the Almighty Father or fathers-in-God) they would be able only to pronounce what was previously pronounced, but the Spirit gives them leave to utter something different. The bishop in the example just cited was actually reprimanding me for stating the doctrine and holding to the liturgy which he was himself ordained to state and uphold. But armed with the Spirit he was able to ease himself into a new position. The advantage of appealing to the Spirit is that He can release you from the letter, as and when you need it, and be mobilised behind a vagueness of which the bishop is the designated interpreter.

I used the word 'mobilisation' because I am talking of moves, both political moves and theological shifts. A new authoritative 'move' finds the invocation of the Holy Spirit (or just the 'spirit' of the text of a founder or saint) very useful. Those intent on destroying the substance of Cranmer's great liturgy appealed to the Holy Spirit, as guiding them, and to the 'spirit' of Cranmer. They also appealed to the importance of the spirit in which words are said as distinct from the form and substance of the words. The Spirit can, therefore, legitimate both authority and subjectivity, and especially the subjectivity of those set in authority.

From the point of view of ecclesiastical authority, 'the Spirit' is an all-purpose legitimator. He is discerned 'at work' in committees, even according to one bishop, in bodies like the Liturgical Commission. A decisive alteration can be achieved by asking the Spirit to brood over his previous authoritative revelations, and select those which remain true. The Spirit leads us 'into all truth', and this means that He can reveal which of His previous revelations were really true, or true for us in our time, supposing we have given up the concept of really true. For example, he can direct us to find an authoritative pronouncement in the eucharistic prayers of Hippolytus Romanus, on the ground that he is 'early' or primitive, and simultaneously release us from some of the pronouncements of St Paul on the ground that he is so very early and uncomfortably 'primitive' that he may be ignored.[4] The Holy Spirit can cancel St Paul's revelation, even though it is the earliest we have, on the ground that it is 'distorting' and 'culture bound'. This is very advantageous for an authority seeking *aggiornamento*, since it allows a cancellation of culture bound revelations in the past in favour of the revelations of our own culture. In this way the Holy Spirit of truth may be invoked to secure the undisturbed reign of *Zeitgeist* i.e. the spirit of the age against which the New Testament inveighs so ceaselessly.

The Spirit of Truth is the Spirit of Wisdom, or Sophia, and he (or she) shows the wisdom of ecumenism in the role of Spirit of Unity. It can be argued first of all that we are all unified in the spirit, or alternatively in spirit. I make the distinction between 'in the Spirit' and 'in spirit' because all sorts of subtle shifts are associated with the removal of the capital 'S' and the definite article. For example, as we move away from 'It seemed good to the Holy Spirit and to us' we gradually find ourselves 'agreed in spirit' after the fashion so magnificently set out in John Wesley's sermon 'On the Catholic Spirit' where he says 'Is thine heart as my heart?' Defined dogmas here dissolve into warmed hearts. This makes for tolerance and ecumenical progress, but it means that the Spirit of Truth i.e. orthodoxy, becomes the 'truth' which we subjectively share 'in spirit'. The Spirit of Truth is then made to serve the cause of ecumenism by losing his capital letter and the definite article.

The Roman Church can deploy the Spirit (or the condition of being 'in spirit') to achieve whatever ends and conclusions authority may desire. Newman, for example, showed how the whole extended growth of Roman doctrine was to the New Testament as oak is to seed. The 'development' from seed to oak by the directing energies of the Spirit of Wisdom, Unity and Truth was inevitable. This has the rhetorical advantage of enabling extremely tiny seeds in the New Testament to become by far the largest oaks, overshadowing the other oaks, and quite altering the weight and principal direction of the original documents. Alternatively, when this 'development' becomes ecumenically inconvenient, or somehow not quite right by the standards of some localised *Zeitgeist*, the Spirit of Truth can lead sophisticated searchers to discover that the Roman Church never really claimed to say this or that, or to find (say) that the word 'sacrifice' applied to the eucharist, never really meant what it appears to mean. Thus the Church is not only able to make 'real' the divine presence, but is also able to show that what it taught previously was not what it really meant. This singular ability, embodied in a subtle polity, may be thought to account for the survival of the Roman Church, as indeed Lord Macaulay claimed in his Essay on von Ranke's *History of the Popes*. (The Anglican Church has proceeded somewhat differently by setting store on ambiguous formularies, susceptible to a rather wide range of interpretation. This also assists survival, though at a certain price in social and intellectual coherence.)

The Spirit and the Sects

When I turn to the spirit as it is held to work in the 'sects', I have no tight definition in mind as to what 'sectarian' connotes. I merely want to indicate *gemeinschaftliche* groups of a voluntary kind, especially those which stress conversion into tight cells of committed Christians, or else lay stress on the elect who are to be saved in the great and terrible day of wrath.

Sects often begin by using or invoking the Spirit to modify or reject tradition. However, the Spirit which legitimates such change is not always invested in a collective hierarchy but in individual leaders, around whose successive and even contradictory revelations the faith of the whole group may pivot. Characteristically an individual receives a peremptory invitation by the Spirit and he (or quite often she) reluctantly obeys. The Spirit acts as a spontaneous insertion into the inert body of tradition, and takes particular persons out of themselves to proclaim a new gospel. In this way, Joanna Southcott, for example, obeyed the leadings of the Spirit. For that matter, the New Testament opens with a new birth in the Spirit (*de spirito sancto*) announced by spiritual messengers. The gospel opens with the claim of Jesus that 'The spirit of the Lord is upon me', just as the disciples on the day of Pentecost began by referring back to the prophecy of Joel about a pouring out of the Spirit on all flesh. Thus the freedom of the Spirit as embedded in scripture is used to widen the range of options to include a new revelation.

The re-reading of tradition or of an 'old' testament has to be done 'in the spirit'. Sects and new movements derive their justification from a selective re-reading of a revered text and this is made acceptable by appeals to 'the spirit' of that text and to whatever invocations of a free spirit are embedded in it, as well as to 'signs' of the spirit which can be taken as accreditation. The new revelation has to locate itself and find its sense of direction by a careful placement of the new charisma in the context of the old. Thus Jesus was taken up in the spirit and conversed with Moses and Elijah whom Jewish tradition defined as representing the law and the prophets. In exactly the same way, Mr Moon claims to have had spiritual converse with Moses, Buddha and Christ, in order to place himself at the strategic convergence of distinct genealogies. The Spirit usually insists on placing a new revelation 'in line' i.e. in a historical genealogy.

Since the sect or new movement cannot usually be as relaxed as the Church, which broods very slowly over traditions placed in hierarchically ordered strata, the re-reading tends to become stereotyped. The text, momentarily warmed up and fluid, sets again, even harder than before. Key phrases are iterated which firm up and establish the character of the new revelation. This also provides a stereotyped vocabulary, key phrases, passwords and a selection of proof-texts which serve to identify believers and exclude the uninitiated. Discussion is reduced to the swapping of proof-texts. (This, however, is by no means confined to sects. Jewish and Catholic disputations in the Middle Ages also turned to a considerable extent on proof-texts).

Those who are initiated into the vocabulary are implicitly examined for the right use of passwords. Some of these may well be pious ejaculations, emitted at the height of collective fervour. These phrases, repeated in unison, work up through a kind of stylised cadenza and easily become hypnotic chants and incantations. At this point a common ecstasy may seek to rise above the text, and even to dispose altogether with a settled verbal sequence. Utterance shifts away even from ejaculations with distinctive meaning, like 'Allelujah', or 'Praise Him', towards huge portentous syllables. These are sibylline prophecies, hidden from the wise and initiated, revealed to open hearts, and interpreted by love.

It is almost as if the high poetry of liturgy composed in a sacred language, such as Latin, Old Slavonic, Arabic or Elizabethan English, has gone one stage further into an uncluttered empyrean where it is pure sign. This level above language (which is also, as I will suggest, below language) serves as a vehicle of spontaneity, though there are fairly strict rules as to who is to be spontaneous, when, and for how long. The spinning rota of spontaneous utterance allows each person to give free passage to 'the Spirit' and to play their own cadenza.

Babel is reversed, and the universal speech of Pentecost is achieved by a return to an analogue of baby-talk. Those who give way to this baby-talk may even be seen as simply babbling. Thus pure spontaneity is open to various interpretations. It could be the triumphant but entirely subordinated 'I' which the executant experiences after he has appropriated a musical score so that he becomes a free re-creator, momentarily restored in the divine image. It could, however, be that collapse of all levels of rationality which takes the 'child' back to a total dependence. This collapse, which is really a melting down of the psyche, allows the group to imprint its seal indelibly. The soul of the neophyte is imprinted in a manner which seals him away from all exterior influences and doubts.

The molten wax hardens in the image of one sole seal. Here then, we have a power of speech which holds a group together by the bonds of the Spirit: an *esprit de corps*. The rational sequence of ordered liturgical speech may indeed mark the soul, but boundaryless babble can finally seal it.

The power of stamping and sealing the soul is also redeployed as the stamp and seal of authority. The group imprint, which looks as if it is democratically placed on all, is mediated by group leaders armed with a word of power. The power of the word, which makes the speaking of man or woman impressive and forceful, is translated into social power and force. All charismatic speech and all powerful exhortations are equal, but the words of some are weightier than the words of others. Even in the Society of Friends the egalitarian eloquence of a shared silence is most often broken by those who are known to be 'weighty Friends'. In the prayer meeting there are those who sway the other brothers as the Spirit gives them utterance.

This power of exhortation or sheer charismatic force, is intuitively recognised and leads to concentrations of authority more individual and therefore more arbitrary than the authority vested in collective hierarchies. In many groups it is precisely those whose tongues have the power of utterance who act as keepers of the house, inducting, controlling and expelling. Thus egalitarianism, as so often, contains and to some extent, creates authoritarianism.

One key technique of an authoritative person with a 'strange gift' is the rapid deployment of selected texts against dissidents. Often some quirk of individual behaviour can be eliminated by an appeal to these texts. The 'pride' of individuality can be quelled by a barrage of quotation. Appeals to humility and meekness as necessary virtues are useful cloaks for a demand that others submit. As in churches so in sects submission to God is subtly re-used to ensure submission to his appointed messengers. Docility literally means teachability and it is docility which ensures doxological conformity, or sheer obedience.

People in such groups are made docile, even as they are also 'given a voice' (or a tongue). They may, of course, exchange pious thoughts within the marked out ambit of texts, and they will ponder the scripture in their hearts, but the open, individual use of discursive reason, especially a use which arrives at new combinations outside the charmed circle of accepted ideas, must be *anathema Maranatha*! The guardians are armed with terrible words to anathematise those who desire free use of mind and imagination. The terror of inquisition, which means the right to cross-examine, is revived in the small religious group. Thus, when my daughter, aged sixteen, was inducted into such a group, and then proceeded to use her accustomed freedom of imagination, the woman on whom charismatic power had settled, identified in her a liturgical 'spirit of contentiousness'. The rampant will of the group was then displayed in prolonged prayer, which they called 'exorcism', supposedly 'for' her, but effectively against her. In the group view, she did not have the 'right spirit', and they were determined to 'renew a right spirit within her'. To the outside observer this may seem a paradigm case of charisma turning graceless. The woman's name was Grace. The injunction 'Quench not the Spirit, despise not prophesyings' is used precisely to quench the spirit.

Here, of course, we enter that dark area which the New Testament describes as 'discerning the spirits'. God and the devil change places and faces, good switches with evil, without an obvious change of vocabulary. (Indeed, my daughter commented that the identity of their vocabulary with what she was familiar obscured the way the 'spirit' had acquired a malign countenance). Even the idea of exposing a counterfeit is used by counterfeiters to buttress threatened power. The reality of counterfeiting cannot be shown by sociology, since it is as invisible to science as is 'bad faith' or 'false consciousness'. Nevertheless, it is a crucial question as to when seeming charisma has become counterfeit force. The express image of God, implanted in the soul, can be the visage of Satan. The highest moments and manifestations allow precisely this switching and terrifying ambiguity. When is God really 'Old Nobodaddy' in disguise?

The authorities in religious groups claim the right to decide this very question. They question the spirits and cast out devils, and show no doubt that they act 'in his name'. The name they appeal to is a power as strong as the formalised *In Nomine Domine*, 'In the Name of the Father, the Son and the Holy Ghost', spoken by ordained priests, and their excommunication is just as real. To exorcise devils and demons is their right, though it is as dangerous as the power of inquisition. Docility before the chosen interpreter is pushed one step further towards absolute obedience.

A figure of authority, charismatically endowed, steps into the arena of the soul to challenge a resistant demon, who could be a split mind or a dormant faculty of reason. At any rate, devils cry and cower at a name which could be divine or could equally well be that of Beelzebub, the prince of devils. Sometimes the pathology of the soul is under threat from a pathological authority. Huge figures of arbitrary evil emerge, paralleling the exemplary figure of authoritative goodness. What in the Church is the canalised authority of the keys, switching the role of vicar of Christ and anti-Christ, becomes in the sect individual capacity for immense good or evil. Perhaps that is why Anselm, commenting on Christ said *aut Deus aut homo non bonus*, either God or not a good man.

These unearthly powers are obviously dangerous. Communication with spirits has always been seen as ambiguous at best, and the power of the Roman Catholic Church has been used to prohibit such communication. The untrammelled imagination finds all kinds of spurious validation in what it takes to be converse with the forces and spirits of the air. To command in the spirit world, to call up spirits from the vasty deep or from the bowels of the earth is a kind of hubris. One speaks, of course, in symbolic terms of realities which are given non-Christian names by psychology. Anthony Burgess has given plenty of warnings about this area in his *Earthly Powers*, and Robert Browning long before him rebutted counterfeit claims in *Mr Sludge the Medium*: 'But for God? Ay, that's a question!'

The Spirit of the Sects now in the Churches

So far, I have described some of the ways the Church may deploy the authority of the Holy Ghost and the manner in which some sectarians have invoked and utilised what they claim is His divine power. But I must conclude by noting the way those phenomena which for convenience I call 'sectarian', have appeared in the 'Church' of recent years. Everything I have said about the dangers of unbounded 'spirit' amongst sectarians now applies to parts of the traditional churches.

Alongside the canalisation of the Holy Ghost to subserve the hierarchies of ecclesiastical power, there now runs a sort of electro-convulsive therapy, both clearing the brain and destroying some of the crucial networks of cerebration. The old cure of souls, which is the work of compassionate persons — or parsons — ordained to celebrate, admonish and absolve, has broken out in a new kind of cure, working by contagious excitation. This can show itself in speech which radiates personal authority, or spill over in a flow of grace which shakes the whole body. It can undermine the centres of reasoned control and criticism, and lay claim to powers which expel demonic forces.

These outburst of primitive energy in all their potent ambiguity are quite intimately related to the liturgical dislocations of the last two decades. The traditional liturgy of the English church was a conductor of energies and exhibited them in disciplined shapes. The familiar recitations and even incantations conveyed an incandescence which was tempered by rigorous intelligence and imaginative genius. Every sentence, every sequence of thought, lived, moved and worked by a high and constant pressure. Now, however, the pressure has been slackened and a bland surface has replaced shapes which held iconic and archetypal power. The new liturgy considered as text has become dispirited, and spiritless. Being 'constructed' it doesn't recognise that 'the communication of the dead is tongued with fire beyond the language of the living.'

A dislocation of the liturgy is a dislocation of a profound human desire for a succession and a genealogy. A whole line of fraternity is disrupted. But the doctrinal disturbance is equally important because a break in the visible line of the fathers has been complemented by an uncertainty about the authoritative Father, *Pater omnipotens* and a parallel uncertainty about all analogous authorities, the 'Holy Father', fathers-in-God, padres in general. People who had been obedient and inclined to trust established paternalisms, metaphysical and ecclesiastical, became disoriented.

With the liturgical words, literally, taken out of their mouths, the continuities gone, and the authorities somehow naked, many Christians were ready for an invasion of the Spirit. He was, after all, defined as free, spontaneous, creative, capable of breaking in or breaking out. With the old boundaries gone the Spirit might blow where He listed. For some He was a sense of warmth breathing new life into themselves and into old formulae. Many have testified as much. For others He was the enticing, inviting religious equivalent of the encounter group, capable of touching all, and making all touch, with a spirit which broke down all divisions, including the partitions or spaces between people. He could break down 'defensible space' and open up the tight-lipped so that they could speak freely. For yet others the Spirit could be assimilated to a new 'process theology', since He was the vital breath animating all sentient life. His vesture was the created world, his creatures and instruments the imaginative geniuses of science and art. The fixity of the Father-God, out or up there, became a new fluidity and plasticity realised in the spirit. The spirit was understood panentheistically, struggling for release and expression in and through the resistant stuff of the visible world.

So for some new life was breathed into old formulae and for others fixity dissolved in animated fluidity, whether that fixity was the psyche or the whole universe. Both the reanimated, orthodox, and the liberal proponents of the universal spark, saw in the Spirit, with or without a capital 'S', a vehicle of unity. 'Names and sects and parties fall' proclaimed Charles Wesley, and for warmed hearts two centuries later, the Spirit was the power which ended denominational boundaries. He leapt over the partitions, uniting denominations as well as banishing the spaces and reticences which separated people. Here one aspect of the evangelical revival came to a late fruition. John Wesley in his great sermon 'The Catholic Spirit' spoke of the love which generated a catholic spirit so that a man might give 'his hand to all whose hearts are right with his heart'. Here, the subjective union of warmed hearts is clearly paramount. It found religious and secular echoes in the spirit of the sixties. People in the sixties were above all against objective, classical form, such as would discipline and inform the psyche, and against everything which could separate men and women from 'their even Christians'. Within the upper echelons of the Church a newspeak, slippery and subtly manipulative, was developed and proclaimed as a 'language of reconciliation'.

Clearly, one may think that there are both gains and losses. Certain people hitherto dumb or tongue-tied found their tongue and felt they had a voice in the Church; or they simply believed they had discovered a new self outside the limits of manners and ritual restraints. The charismatic buzz of the kiss of peace would break things down. On the other hand, the mandatory embrace of smiling enthusiasts was a sort of organised invasion of other selves. If that was not particularly disturbing on its own account, the new communalism served to induct individuals into happy, holy, healthy cells of the like-hearted. The openness of the saved (or of the liberated) towards each other had closed off the outside world. Within these cells the reticence of reason or of personal meditation was disallowed. Awareness of God became a clerically-orchestrated group consciousness.

The older, and cooler, liturgy had allowed space to persons without being intrusively or impertinently personal. Victor Turner, the Roman Catholic anthropologist, has commented on the importance of this space. A person attending the Tridentine Mass might be in a church thronged with people, but his eyes would not be on them, but directed towards the objective action of the Mass. He would move between the reticence of his own personal space, and collective affirmations, without thrusting his own selfhood on others or they in turn pushing their personalities at him. The new liturgy broke all this down, and insisted on the spirit of the communal circle. With the spirit evacuated from the words it had to be renewed in communal actions.

So, in various ways the traditional churches became simultaneously more ecumenical and more sectarian. Sometimes this meant spontaneous joy, sometimes mandatory jollity. It is, of course, characteristic of the sectarian smile that it becomes fixed. The liberating rush of the spirit degenerates into an emotional fix. The urge to rejoice ends up as a vogueish insistence on 'celebration'. A 'warmed heart' such as Methodism celebrated settles down and becomes merely methodical. The warmth of united hearts shifts towards fission and towards the heated disputes of rival claimants to the one true Spirit.[5]

It has all happened many times before. Primitive energy rushes up through all the vents and apertures, and produces Holy Rollers, Quakers and Shakers. In the upshot the balanced incantation of the liturgy is often reduced to one or two hypnotic basic rhythms, gut responses, holy ejaculations, existential grunts and signs. The supposed 'vain repetitions' of classical liturgy becomes a few stereotyped phrases passed around like so many passwords, and providing substitutes for thought. Of course, it can sometimes come close to a profound meditative mysticism, so that one sees a link between the invocation of 'Jesus, Jesus, Jesus' and the Jesus Prayer of Eastern Orthodoxy. But it can also come close to an inward-looking cant, such as Ben Jonson satirised in *The Alchemist*. How you judge these alternative possibilities is how you will

judge the contempoary outbreak of strange gifts. Whichever way the
judgement goes, the diversion of these gifts for the purposes of authority
is clear, whether it is exercised in traditional hierarchies or by the
charismatic leaders of enthusiastic cells.

Conclusion

At best, we might conclude with Augustine of Hippo,

> So men who sing like this — in the harvest, at the grape picking, in
> any task which totally absorbs them — may begin by showing this con-
> tentment in songs with words; but they soon become filled with such
> a happiness that they can no longer express it in words, and tearing
> aside syllables, strike up a wordless chant of jubilation.

At worst, we might conclude with Shakespeare 'the Devil hath power
to assume a pleasing shape.' Shakespeare gave these words to Hamlet
when he saw a ghost which might have been far from holy. Unholiness
is one of the major hazards with ghosts.

Notes

1 *Hoc est corpus meum* is one disputable derivation for the term hocus-pocus.
2 R. K. Fenn, *Liturgies and Trials: The Secularization of Religious Language* (Blackwell, Oxford,
   1982).
3 Technically, this invocation is known as the epiclesis.
4 The *Pax* may be legitimated as third century practice, but the first century practice of not
   allowing women to speak in church can be passed over.
5 Although from time to time I have indicated the problem which arises as we move from Spirit
   with a capital 'S' to spirit without one, there is a further important area which has been altogether
   omitted: spirit possession in African 'spiritist' churches, where such possession, and the healing
   powers associated with it, lie part way between indigenous religions and Christianity. (There
   is yet another area which has to do with spirit possession or commerce with 'spirits' in, for
   example, Brazil where the spirit cults form a kind of localised alternative source of 'power'
   to Roman Catholicism.)
       However, it is useful to make one or two observations by referring to the study by Robert
   W. Wyllie, *Spiritism in Ghana* (Scholars Press, Edwards Brothers, Ann Arbor, 1980). First,
   the genealogy which traces developments in Latin America and elsewhere back to Methodism
   is also traceable in Ghana. Second, although gifts can in theory be bestowed on anyone,

in practice they are claimed only by pastors, the local prophets, and a few of the more 'gifted' members. (These gifts, incidentally, are not primarily manifested in speaking with tongues or interpreting them.) Third, whereas Sundkler notes how in Zionist churches 'the serfdom of the formula' is established in the name of the freedom of the spirit, a process I have noted above, this does not occur in these Ghanaian groups. Nevertheless, it seems to me to be a very widespread tendency in 'spiritual' religion.

Speaking in Tongues

C. G. WILLIAMS

Speaking in tongues, or, to give it its technical name, glossolalia, has attracted much attention recently. It has been central in the worship of Pentecostalism and prominent, though perhaps in less exuberant fashion, in the contemporary Charismatic Renewal, which was formerly in fact referred to as neo-Pentecostalism. Speaking in tongues consists in the utterance of unintelligible sounds, often in rapid sequences, by persons who seem to be in conditions of varying degrees of dissociation. The utterance is attributed by those who practise it to divine inspiration and identified with the phenomenon described in the narrative of Pentecost in Acts 2 and in St Paul's first letter to the Corinthian church (1 Cor. 12-14). However, there has been no dearth of critics and no lack of disapproval. It has been dismissed as incoherent gibberish, described as the vomit of Satan, categorised as the emotional extravagance of the socially deprived or as the morbid outbursts of psychological misfits. Others regard it as an attempt at pseudo language. The curious may ask quite bluntly whether this strange phenomenon is of God, of man, or of the devil, but before we attempt any answer, an indication must be given of some of the implications of the question.

Any study of glossolalia needs to take full cognisance of how glossolaliacs themselves understand the phenomenon. Modern research, which has too often neglected this phenomenological principle, has extended into many areas of investigation such as psychology, anthropology, sociolinguistics, and the study of related phenomena in cultural studies by historians of religion. Obviously no one can be expert in all these fields but some attempt needs to be made to correlate the findings of these different approaches and the biblical scholar and the theologian likewise need to be aware of some of the most important work in these areas. This is not so as to follow the most recent fashion but in order to be able to focus more deeply on what, if anything, is peculiarly and distinctively Christian in the glossalia of Christian groups; to realise, with firmer conviction, the dangers of reductionism; and to dispel or affirm notions of the elusiveness of the inner experience.

Glossolaliacs contend that the mind is passive in the act of speaking with tongues, that is, the utterance is unrelated to the intellect and linguistic ability. But while the speaker has no control over what is said, the act of uttering itself (in contradiction to many accounts by outsiders) is not involuntary. However, on occasion, particularly in instances of initial manifestation, the urge to speak may come with irresistible compulsion. At the same time it is not unknown for leaders to teach beginners to emulate a few sounds which the initiate is encouraged to repeat in the effort to release a 'tongue' (*glossa*). Yet it would be wrong to give the impression that training is the rule. On the contrary, the characteristic of speaking in tongues is spontaneity, a feature associated with inpsired states, particularly in Pentecostal circles. Many glossolaliacs would go as far as to say that both in speaking with tongues and the interpretation of tongues the Holy Spirit actually manipulates the human speech organs. The more perceptive, however, while regarding the Holy Spirit as the ultimate source of glossolalia, will not ignore the role of the subconscious or the depth of the human spirit as the immediate source.

What is gobbledegook to the sceptic is regarded as a special kind of language by the believer and held to be a more adequate instrument of praise and worship than the speaker's normal tongue. It is said to be directed to God, not to people (1 Cor. 14:2) and the believer will refer to St Paul's expression 'tongues of men and of angels' (1 Cor. 13:1) and praying in the power of the spirit (Eph. 6:18). Glossolalia is also associated with the gifts of healing (1 Cor. 12:9), when the sick are prayed for in the spirit. This association sometimes occurs both in Pentecostalism and in the Charismatic Renewal.

Both in Pentecostalism and in the Charismatic Renewal, tongues are regarded as one of the gifts of the Holy Spirit, but Pentecostals have distinguished between tongues as a 'sign' of the individual's initial baptism in the spirit (which is regarded as an experience that is quite distinct from conversion) and subsequent manifestations in which the 'gift' of the Spirit is at work. Tongues can be employed in private or in the worshipping community. In the latter they can contribute to the edification of the church when interpreted. Interpretation is also understood to be an inpsired communication and sometimes the tongues-speaker is also endowed with the gift of interpretation, but in practice, more often than not, the two will be separate. The glossolalic utterance can also be a means of mediating a 'prophecy', which needs interpretation. The 'speaker' knows when his utterance has a prophetic content for the physical force felt on such occasions, it is said, differs from other occurrences. Prophecy however is listed in its own right as a separate vocal gift and will be given, on most occasions, in the language of the congreagation. Indeed its intelligibility is contrasted by St Paul with the unintelligibility of glossolalia and for this reason he regards it more highly. Even so it is important to remember that genuine prophecy, like glossolalia and interpretation, is charismatic, that is to say it is not considered the product of the human intellect and insight, but the direct, spontaneous inspiration of the Holy Spirit.

Claims are sometimes made by glossolaliacs that their 'tongue', though unknown by the speaker, has been identified by listeners as a known language. This phenomenon is referred to technically as xenoglossy. In early Pentecostalism some believers went to mission fields abroad with no knowledge of the native tongue, confident that God would make their glossolalia intelligible to their audiences. Generally, however, glossolalia is not regarded as a vehicle of communication but a means of enhancing the spiritual life of the individual and, when interpreted, of building up the church.

Occasionally, in glossolalic circles there occurs what is described as 'singing in the spirit' (1 Cor. 14:15) when the worshippers sing their glossolalia spotaneously in unrehearsed melodious harmony with telling numinous effect. Whether praying in the spirit, or singing in the spirit, speakers in tongues find the exercise beneficial in its effect in terms of their well-being and testify also that their worship becomes more meaningful.

In the sphere of denominational worship, what is happening in the Charismatic Renewal is of special interest. Whereas the Pentecostals formerly found that in the end they were led to separate themselves from the churches within main line traditions, the interesting feature of the Charismatic Renewal is that the glossolaliacs remain within their respective traditions whether Catholic or Protestant. Moreover many of them claim that the liturgy and worship of their own church become not less but more meaningful. Their glossolalic experience, we are told, deepens their understanding of the teaching of their church and strengthens their commitment to it. Some, however, find they become uneasy about reconciling doctrines previously accepted on the authority of their church and their new understanding of scripture. All are agreed that a theology of tongues must be based upon a proper understanding of scripture. The situation presents a theological challenge of the first order since the churches have basic doctrinal differences and as yet the challenge has not been taken up in earnest. It is more demanding upon the theologians than for the charismatic circles since the emphasis in the latter is on the experience of direct encounter with the Holy Spirit; doctrinal creedal statements, although not ignored, take second place. But again the more perceptive on all sides will see the need for a continuous dialogue between doctrine and experience and an unbalanced emphasis will always need to be redressed. Before we return to the question of theolgoical evaluation let us turn briefly to note some aspeccts of modern investigations of glossolalia.

How do researchers view the phenomenon of tongues? Very little attention was paid to it in the first half of the present century but the last few decades have seen a growing interest and much serious investigation, not least in the behavioural sciences, resulting in a substantial flow of publications. Unfortunately, so far, while researchers have concentrated upon the field of their own specialisation, there has been little attempt to correlate findings in various fields such as psychology, anthropology, and now sociolinguistics, not to mention comparative studies of religious phenomena and, of course, essential biblical studies. Competence in any one of these fields demands a lifetime's study, yet the attempt must be made to bring together the results of investigations in several fields. Obviously, this involves the risk of distortion and over-simplification but the theologian who seeks to evaluate a phenomenon like glossolalia needs to be aware of trends and views derived from other avenues of approach. This will not only enable him to appreciate more readily the several aspects of glossolalia but also to know where to focus his concentration if claims of distinctiveness are to be made for the Christian glossolalic event. It is well known for instance that many physical and emotional effects, manifest in both Pentecostal and Renewal glossolalia, can be encountered in non-Christian ecstatic religions ancient and modern or indeed in non-religious contexts. The theologian has to consider the implications of such empirical data in his endeavour to understand the phenomenon of glossolalia as fully as he can.

Theorists of the early part of this century presented glossolalia as a regressive pathological experience but recent researchers, in the main, offer explanations in terms of health, maintaining that glossolaliacs are no more likely to be maladjusted or inadequate community members than any other random group. Indeed, the experience is seen by a good number of investigators as a means of integration and therapy, imparting hope and confidence and other positive benefits to the individual. But assessments of the influence of glossolalia on the personality would be more convincing if studies could be diachronic, embracing observations of the subjects before their glossolalia as well as during their practice of glossolalia and, where appropriate, afterwards. Some psychological studies refer to the way in which tongues-speaking is a means of discharging energy and releasing inner conflicts which have not been faced at a conscious level, with consequent beneficial results. Others maintain that it is not the actual experience of speaking in tongues which promotes therapy but the fact of the individual's association with a group. It is the group experience, they say, which is the key to personality integration. There is no need to play down the benefits of group acceptance, but the charismatic group is not 'any' group and other factors need to be recognised. For instance the beliefs shared by the group no doubt affect the inner experience which in turn provides as it were dramatic affirmation of the correctness of the belief. The cognitive and non-rational interact and the individual is filled with a glowing assurance, which has a beneficial effect on both the attitudes and character of the individual and the cohesiveness and shared convictions of the group.

Students of the history of religions will draw attention to seemingly parallel phenomena to glossolalia in the classical world, for example at Delphi, or in the ecstatic worship of Dionysus, in shamanism, or in some eastern religions where unintelligble utterance is associated with possession states. But can we do justice to glossolalia by isolating the external somatic effect or divorcing the vocalisation from the totality of the event? Much can be learned by examining the vocal forms of glossolalia, provided one allows that other factors cannot be ignored. One of the most important contributions to the modern research on tongues-speaking is that of the sociolinguist W. Samarin.[1] He looks at the form of the glossolalic utterance which he declares has nothing mysterious or miraculous about it. In fact, according to Samarin, anyone can produce glossolalia and he rejects the thesis of Felicitas Goodman,[2] another important investigator, namely that glossolalia is an artefact of hyperarousal in an altered state of consciousness.

Glossolalia, says Samarin, is fundamentally not 'language', but he describes it as a linguistic symbol of the sacred. I do not share his view that glossolalia can be produced by anyone, at least not the genuine article, for spurious samples have been detected by glossolaliacs. At the same time I concur with his view that it has value as a symbol of the sacred, and I can agree to some extent with Goodman that there seems to be evidence of dissociation and some change of consciousness in the glossolalic condition. This does not mean that in each case one has to deal with the extreme form of ecstasy. Indeed in the case of experienced glossolaliacs there appears to be scarcely any change at all from the normal condition and a calm serenity prevails. The experienced practitioner can switch from normal conversation to glossolalia and vice-versa when outwardly there seems to be no change in the subject. It would appear perhaps that what we have is partial disorientation when the speaker is quite aware of his environment and yet can dissociate part of his consciousness.

The degree of emotional impact may differ from individual to individual and on different occasions in the case of the same individual. The term ecstatic will therefore invariably need qualification for it has been used in the past to denote conditions ranging from mild dissociation to the wilder extravagances of dervishes. The translators of 1 Corinthians in the New English Bible used the term 'ecstasy' or 'ecstatic' whenever the word *glossa* (tongue) occurs in the text whether in the singular or plural (1 Cor. 13:8; 14:2, 4, 5, 9, 18, 19, 23, 26). This might give the impression that the manifestation always exhibits some ecstatic characteristics. But as we have already mentioned there is generally a calmer atmosphere in contemporary tongues groups compared with the more explosive experiences of earlier Pentecostal churches, or indeed with the Corinthian experience. What is clear is that a single paradigm will not provide the model for all instances of glossolalia.

Somatic effects which can occur in glossolalic conditions include trembling and shaking, yelling, dancing and rhythmical movements. In revivalist settings, clapping of the hands, waving the arms, repetition of phrases such as 'Praise the Lord', chanting — all can combine to produce an atmosphere of intense excitement and rapture. In early Pentecostalism glossolalia flourished in such an environment. Not infrequently crying and laughing accompany the tongues experience, features which have strengthened the conviction of sceptical critics that the persons involved are psychologically deficient, an inference which in my view is too simplistic.

In a recent article, R. A. Hutch[3] describes glossolalia as a ritual process. The charismatic prayer meeting may proceed from scripture reading, at the semantic level, through what the writer calls 'liminal non-semantic utterances', meaning glossolalia, and the whole results in reinforcing the personal, social and cultural meanings of the speaker's faith. The speaker, we are told, becomes an explorer of the linguistic symbol of the sacred, namely his or her 'prayer-language'. He makes the interesting point that the ritual process contains and enters into the meanings associated with the most basic of expressive utterance, namely crying and laughing. The physical act of crying is seen as a response to a sense of hurt pointing 'beyond the situations of hurt to their source, namely to the end of the life cycle and to the inevitability of one's own death, however disguised'. On the other hand laughing is seen as a physical response to intense joy, reflecting the possibility of moments of symbolic rebirth and has as its corresponding emotional element 'a sense of goodness in the world, or the "holy" aspect of sacred power'. This thesis is attractive enough but while one can accept that there is a correlation between physical manifestation, the emotional element and what they point to or reflect, it is highly speculative to specify what the latter is. We must also be reminded that crying need not be associated with the hurtful but with the joyous. We may for instance think of the 'tears of joy' of an athlete who has won a championship race or of a St Ignatius of Loyola in the thrill of spiritual meditation, and many other instances. Where we can readily agree however, is over the contention that tongues-speaking can bring about a deepening of the spiritual dimension of human existence.

This is a convenient point therefore to raise the question of the theological status of glossolalia. Glossolaliacs have no hesitation in attributing their tongues to a divine source and a theology of glossolalia would need to consider the wider context of the doctrine of the Holy Spirit. This would involve a minute examination of the relevant biblical texts as well as a discussion of the doctrines of Pentecostalism and the views of Renewal groups, which assume that contemporary glossolalia is the same phenomenon as the tongues of apostolic times. Such an exercise would be far beyond the scope of this chapter, but the reader may be directed to the well balanced investigations of James D. G. Dunn.[4] However a few observations can be made.

The most relevant New Testament passages which would have to be scrupulously examined would be the account of Pentecost in the Acts 2 narrative and the first letter to the Corinthians. Luke writes of 'talk in other tongues' (Acts 2:4) and exegetes have focused on the question whether the explanation of this Pentecost phenomenon should be in terms of a miracle of speech or a miracle of hearing. The present writer's view (discussed more fully elsewhere),[5] is that the experience behind the Lukan narrative concerning 'other tongues' (*heterais glossais*) was not speaking in unlearned languages, xenoglossy, but glossolalia, similar to the Corinthian manifestation (1 Cor. 12:28, 30; 13:1, 8; 14:2, 4, 5f., 9, 13f., 18f., 22f., 39). Some of the sounds may have evoked memories of words in known languages or dialects identified by some listeners as languages of their homeland. In the ecstatic atmosphere such claims multiplied and the miracle was enlarged. We must not forget, however, those who were not so impressed and heard only the babblings of drunken persons. Whatever the explanation, unless one accepts the view that Acts 2 is a purely Lukan aetiological construction, that is 'a mythical narrative to explain the unknown origin of the church',[6] one must agree that the narrative indicates a momentous experience which the early church attributed to the visitation of the Holy Spirit.

In the Pauline epistle, greater store is set upon intelligible prophecy than glossolalia (1 Cor. 14), but one must remember that both are charismatically given and in the Corinthian context both probably had ecstatic features, even though the New English Bible seems to give the impression that glossolalia alone was ecstatically produced. True, the one is 'speaking with the mind' and has a rational communicable content while the other, presumably like the 'unutterable utterances' of 2 Cor. 12:4, is devoid of semantic value, but as we have emphasised, both are claimed as charismatic, being the work of the Spirit. According to St Paul glossolalia edifies the individual but unless interpreted it does not build up the Christian community (1 Cor. 14:4). Edification in the case of the individual is a 'spiritual' benefit, but certainly non-rational. Interpretation involves 'translation' into rational terms for the edification of the congregation. We must not think of this 'translation' as a word for word translation in the usual sense, or as indicating any linguistic ability. What seems to be conveyed is a message in close touch with the spirit of the glossolaliac, who is likewise inspired by the spirit. Why there is this roundabout way of edifying the church is of course a mystery. A prophetic message may sometimes be received in this way, but it is more customary for a prophecy to come directly through an individual charismatically endowed.

St Paul speaks in enigmatic terms of glossolalia as a sign for unbelievers in an obscure verse, 1 Cor. 14:22, 'Clearly then these "strange tongues" are not intended as a sign for believers, but for unbelievers, whereas prophecy is designed not for unbelievers but for those who hold the faith.' (New English Bible) It is enigmatic for the very sign which is supposed to convict unbelievers makes the assembly appear mad in their sight, whereas prophecies will cause the unbelievers to 'fall down and worship God' (1 Cor. 14:24-5). I have found no satisfactory explanation for this passage but what emerges clearly in the letter to the Corinthians is that St Paul favours intelligible communication above unintelligible utterance in church. And yet it seems, judging by various other oblique references in the New Testament (e.g. Rom. 8:26; Eph. 6:18; 5:19; Col. 3:16, 1 Thess. 5:19; 2 Cor. 5:4) that glossolalia flourished in the early Christian communities. Mark 16:17 is more explicit, but it is a later addition to the gospel, and this would suggest that glossolalia was prominent and significant in the mission of the early church.

Turning to the present century, classic Pentecostalism made experience essential while doctrine was not given the same respect. Theology was viewed with suspicion as a threat to the living encounter with the Spirit, giving pre-eminence to the opinions of men rather than to the vitality of first hand experience. But in fact Pentecostalism developed its own body of doctrine with a rigidity equalling any creedal system. Doctrines held to be merely secondary became the charter of spiritual progress. The manner of the operation of the Holy Spirit was set out with confidence. To the work of the Spirit in the conversion and regeneration of the sinner was added the further experience of baptism in the Holy Spirit. Speaking in tongues was seen as the initial evidence of this experience, and referred to as a 'sign' of Spirit baptism, while the subsequent manifestation of tongues, where it occurred, was regarded as a 'gift' of the Spirit. It is, however, fair to say that not all Pentecostal leaders shared this view. In the Charismatic Renewal, on the other hand, baptism in the Spirit is not regarded as a separate spiritual experience subsequent to rebirth and it is not thought of as being necessarily accompanied by glossolalia. Yet the significance of tongues-speaking is by no means minimised and the Christian who does not experience tongues is considered somewhat incomplete. The experience, it is held, makes God more real to the speaker and strengthens his assurance of the divine presence.

While one can accept that the glossolalia of modern Pentecostalism and the Charismatic Renewal is of the same genre as the glossolalia of apostolic times, one feels that to focus unduly on this gift, to the neglect of other gifts of the Spirit, is not commendable. Moreover, it seems to me that the work of the Holy Spirit must be seen to extend beyond the worshipping community and the circle of confession. God's gift of the Spirit is measureless and not restricted in operation or manifestation. Where the Spirit works, distinctions such as sacred and secular are transcended and it seems inappropriate to restrict the gifts of the Spirit in too limiting a fashion to those nine gifts listed by St Paul in 1 Corinthians 12:8-11.

The fact that glossolalia has only erupted sporadically throughout the centuries in the history of the Christian church should make anyone pause before insisting that it is of the *esse* of the church or even of the *bene esse*. Whether or not the pattern of the early apostolic church is normative for all times has been much debated in theological circles, but irrespective of that question, the fact that glossolalia was assigned a lower position than intelligible prophecy by St Paul, is invariably deemed to be still relevant, not least by those who would reject tongues-speaking absolutely in congregational worship. They conveniently ignore that, as stated previously, in the Corinthian context, prophecy was not considered the product of the intellect, intelligible though it was and subject to evaluation by the congregation, but was regarded as inspired speech uttered possibly in an ecstatic condition. Spontaneity was a feature of the charismatic scene, and while it would be improper to equate spontaneity and inspiration, it is salutary to remind ourselves of the varied nature and vitality of the charismata when compared with the formalism and rigidity of much contemporary traditional worship, which can stifle the Spirit, the *esse* of the Church. To understand the place of glossolalia in the life and worship of the Christian, I repeat that factors beyond the actual utterance need to be taken fully into account. The total experience, we are told, strengthens the believer's sense of belonging to the group, activates his or her faith and deepens commitment to Christ as the living Lord. This Lordship of Christ is then expressed more readily and joyously in a quality of life lived as if in His constant presence. It is these associations which must be taken into account when considering the glossolalic event. Helpful and desirable though our studies may be of external aspects, the environmental factors, or indeed, as far as we are able, the psychological processes at work in the subconscious, none of these singly or even when taken together can rule out all possibility of an ultimate transcendent source. It is believing in the transcendent source of his glossolalia that gives it such deep significance for the glossolaliac. Likewise comparisons with similar vocalising and ecstatic features in religious and non-religious behaviour elsewhere do not impress the believer, for the validity of the experience for him resides in its source. The experience is self-authenticating, and so real that its reality is beyond question. For those of us who are outsiders as far as glossolalia is concerned, the inner experience of the glossolaliac must remain elusive, but for the one who knows, it is where reality impinges with compelling force upon the inner being. No wonder it leads to greater dedication and fuller commitment to discipleship and service. Divorced from such commitment, glossolalia could be entirely of man. Where it is present, the claim that glossolalia points beyond itself to its ultimate source in divine authorship, need not be questioned. If St Paul, though critical of abuse, valued speaking in tongues as a divine gift and a method of prayer (and wrote, 'I thank God I speak in tongues more than you all'), those who would dismiss glossolalia as 'gibberish' need to think twice!

Notes

1 W. Samarin, *Tongues of Men and Angels* (Macmillan, New York, 1972).
2 F. D. Goodman, *Speaking in Tongues: A Cross-Cultural Study of Glossolalia* (University of Chicago Press, 1972).
3 R. A. Hutch, 'The Personal Ritual of Glossolalia', *Journal for the Scientific Study of Religion*, vol. 19, no. 3 (1980), pp. 255-66.
4 James D. G. Dunn, *Baptism in the Holy Spirit* (SCM, London, 1970); *Jesus and the Spirit* (SCM, London, 1975), which has a useful bibliography.
5 Cyril G. Williams, *Tongues of the Spirit* (University of Wales Press, Cardiff, 1981).
6 For a discussion see Dunn, *Jesus and the Spirit*, p. 150.

An Impressionistic View of the Influence of the Charismatic Renewal in the Life of the Church of England

JOHN GUNSTONE

I define the influence of the Charismatic Renewal in the life of the Church of England as the attempt by those Anglicans whose Christian lives have been revitalized by Pentecostal spirituality to apply the lessons of their experiences to the parishes, deaneries and dioceses to which they belong. In this essay I have used Pentecostal terminology without attempting any theological critique of it — terms like 'baptism in the Spirit', 'the every-member-ministry', 'deliverance ministry', and so on ('ministry' being used in its scriptural sense of *diakonia*). I have used 'charismatic' to apply exclusively to those involved in the movement we are concerned with, 'prayer group' to refer to small gatherings of up to a dozen, and 'prayer meeting' to describe any number assembling for prayer, praise and ministry.

Individuals

While the proportion of young Anglicans involved in the Charismatic Renewal is high (especially in some university chaplaincies and societies and in theological colleges), it touches people of all ages. In the sixties it seemed to influence mainly Anglicans from the evangelical wing of the Church, but in the seventies Catholic Anglicans have been influenced as well. Among the latter, interest in the Renewal has been apparent among those who support the 'Catholic Renewal' movement stemming from the 1978 Loughborough Conference. An annual Anglican Catholic Charismatic Convention which started some years ago to meet at Walsingham has grown so large that in 1979 it shifted its venue to High Leigh. My rough guess (unsubstantiated by any research) is that about ten per cent of Anglican communicants are baptised in the Spirit, and perhaps a slightly higher proportion of the parochial clergy.

There is a saying in charismatic circles that when someone is baptised in the Spirit they should be shut away for six months! Their new enthusiasm for the things of God can create strains in a Church of England congregation, whose faith in Jesus Christ (though it may be just as real) is expressed less exuberantly. With pastoral care and spiritual direction, however, most Spirit-baptised Anglicans settle down as more committed churchmen with a growing appreciation of what is God's gift in the characteristic worship, spirituality and activity in the Church of England.

Difficulties occur when this pastoral care and spiritual direction are lacking. When an individual becomes more open to the Holy Spirit, he finds himself called on by God to accept a fuller personal cleansing and healing than he has known before, and this can cause a crisis in his life. Some refuse to accept what God offers and become rebellious; they are the charismatic nuisances who are highly critical of their church and its clergy and who wander restlessly from one charismatic meeting to the next. Some find the encounter with certain Pentecostal ministries (tongues, prophecies, deliverances) a threat, exposing weaknesses in themselves that they had not recognised before, while others — used to a comfortable religion that made little demand for change in attitudes and behaviour — are disconcerted and challenged. It is in these circumstances that the wise guidance of pastors (ordained or lay) is required.

It is not only the laity who are affected in this way. In recent years I have met the partners in two clergy marriages whose relationships have broken down after some involvement in the Charismatic Renewal. Unfortunately reconciliations have not yet been made because in each case one partner is not prepared to wait for the healing which God's grace brings. Charismatics tend to blame such things on the work of the devil, but I am inclined first to look for mental and psychological causes, along the lines hinted at in the previous paragraph, and to suggest that, in these marriages, the poverty of existing relationships was hidden beneath the busyness of vicarage life, until the Spirit exposed it.

But these are shadows cast by the Charismatic Renewal. In its light there is much to welcome: a greater love that is manifested in all sorts of ways among Anglicans after they are baptised in the Spirit; a firmer confidence in the presence, power and guidance of God; a more spontaneous joy that bubbles over in worship as well as in daily living; a deeper appreciation of other Christians' response to the gospel of Jesus Christ; and a bolder readiness to embark on projects requiring degrees of self-sacrifice unthinkable before. For all their faults (and few would claim sinless perfection for charismatic Anglicans, as a minority of Pentecostals did for themselves at the beginning of the century) there is a lively sense of the accompanying presence of the risen Christ among those who are baptised in the Spirit when they begin to mature in their experience of God's ways. Gifts of wisdom, knowledge and discernment become evident in a manner that has not always been noticeable among the ordinary members of the Church of England, coupled with what might be called a 'Bible-orientated' view of life — an acceptance of certain fundamental scriptural attitudes without necessarily becoming what theologians call 'fundamentalist'.

Evangelicals and Catholics

The effect of the Charismatic Renewal on the Church of England's own domestic ecumenical movement is worth a note. While in recent years the mutual respect of Evangelical and Catholic Anglicans has been more marked than their mutual hostility, and while the two parties often find themselves more as allies than as foes, yet I think it is true to say that we have had to wait for the Charismatic Renewal for Anglicans in the two streams to find a spiritual unity with each other that is stronger than their doctrinal and devotional emphases. It is remarkable how, as a result of the renewal, the evangelical seems to be drawn towards a more Catholic understanding of the nature of the church and the sacraments (especially the eucharist, the laying on of hands, and the anointing with oil). And it is equally remarkable how the Catholic seems to be drawn towards a more evangelical understanding of the Bible as the Word of God and of the value of personal testimony to Jesus Christ as Lord and Saviour. This is not to say that there is a merging of the two streams. Rather, each is widening to include the other. The effect of this is to make 'non-charismatic' Evangelical and Catholic Anglicans suspicious of their fellows — a reaction clearly seen both at the Nottingham Evangelical Anglican Conference in 1977 and at the Loughborough Conference in 1978.

This ecumenical fruit of the Charismatic Renewal is, of course, appearing far beyond the membership of the Church of England. The local moves towards ecumenism that have been a feature of Church life since the end of the Second World War, and especially since Vatican Two, have been a breath of the same Spirit who is now gusting through the renewal. At a time when it has become a cliché to say that 'ecumenism has run out of steam', there is plenty of evidence that the Charismatic Renewal is bringing Christians together locally in a desire to be more open to God in company with each other. The Rev. John Nicholson, when he was Ecumenical Officer for England, reported that two local ecumenical projects, one in Southampton and the other in Sheffield, had been given a new impetus through the renewal. The city mission celebrations, led by groups such as those from St Michael-le-Belfrey, York, have brought Christians together in ways that have continued long after the actual festivals are over. And in my own experience in Greater Manchester, many of the worthwhile local ecumenical initiatives, inside as well as outside councils of churches, seem to come from groups inspired by the Charismatic Renewal.

As far as I can tell, the renewal does not seem to have influenced the radical/liberal stream in the Church of England. The response from that quarter has been cool. Radical/liberal Anglicans seem to regard the renewal as evidence of a Christian conservative backlash against the contemporary religious scene, to be associated with such phenomena as the Festival of Light and Mrs Mary Whitehouse.

Worship

One place where the Charismatic Renewal is having a wide influence is in the worship of parish churches. The renewal has, through its prayer meetings, introduced Anglicans to forms of praising, praying, singing and sharing which most of them had never experienced before. The worship of the prayer meeting, through which the renewal has spread, traces its ancestry back to the evangelical revivals of the nineteenth century in Europe and America. It was adapted as the normal form of Sunday worship in the Pentecostal Churches at the beginning of this century. Chorus-singing, testimonies, gifts of tongues and interpretations, prophecies and singing in the Spirit, ministries of healing and deliverance carried out in the midst of the congregation — such things were quite unknown to Anglican clergy and laity until they began attending prayer meetings to find out what the Charismatic Renewal was all about. For some, the religio-cultural shock has been too much and they have vigorously opposed such influences. But others, associating this form of worship with considerable spiritual transformations in their own lives, have found a reality and a relevance within it that has had a profound effect on them and on the way they want to worship.

It is now common to find prayer meetings organised by parishes or groups of parishes. The Stockport Deanery has its own bi-monthly prayer meeting presided over by the rural dean. The Southwark diocese has similar meetings attended by the bishop and the archdeacon. In parishes such meetings take the form of a weekday fellowship. In several churches I have found this kind of a programme on a weekday evening: meal together; division into interest groups; re-assembly for praise (plus sometimes eucharist), the whole event lasting from about 6.30 to 10.00 p.m. Many towns and cities have prayer meetings to which they invite visiting speakers known for their involvement in the Charismatic Renewal. One important by-product of these meetings is that parish priests and a few laity have been given an opportunity of presiding over worship that was open to a far greater degree of spontaneity and participation than is usually experienced in the Anglican liturgy. So they discovered what was possible when they forgot they were Anglicans!

But it would be an error to suggest that there is a deep gulf fixed between the worship of the prayer meeting and that of the Church of England. The work of the Liturgical Commission has been based on the assumption that more spontaneity and participation should be expected in Anglican worship than has usually been the case until recently. Indeed, they have created a eucharistic liturgy that is so flexible that Anglicans used to Prayer Book conformity have been lost in it. But not the charismatics! On the contrary, they have found the Rite A in the *Alternative Service Book* an admirable framework within which to celebrate what they call 'an extended eucharist'. What this means is that within the parts of the rite provided by the Commission it is possible for charismatics to introduce most of the elements learned from the prayer meeting and create inspiring celebrations. A memorable example of this was the eucharist in Canterbury Cathedral which took place during the first International Anglican Charismatic Conference in 1978, presided over by the Archbishop of Cape Town and thirty bishops.

Yet it must be admitted that an insensitive attempt to introduce Pentecostal elements into the ordinary worship of a parish church can cause trouble. There are many Anglicans who by temperament and up-bringing prefer the more formal and more aesthetically acceptable services that are part of the Church of England's liturgical tradition. Such individuals are not attracted to loud and prolonged chorus-singing, extemporary prayer, hands-lifting and neighbour-embracing; and not a few organists have resigned when the vicar introduced a guitar group and *Sounds of Living Water*.

These tensions are not unfamiliar to members of the Church of England. The student of Anglican history who has followed the story of the ritual troubles of the last hundred years will have the feeling that he has heard all this before! But just as the worship of Catholic Anglicans has influenced many parish churches, including large numbers who would never claim to be 'high church', so the Charismatic Renewal is influencing many parish churches, including those who would never claim to be Pentecostal. The popular, scripture-based choruses, which have been the voice of the Charismatic Renewal in worship, are heard everywhere, and there is a more relaxed freedom in the conduct of worship nowadays. Evangelicals have discovered the liturgical dance and Catholic Anglicans the personal testimony. It is interesting to compare (and contrast) the liturgical and devotional expression of the beliefs of the Oxford Movement with the liturgical and devotional expression of the beliefs of the Charismatic Renewal. The lessons of the past then become very relevant.

Charismatic Groups

Charismatic prayer groups are legion, and the quality of leadership and of fellowship they experience varies enormously. Every story of a blessing in one group can be matched by a story of a disaster in another. Nevertheless, the prayer groups are extremely important features of the Charismatic Renewal, for they provide the opportunity for the individual Anglican to explore the practical application of the renewal's lessons and to begin to take part in the every-member-ministry which is at the heart of Pentecostalism. It is in the prayer group that the shy layman or laywoman can pray aloud spontaneously for the first time. They can speak in tongues and seek interpretations. They can listen to the concerns of others and intercede for them. They can lay hands on one another. They can move out in initiatives of mission and service beyond their own circle in the name of the congregation. The prayer group can give them a deeper sense of Christian fellowship than they usually find in the congregation, and encourage them to exercise spiritual gifts, of witnessing to Jesus Christ and helping others, that they have not been aware of before. Recently two visitors from Papua New Guinea spent three months in England going to different churches. It was in a charismatic parish that they reported they experienced an authentic sense of Christian caring and concern both for the Church and for society.

If there is some justice in the commonly heard accusation that charismatic groups are divisive, it is equally just to say that such divisions only become serious when the pastoral leadership in a parish is weak and divided. Many Church of England clergy and parochial church councils have given little consideration to the nature of pastoral leadership in a congregation or attempted to discern where the spiritual gifts for this ministry are being manifested. There is a basic assumption that the plenitude of pastoral leadership resides within the person of the vicar. There is another basic assumption that the ministry of the laity is largely to do with the administration and maintenance of all that happens in and around the parish church building, particularly on Sundays (the names of the officials demonstrates this: churchwardens, readers, organists, choirmasters, choirmen and women, sacristans, servers, sidesmen, Sunday School superintendent). The individual who emerges as a pastoral leader in a prayer group, although he may hold one of the offices listed, does not fit into this structure, and the life of the group is usually centred on its members' homes, not on the church. It is in this situation that the divisive forces are magnified.

It is to meet this need that 'elders' have appeared on the Church of England parochial scene. They act as mini-pastors in groups, and the unity of the group with the congregation depends almost entirely upon the way in which the elder and the vicar trust and support one another. In parishes where there are a number of groups, the elders form a pastoral team round the vicar. Then the vicar's task in the parish becomes one of 'oversight' to the groups with their elders, rather than of direct pastoral care to each individual who is a member of the groups. The diocese of St Edmundsbury and Ipswich has a scheme for the selection and training of elders. The diocese of Derby recently debated the value of elders in its deanery synods. Some elders are commissioned with prayer and the laying on of hands by the vicar and/or the bishop. It will be necessary to discuss the relationship of these elders to the Church of England parochial structure. Are they to be identified as an extension of the clergy, as readers tend to be, and therefore regarded as suitable candidates for ordination through the auxiliary pastoral ministry? Or are they to be identified with the laity, as churchwardens and Sunday School teachers are, and prevented from being regarded as 'semi-ordained'? Obviously much depends on the way in which individual groups evolve and the kind of corporate ministry they follow.

Divisions in a parish experiencing charismatic renewal can sometimes take an unexpected turn. In one parish in Sussex the vicar and the Parish Church Council became so involved that they virtually formed the charismatic prayer group. The result was that the rest of the congregation, delighted that they had in their midst such a dedicated PCC, tended to sit back and let the vicar and the PCC get on with the whole job of running the parish! But in another parish in Cheshire a charismatic group that had been rather loosely connected with the church because of the ecumenical nature of its membership, gradually became more identified with the congregation when a charismatic auxiliary pastoral curate moved into the area and was accepted as its leader.

The Ministry of Healing

Through the encouragement given by groups like the Guild of St Raphael, the Church of England has never lost her sense of having spiritual gifts of healing to offer the sick; but it is probably true to say that those who acted on this belief were in a tiny minority among the clergy and laity until the Charismatic Renewal gave Anglicans a fresh expectancy in the spiritual gifts. As a result, services of prayer for healing with the laying on of hands and anointing are appearing as a regular feature in the parish programme. Often they are held on Sunday or week-day evenings every month or two months. With them has come the need for the after-care of individuals, in co-operation with the medical profession, and a number of communities have been established with the intention of providing the support of the Christian group for people in need. The PCC at Littleborough near Rochdale has recently acquired premises for this purpose and has committed itself to the support of the community there.

Stories of healing abound in the wake of the Charismatic Renewal. Perhaps some of them owe more to the medical-psychological gifts of God rather than to Pentecostal charismata, yet the effect of the ministry in the Church of England generally is considerable. Numerous clergy and laity who are suspicious of tongue-speaking and averse to choruses are nevertheless deeply appreciative of this aspect of the renewal and willing to learn from it. There are also indications that members of the medical profession see the need for the deeper, personal healing that is associated with this ministry. One general practitioner I know leads servics of prayer for healing in churches in Lancashire, as a result of his encounter with the Charismatic Renewal in the Anglican cathedral in Hong Kong, and he affirms that in them he has found a fulfilment of his work as a doctor.

After the Second World War the Church of England grasped the importance of pastoral counselling and learnt much from bodies like the Clinical Theology Association in Nottingham. This prepared the way for the prayer counselling and deliverance ministries that have been introduced through the Charismatic Renewal. Through these ministries a troubled individual is encouraged, aided by the prayer of one or two others, to seek God's healing for the hurts in the past that contributed towards his problem, or to find deliverance from the devil through claiming the power of Christ's cross and resurrection in that part of his life. There are obvious dangers in these ministries and, where possible, they should be pursued in co-operation with the members of the medical profession. On the other hand, there are a number of cases where healing has only come through these ministries, when the medical practitioners were not only unsuccessful themselves but sceptical of the charismatic gifts employed.

The ministry of healing should be seen as the spearhead of the Church's mission to proclaim the kingdom of God to a sick and sinful society, and in this respect the Charismatic Renewal has rescued the Church of England's mission from an over-dependence on the radical theology of the sixties to a more scripturally-based conception of what the gospel can do for men and women. It is not fair, however, to accuse the Charismatic Renewal of being concerned largely with the conversion and the sanctification of the individual and ignoring the social environment within which that individual lives. Charismatics are learning to follow the Lord's leading in the industrial, commercial, government and educational institutions within which they live and work, and I have known many incidents of Anglican charismatics attempting to invoke the power of the Holy Spirit when they encountered problems in these situations. To take one example, a director in a multi-national company asked his prayer group to pray that the Spirit would equip him, so that he could fight a decision the board was to make that would throw six thousand people out of work.

Agencies for Renewal

The Charismatic Renewal is encouraged and informed in England by a number of agencies, of which the Fountain Trust was foremost in importance. From its foundation it has had wide support from the Church of England (three of its four full-time directors have been Anglican priests). Its festivals, conferences, courses and publications (the periodicals *Renewal* and *Theological Renewal* and its library of cassettes) have assisted thousands of Anglicans to apply the lessons of the movement to their own groups and parishes. The Fountain Trust's policy was always to strengthen charismatics' allegiance to their own churches and it avoided creating a para-denomination among them. Until it was disbanded in 1980, it was concerned to form links with other bodies (like the British Council of Churches) and urged charismatics not to think they have a monopoly of the Holy Spirit.

> It is time for the charismatic renewal to divest itself of all exclusiveness and to make it clear that we are ready for fellowship and co-operation with all shapes and sizes of our fellow members within the body who share our confession in the Spirit that Jesus is Lord. We do that in practice when we are as ready to listen to and receive from others as we are to witness and minister to them.[1]

Other agencies are to be found among the communities that have sprung up in England in the last decade under the inspiration of the Charismatic Renewal. The Episcopal Church of the Redeemer, Houston, has been taken as a model for this development (rather as Catholic Anglicans used to model their churches on All Saints', Margaret Street) and many groups of charismatics have begun living together in different parts of the country — the Community of Celebration at Post Green, Poole, the Barnabas Fellowship at Whatcombe House, Blandford, Fellowship House, Brentwood, Lamplugh House near Hull and the Sacred Dance Group near Dorchester. Lee Abbey and Scargill have been influenced by the renewal as well as some of the traditional religious orders. These communities have the resources to mount conferences and conduct courses in parishes to teach and demonstrate the lessons of the renewal in parish life.

Out of this has also come a parish-to-parish ministry. The initiative was taken by St Michael-le-Belfrey, York, but now a number of parishes send teams of lay folk to other parishes for 'sharing weekends', expressing a corporate version of the every-member-ministry. St Andrew, Chorleywood, can bring together 'faith-sharing' teams of thirty or forty for this purpose. It has been discovered that ordinary Anglican parishioners can be highly effective as encouragers and evangelists when provided with these kinds of opportunities.

Causes of Tension

All movements in the church for renewal or reform create tensions as enthusiasts encounter the immobility of the institution, and many of the tensions felt today by charismatics in the Church of England are no different from those felt by Anglicans in movements in the past. But perhaps it is worthwhile singling out a few causes of tension which arise from this distinctive thrust of the Charismatic Renewal, as the charismatic feels them within himself or herself.

Dissatisfaction is felt with infant baptism and confirmation administered after a course of instruction unrelated to any personal experience of the Holy Spirit. There is an increasing tendency among Anglican charismatics (even among those with a high sacramental doctrine of baptism) to postpone the baptism of their children until they are old enough to confess a personal faith in Jesus Christ, and some clergy attempt to make their confirmation classes like 'Life in the Spirit' seminars.

There is disappointment that many Church of England clergy will not administer water baptism after a baptism in the Spirit experience, if the charismatic has been christened in infancy. In such cases some Anglican charismatics seek baptism (usually by submersion) in a Baptist or Pentecostal church.

Distress is caused by the fact that some clergy and laity in the Church of England seem to reject the suggestion that the spiritual gifts listed in the New Testament are relevant today, and also appear to disregard the dangers linked with practices such as the occult and spiritualism. The charismatic usually has a vivid sense of the reality of the devil, and it is not easy for him to work with those who dismiss this belief as a relic of medieval mythology, especially when ministering to an individual who has spiritual problems.

An impatience is felt with the formalism of the Church of England, from its traditional worship to its hierarchical structure. It is difficult for the charismatic to accept that the only ministries that have mattered from the Apostles' time are those exercised by bishops, priests and deacons, and to believe that the grace of God continues with those who, while holding offices in the church, have apparently lost the spiritual gift that equipped them for that ministry.

There is a reluctance to divide parishes into 'charismatic' and 'non-charismatic' categories. Yet this is often forced on ordinands seeking a title in a parish which is open to the Spirit in this way, and on Anglican charismatics when they are moving their home into a new area.

Conclusion

In spite of these tensions the vast majority of Anglican charismatics, as I have said, remain loyal to their parish churches as more committed Christians. It is my impression that the recent slight improvement in the number of church attenders and ordinands is due largely to the renewal. And I have noticed that where a fresh vision is seen that leads to new ways in evangelism, in social concern, in community-building, in new expressions of worship in a parish, charismatics are usually involved somewhere in them.

Finally, it cannot be stressed too strongly that Anglican charismatics have no other objective than that the Church of England should realise what they believe is her true nature as part of the family of God in the world — the family that God creates out of the sacrifice of Jesus Christ and the outpouring of the Spirit at Pentecost.

> The Charismatic Renewal does not seek to create a special group within the church which specialises in the Holy Spirit and his gifts, but rather the renewal of the local and the universal church through the rediscovery of fullness of life in Christ through the Spirit, which includes the full spectrum of the spiritual gifts.[2]

Indeed, the Anglican charismatic will be deeply relieved when the phrase 'Charismatic Movement' can be forgotten, because it is clear to all that the phrase is just another name for the church of Jesus Christ.

Notes

1 Editorial by Michael Harper in *Renewal*, no. 81, June/July 1979, p. 3.
2 *Theological and Pastoral Orientations on the Catholic Charismatic Renewal* (Malines, Belgium, 1974), p. 61.

Confusion Worse Confounded

PETER MULLEN

> Confusion is horror and nothingness.
> D. H. Lawrence, *Twilight in Italy*

> They are a narrow ignorant set, and do more to make their neighbours
> uncomfortable than to make them better. Their system is a sort of
> worldly-spiritual cliqueism: they really look on the rest of mankind as
> a doomed carcase which is to nourish them for heaven.
> George Eliot, *Middlemarch*

Any lively, innovative movement is bound to have its detractors and
the Charismatic Revival is no exception. Some of its critics are merely
too hidebound and dyed in the wool to appreciate anything new. I would
even say that others are only envious: and envy, uninformed criticism
and prejudice are simply irrelevant to a proper assessment of the strengths
and weaknesses of the movement. But there is widespread and, I believe,
not entirely misplaced alarm about some of the phenomena which make
up the Charismatic Revival. I will give one or two examples.

First, the practice of exorcism. I have had first hand experience of
the suffering which this can cause. A middle-aged woman came stumbling
into my evening class to unburden herself of an alarming story of how
she was exorcised against her will. She had only recently moved to York
and begun attendance at a famous — some would say notorious —
charismatical church called St Michael-le-Belfrey. She was recommended
to attend a mid-week prayer group — a 'cell' as they call it of the whole
congregation. This group was discussing the problem of evil and the
devil. When asked for her opinion, the newly enrolled woman — an
educated person with a first class honours degree in philosophy — said
that while she would admit there was much suffering and evil in the

world, she could not bring herself to believe in the existence of a personal
devil. This confession caused a stir among the guitars and the song sheets.

The leader of the group, utterly certain of the truth of his own belief,
reasoned as follows: 'I know that there exists a real, personal devil. This
woman denies the existence of the devil. Therefore, it must be the devil
himself who is prompting her.' The logic ran on inexorably to the
prescription of exorcism. The result was that the 'possessed' woman
became acutely and then chronically disturbed to the extent of requiring
treatment of a psychiatrist. For the exorcism was peremptorily inflicted
upon her despite her protestations. And, with due irony, the last state
of that woman was worse than the first.

Nor is her story the only one to come to my hearing. Problems
following exorcism have become so common that they have attracted
warnings and cautions from that erstwhile supporter of the Charismatic
Revival, Cardinal Suenens in his recent book *Renewal and the Powers
of Darkness*. What is modern, secular man to make of these claims that
human beings can be possessed by evil spirits? It would take more than
one article to conduct a thorough analysis, but one aspect of demonic
possession is, to say the least, interesting: it almost always only occurs
in connection with charismatic sects. The reason for this is not hard
to find, since any diagnosis will always include the symptoms which
the one who makes the diagnosis will hope to alleviate. 'Create a language
and you create a world,' said the philosopher Wittgenstein. The world
created by the jargon of the Charismatic Revival is one which is peopled
by supernatural forces, spirits both bad and good. A Freudian psychiatrist
faced with similar clinical manifestations might prefer a vocabulary which
includes words like 'neurosis', 'repression' and 'hysteria'. A Jungian
would want to talk about 'the archetype of the shadow'. A Behaviourist
might try to reduce the subject's anxiety by a carefully measured
programme of 'operant conditioning'. And so on.

Charismatic revivalists, spiritisers and impromptu exorcists will have
none of this 'relativising' and 'reductionism'. They believe not that they
possess one of many possible interpretations, but that they have the
absolute truth. Their grounds for this belief are a fundamentalist interpretation of the passages concerning demons in the New Testament.
Anyone who does not share their view is regarded as a blasphemer or
worse. Hence the 'cure' inflicted upon my friend the middle-aged

philosophy graduate. It is notoriously difficult to teach enthusiasts that their misplaced fundamentalist doctrines are erroneous, that the absolute certainty which they claim is itself a neurotic symptom of insecurity. But the doctrines are erroneous nonetheless — erroneous because 'culture bound'. This is an expression developed from the understanding that certain ideas belong to certain epochs and not to others, and that a culture is made up of many beliefs, attitudes and behaviour patterns that are coherent only when they are seen together. To take exorcism out of its first century biblical context and place it uncritically in the world of the twentieth century is as useless an action as it would be to take the television set to St Paul's unelectrified Corinth. The absurdity of this sort of selective fundamentalism — i.e. it is not really fundamental at all — is shown by the revivalists' own refusal to import the first century lock, stock and barrel. They pick and choose where it suits them, preferring their motor cars to St Paul's method of transportation, their electric light to the old candles and in general the values of bourgeois society to the more rugged social practices of New Testament times. There is something more than faintly ridiculous about someone who believes in literal and physical resurrection from the dead and demonic possession, also looking for a nice apprenticeship in Marks and Spencer for his daughter or a studentship in microbiology for his college-educated son. The fact is that elements of different cultures and epochs — in the Wittgensteinian sense different 'languages' — are not so interchangeable. And there is nothing commendably religious about so imagining them. What was the point of all that advanced study of microbiology if, in the interests of religious fanaticism, it is to be tacked on to first century psychology? But the two worlds are incompatible. No wonder so many of the revivalists exhibit dissociative tendencies. I am not saying that our culture is 'superior' to that of New Testament times; in fact, as an admirer of D. H. Lawrence, I might argue the opposite. What I do say is that the methodological presuppositions of the two ages do not mix, and that, surrounded by the whole paraphernalia of modern technological civilisation, there is nothing to be gained by turning back the clock except confusion. Confusion is something so much seen among the revivalists as to be almost a trademark.

Secondly, there is confusion over the issue of supernatural healing, another doctrine and practice which is popular among the revivalists.

Peter Mullen

I was once asked by our Suffragan Bishop to visit, for my edification, a certain Home of Healing, so-called. I stayed there for a fortnight. My impression was, once again, of confusion and dissociation. On the one hand, this home was a place where the chronically sick, disabled and mainly elderly could come for some peace and quiet, four square meals a day, fresh air and regular worship in the little chapel. But these modest, worthy values were set against a background of the most lurid super-naturalist kind. There were services of laying on of hands. There were talks and filmshows in which folk were encouraged to expect miracles of divine intervention. Most noticeable of all was an atmosphere of acrid and petulant sectarianism. Could other denominations (such as Spiritualists) claim to heal? Their healing was not considered divine; it was a demonic trick to seduce the faithful into heresy, idolatry and faithlessness.

There was the same confusion of thought: I was encouraged to regard instances of wonderful healing (I did not see any — but I was there for only two weeks) as evidence for the truth of revivalist doctrine. 'But,' I said, 'suppose a Red Indian rain dancer or even a Spiritualist were to replicate these miraculous signs — would that be evidence for the truth of their doctrine?' The value of this home lay in its function as providing the same facilities and care as a score of other homes for sick gentlefolk, but when those ordinary ministrations became mixed up with crude supernaturalism then there was confusion among the guests — disappointment and confusion.

But that whole doctrine of supernatural healing is shot through with inconsistencies and false expectations. 'It is always God's normal will to heal,' says Francis MacNutt OP in his classic text on the subject — a book which even the Archdeacon of York has called 'sane'. But then MacNutt goes on to give 'eleven reasons why God does not always heal'. This is a complete theological failsafe being full of so many pleas for excuses that the original bold statement about God's 'normal will' is rendered meaningless. And this is not a book 'on the fringe': it (*Healing*) claims on its cover to be 'the first comprehensive Catholic book on healing by the foremost authority on the healing ministry in the Roman Catholic Church today'. This foremost authority says:

Some healings are instantaneous.
In some healings there is a delay.

Some healings occur in a process gradually.
Others do not seem to occur, at least on the physical level, at all.[1]

The author compounds the incoherence by telling us that God sometimes heals us by death. He does not see that these options exhaust all the possibilities in any situation, so that any and every outcome is to be allowed to count as a healing. And that only means we cannot talk about healing at all in any coherent way. Once more it is all incoherence and confusion. MacNutt juxtaposes two cases of the divine healing of babies: in the first case the infant was cured of nappyrash — not an inconsiderable relief I imagine; in the second case a dead baby is raised to life again through the administration of baptism.[2] It is not my fault if this essay invites incredulity; the examples are all MacNutt's.

The obsessions with exorcism and miraculous healing betray not merely a failure of logic but an alarming lack of faith and trust in the loving wisdom of Almighty God. It is as if the everyday world, created by God though it may be, is not enough for the revivalist; he requires sensation upon sensation to fan his flagging faith and that is why he needs to import, selectively, the cultural motifs of other epochs and to try and force them into contemporary understanding. No one wants to say that wonderful healings are beyond the power of God but, in the light of everyday experience, the claim that it is 'always' God's normal will to heal is just silly, when so many people die and there is so much suffering and disease, and endemic cancer and coronary thrombosis. And then we all eventually have to die of something anyway! The charismatic revivalist frequently replies to this naming of specific diseases by saying that if we lived more faithful, godly lives we would not fall victim to these illnesses which are largely of our making. Well, if that is all he is saying, I agree. But that is not all that he is saying. He claims supernatural intervention as if it were the norm. And that is simply to fly in the face of all our reason and ordinary experience.

Always sensational, the revivalist is not interested in ordinary workaday holiness and the attempt to make such progress towards God as might be achieved by quiet and honest devotion. He wants miraculous signs. But it is a wicked generation which asks for signs. What is required of the Christian is faith and perseverance and that includes faith in the world which the Bible describes as God's creation. Of course the

immature and the faithless will always want the world to be different
from the way it is, in Schopenhauer's memorable phrase, for every dawn
to be cloudless and for chickens to fly round ready-roasted, but faith
demands a measure of acceptance. The maturest and most faithful,
spiritual Christians are always marked by this quality in abundance. They
would not pray to God to change creation but only change themselves.

Whatever is said about spiritual and inner healing, we are never left
in much doubt that the revivalist's preoccupation is with the more
remarkable (because visible) physical healing. Another leaf from my parish
diary will help illustrate my meaning.

A parishioner was told that he had cancer and that he had only three
months left to live. As will be imagined, his distress was acute. At first
he could not believe the doctor's statement. 'He must be wrong! I don't
feel too bad.' As be began to feel worse he also became more resentful.
There was no joy in him, no hope, only a cringing horror of what was
to come to pass. But in the last few weeks of his life he found — I
would say by God's good grace, others are free to judge differently —
some peace and a measure of acceptance. By this time he was, physically,
very ill indeed. But as the life in his body ebbed, the light in his soul
burned more brightly. We sat for hours in his window and stared out
over the countryside as we talked. We prayed. We played Mozart. We
kept silence. He knew where he was going and he was learning to go
not entirely unwillingly. One morning I received a telephone call from
his wife. Some healers from a local charismatic congregation had been
in touch with her to say they had heard about her husband's illness
and that they were coming to pray with him. Did I think it would
be a good idea? There was no chance for me to influence events one
way or the other: the healing threesome turned up at my friend's house
that same morning. They assured him that it was always God's normal
will to heal and followed this assurance with what they called 'praising'
and with an imposition of hands.

My friend's mood had changed remarkably by the time I saw him
that afternoon. He was exhilarated, manic, high. He was sure that God
was healing him. In fact he died not many days later in a state of bewilder-
ment and fear from which I could do nothing to relieve him. All that
faith over the previous three months, all the hard work, the anguish,
the patience, the watching and praying — it had all come to nothing.

And all because of the interference of a bunch of enthusiasts with their glib phrases and their rubbery grins.

Now if one uses a real example like this as support for a criticism of the revivalists, one is always told — as I was told by the Suffragan Bishop — that such examples are not typical but only 'excesses'. Apparently, we should learn to accept the odd 'excess' from time to time, some over-enthusiastic response to the promptings of the Holy Spirit, as an unavoidable by-product of the wonderful blessings which we receive. What blessings? Besides it is easy to show that these so called 'excesses' are in no way excessive; they are exactly what one would expect to happen as a result of ministrations which are based on theological principles which are themselves confused and incoherent.

Thirdly, it is often said that the Charismatic Revival is a breath of life in a rather stale old church. Much more extravagant claims are made on behalf of its supporters: for instance, that the Revival is the work of the Holy Spirit. I do not believe that. I cannot persuade myself that a movement which is so incoherent and self-contradictory, so exclusive in its jealous sectarianism, can be the inspiration of the Spirit of Truth. They speak not in the tongues of Pentecost but in those of Babel.

Moreover, I do not accept the claim to greater liveliness. Much is made of the exuberance, 'the joy' as it is usually called, of charismatic services. But what does it all amount to? Merely a spurt of frivolous excitement to the accompaniment of repetitively unimaginative guitar music and the adoption by the minister of techniques which belong in television's vapid 'games shows'. This is not liturgy — the theatre of the soul. It is not even *Stars on Sunday*; it is *Game for a Laugh* transposed to the sanctuary. Are Thomas Tallis, Orlando Gibbons, Thomas Cranmer and the King James Bible not lively? Come, come! I would hear more — but not, please, of stuff that sounds like failed Andrew Lloyd-Webber and the God-forsaken rhythms of *The Alternative Service Book*. They will say I am being unfair, that style of worship is a matter of taste. And I will reply, yes, indeed, it *is* a matter of taste. Taste consists in this: there are genuine depths of real spiritual experience that simply cannot be expressed in the trivial argot of pop-culture: *Living Waters* or choruses from the appendix to *Hymns for Today's Church* are no substitute for the *Parish Psalter* and the *English Hymnal*. Come, Sir, thou jestest but makest me not merry! The other claim, which we are supposed to take as a sign of tolerance, that charismatics would like to retain the traditional alongside the new, is bound to fail. Any aesthetic judgement, whether this is alleged to be inspired by the Spirit or not, which could place in the pew the *English Hymnal* alongside *Living Waters* immediately shows that 'judgement' is the last quality to be involved. In any case, are we supposed to think that those who have shown an astonishing vacuity of critical insight in the issues of theological principle and of ordinary coherence should suddenly aspire to authority in the aesthetics of worship? If the Holy Spirit is really behind all this jiggery-pokery, why is it all so fifth rate.

Perhaps the most worrying aspect of revivalism is its influence among adolescents, insecure people from many different backgrounds and particularly university students and divorcees — among anyone, in fact, who is especially suggestible and therefore especially vulnerable. The method of procedure in acquiring converts, and in keeping them, is much the same as that of the so-called 'religious cults' and 'fringe religions' — themselves so condemned by many of the senior clergymen who have welcomed the charismatics as a blessing from God. At any rate, the psychological moves and their effects are the same in both cases.

Anyone who is lonely — say a newly divorced person or a young university student in a strange town — stands in need of human companionship. The lively charismatic congregation provides just such an ambience. There is a warm welcome and the feeling of togetherness. These are cemented by a shared belief. It does not much matter what this belief is: it can be the teachings of Guru Bhagwan Rajneesh or of Maharaji's 'Divine Light' — or the amalgamations of half-truths and misapplied scriptural texts which go to make up charismatic revival. All that really matters is the relief of loneliness, via, as it usually is, an appeal to that sense of guilt which is present to some degree in most of us, but particularly present in those who have the sense of having just failed in some significant way such as the divorcee, the half-survivor of a broken marriage, or the student who has just ploughed his first year examinations and split up with or experienced sexual problems with his girlfriend. The choruses, the arms raised, the 'Us versus Them' dogma and the victory of shallow sectarianism over the best side of the human personality is complete. Anyone who seriously doubts this analysis, or who believes that I am exaggerating, need only read that classic study of mental manipulation *Battle for the Mind* by the psychologist William Sargent.

Sadly, for many people it is not necessary even to read this far into reasoned analyses of charismatic revival. I include among these the many parents who, following up critical articles which I have written in the *Guardian* and *Church Times*, have telephoned or else written at length to ask if there is anything they can do to free their son/daughter/wife/husband from the influence of charismatic sectarianism. I have a file two feet thick, filled with such letters.

Would you hear of the man who found that he could not go along with his wife's increasing involvement with the charismatics? The woman was told, by 'elders' at that church, that it was a simple choice: her husband or her faith. There was a similar case in which a wife was told she must be prepared to consign her unbelieving husband to 'the synagogue of Satan'. There was a nineteen year old girl student who had tried to leave the charismatics and had, as a result, suffered constant harassing telephone calls which claimed that her 'friends' were praying for her — the same friends who held a prayer meeting in a suburban semi-detached for the exorcism from her of the 'evil spirit of doubt'. Then there was the case of the charismatic vicar who became incumbent of a village on the edge of a small housing development for commuters. He filled the church with revivalists from among the commuters, thus driving out the original rural congregation who were unaccustomed to the new style of worship, and then this new congregation launched a 'prayer demo' around the village inn to try and get rid of the 'intemperate influence'.

Charismatics themselves and their sympathisers among the hierarchy will tell us again, as they have told us before, that these things are 'only excesses'. What I have tried to show, is that far from being excesses, they are precisely what we should expect to happen given the principles and practices of this incoherent movement. Reasons for the movement's appeal — other than those already mentioned — are not hard to find: the apparent aimlessness and meaninglessness of a society which, as the Archbishop of Canterbury said recently, has all but lost its hold on the distinction between right and wrong; the prevailing attitude of cynicism and the debunking of traditional institutions; the age-old desire for certainty and easy solutions; the equally ancient but widespread aversion

to serious critical analysis; the lure of popular and populist solutions
to problems of social identity and religious persuasion. I have heard it
said, 'What harm does it do? These are bound to be some casualties
whatever course is adopted in this life. Why not leave them to it? It's
their own choice.' Well, apart from the injunction to love our neighbour
and to seek his good, there is the reason that none of our actions is
entirely our own business. As my file of letters from victims shows,
the hurt caused by religious enthusiasm is widespread and not confined
to those who choose to take part. But, perhaps surpassing all these
reasons, there is the cause of mature Christian faith and culture: no
moderate, traditional believer in those things given to himself and to
the whole of our society by the refined and workable tradition of English
Christianity can stand by in silence while that tradition is traduced and
usurped by the incoherence of confused enthusiasm.

Notes

1 Francis MacNutt OP, *Healing* (Bantam Books, Ave Maria Press, New York), p. 259.
2 ibid., p. 293.

Living Liturgically:
the Charismatic Contribution

REX DAVIS

When we have exhausted the virtues that good people should share, loyalty, love, duty, honesty, integrity, obedience, truthfulness and so on, I suppose we have to conclude that what makes a Christian distinctive is not simply his or her effort to sustain or even attempt to win such beautiful characteristics but rather the fact that, at some time or another, the Christian will also worship Jesus Christ as Lord. Worship, of this order, transmutes all these other ingredients into what distinguishes the Christian from so many other good people whose lives can indeed be holy and in their own way uplifting for others. I think it is crucial to grasp this sense of the importance of worship at the outset. If we are to get some impression of what contribution the Charismatic Movement has made to Christian worship and, indeed, the problem it poses, it is necessary to underline that worship of Christ as Lord is what identifies and commits a person beyond levels of decency and sincerity and morality and this should, indeed, be the common purpose of humanity.

So in tackling this question of liturgical style and content we touch a very tender nerve. It is clear that this is so in the churches. Reasonable men and women can negotiate many issues about politics, property, ecclesiastical structures but, when it comes to 'Thee' or 'You', the *Book of Common Prayer* or the *Alternative Service Book*, the Latin of Trent or the Vatican II Mass, the hymns to be sung, the clothes to be worn, the ceremony to be used — then one can discover passions undreamt of and causes almost of life and death significance. It is on the question of eucharistic sharing that the outcome of church unity ultimately depends: that is the final sign of unity. But there remains, nevertheless, considerable confusion about worship. Liturgical style in a classical protestant sense offers something different from a catholic emphasis on the eucharist. And the stuff that goes into worship can differ greatly.

Whether, then, we come across dancing Pentecostals or marching African Christians, singing in tongues or intense personal prayer groups, we need to begin with as open a mind as possible in looking at this question. Christian worship is a diverse and wonderful experience, and not a perfected set of prescriptions and performances.

In September 1977 I met in London Bishop Labbe, president of a consortium of small independent Pentecostal Churches in Chile. He was coming to a small consultation in Rostrevor, Northern Ireland, on the Charismatic Renewal. We had a day to spend together before going on, and it was Sunday. I took him to mattins at Westminster Abbey. I was a little apprehensive as, when we first met earlier that year, I had gone with him to one of the tiny tin shelters on the outskirts of Santiago de Chile to share in a very different kind of worship. Would he find an English choir too much? I feared so. For as we listened to the *Te Deum* I heard him sobbing gently. It was a little unnerving, and his weeping became even more intense at the anthem. Embarrassed, I apologised afterwards, but he then told me that he wept from joy; never, he said, had he thought to hear what the heavenly angels might be like! Later, in 1980, when Robert McAlister, Bishop of an independent Pentecostal Church in Rio de Janeiro, Brazil, visited Lincoln, I was both delighted and surprised at his regularity in attending not only the sung office but also our said services in the cathedral. He was eager to get the new *Alternative Service Book* as well as the weekday *Missal.* Again, the reason was illuminating. He found that the disciplined use of psalm and scripture in the liturgical pattern of worship was so much more rewarding, and sometimes surprising, than the subjectively selected passages which tended to come from a fairly limited and predictable stock among his pastors. Both these stories illustrate the importance of having a sense of discovery about the way others worship; and perhaps encourage us to have a greater respect for the intrinsically valuable elements of our own experience and tradition, sometimes too easily caricatured or dismissed.

In the report *The Charismatic Movement in the Church of England* the authors list five aspects of the charismatic contribution to worship which, they suggest, comes out in style rather than content. The first is in the use of the body, and they point to the uplifting of hands, the linking of arms, clapping and rhythmic movement which might be called dancing. Secondly, they naturally identify the contribution in music, noting especially the impact of *Sounds of Living Waters* (1974) and *Fresh Sounds* (1976) together with guitars and a greater sense of the chorus. Thirdly, they notice the freedom allowed for contributions from the participants, pointing out the elements of prophecy and acts of healing and other forms of counselling which are encouraged. Fourthly, the Report suggests the rally as another feature of charismatic worship: the big meeting and inspiring occasion. Lastly, they indicate what Colin Buchanan has called an 'inchoate sacramentality' in the way in which music, art, healing, and colour are used almost as sacramentalist signs by those who might not have accepted easily such a tradition. This list is indicative but not exhaustive. It also seems to me to run the familiar risk of trivialising the deeper things that have happened. Again and again I am struck by the way the Charismatic Movement's influence is portrayed in disconcertingly obvious ways without much attempt to interpret what is happening in worship at a less obvious level. And there are positive and negative things to be said about that. In this essay I want to try to indicate some of those levels. The Report's analysis also illustrates the limitation of the charismatic experience in Britain, as well as the easy and uncritical importation of North American ingredients in worship.

The argument which follows examines some of the characteristics of worship in a general sense and then tries to see what contribution or problem the Charismatic Renewal has presented or may present. This will try to recognise some of the ambiguities that I belive exist. For instance, if we say that the charismatic style puts a fresh emphasis on 'meaning' in worship, that scripture should be read with great emphasis and care, that actions should not be perfunctory, and that words and actions should match, then the other side of that coin is the risk of artificially intense situations and a kind of exhaustion, which comes from stressing subjectivity far more than objectivity. Balancing between extremes may be a dull prescription for worship. It might be better to struggle with the risks.

Some Functions of Liturgy

What is worship? What does it do? If we take the classical word, liturgy, we find it means what the people owe, or should do, as a public service to God. Worship is about what people do together to proclaim Christ as Lord. I see a number of functions or elements in worship, of which not all may be necessary for liturgy, though one or another is always present. By looking at these individually I think we can identify the positive and negative aspects of the Charismatic Movement's influence. There are six functions we will look at: the nature of communion, or communication; the task of proclamation; the exercise of prophecy; the art of healing; the practical outcome in service to others and the need for praise and wonder. This list is not of course intended to be exhaustive.

In his first letter to the Corinthians, Paul writes, 'To sum up, my friends: when you meet for worship, each of you contributes a hymn, some instruction, a revelation, an ecstatic utterance, or the interpretation of such an utterance. All of these must aim at one thing: to build up the Church' (1 Cor. 14:26). This prescription is more suited to a Pentecostal church than some of the labyrinthine liturgies of orthodoxy. But it is the edification of the Church which is essential in this notion of communication. The word offers a double meaning as it implies communion — with God and between persons. Of course the eucharist is the *sine qua non* of Christian worship, and holy communion is evidently that unique service which can involve all the elements of worship. With the Liturgical Movement in this century there has been an increasing awareness of its importance in all churches, and a greater yearning to see Christians free to share in the one bread of thanksgiving, but it remains a stumbling-block. The Charismatic Renewal seems to have shared in several notable influences. First, there is in charismatic circles a much greater willingness to share the eucharist with other denominations. This may be frowned upon, but it happens. A wildfire ecumenism around the eucharist is probably the most necessary thing for the churches today: people should feel free to neglect ecclesiastical inhibitions and discover that the ground will not swallow them up if they share openly and happily. Here church order is threatened. It is a good threat. Secondly, there is an invitation for greater participation by more people in different ways. This happens with other kinds of services, but it is itself a new kind of 'communion'. More importantly, a wider involvement of people who confess the authority of the Holy Spirit, and who, in a sense, assert their baptismal power, leads us rapidly towards a newer understanding of the priesthood of all believers. This has tremendous importance for lay people and especially for women. There are, obviously, many in charismatic circles who are worried about such a trend, especially when it leads to the ministry of women. In fact, the antipathy to women in some charismatic circles is one of the sadder effects of a neo-fundamentalism which is discussed later. In Roman Catholic charismatic circles there is a sensitivity to the eucharistic question, and the need for due church order regularly reasserts itself. Is the Charismatic Renewal strong enough or courageous enough to pursue these lines of development to their ends? Probably not.

Thirdly, within this liturgical context another thing has emerged. That is prayer itself as communication. Prayer to God which points out who is in trouble, what anxieties there are, and which therefore exceeds the boundaries set by formal collects or traditional set piece, so-called 'extempore' prayers, introduces a new and very important element in worship. Such communication can risk banality, but it can also be edifying, threatening, clarifying and hopeful. Within eucharistic worship intercession has become more open; there is a greater degree of secularity in prayer which could lead us to a richer mysticism. This aspect of prayer brings many risks. But the vestigial formality of prayer style may be a healthy element in letting the people of God discharge their emotions over major or minor issues. The prayer group is, certainly, the most usual centre for this. And charismatic groups have found this a major point of growth and insight. Can such prayer go a step further? That is to say, is the communion we see in a stereotyped way capable of being something deeper, which is hinted at in the letter to the Hebrews, 'Remember those in prison as if you were there with them' (Heb. 13:3)? Such solidarity is perhaps the highest communion and so one wonders if in the churches there is truly a yearning for its pain and its potential. Time and time again one feels that in the insights of the Charismatic Renewal there are hints, signs and gestures pointing towards something more important about our worship but which all too often remains elusive.

Such freedom is bought at a price. Many feel that charismatic tendencies such as these challenge too far the spectator quality of a lot of religious services. There is a yearning by many for a deeper individual response to God which can be quenched by an open and gossipy style of service. There is a respect and admiration for the cadences of liturgical language and its profound objectivity which chatty and windy prayers obliterate. There is a desire for a communion with God which is deeply private and which is somehow challenged by the sheer banality of much that is taken as characteristically charismatic. So there is a need for discipline and a liturgical style which does not encourage anarchy. In my experience many of the most demanding leaders of liturgy are found in Pentecostal churches; the apparent freedom is a liturgical style which works within a firm structure for organised spontaneity. The first-timer at such a service can make mistakes of judgement about this.

Proclamation of the Word

If the eucharist is the kernel for Christian worship it is also the place where the Word of God is read and expounded. In characteristically Protestant services the Word of God has become the centrepiece, with the sharing in communion occurring less frequently or, indeed, not at all. This brings into focus the key role of proclamation in any act of worship; the distinguishing mark of the cry 'Jesus is Lord'. So there has been in recent decades, and again reflecting the general impact of the Liturgical Movement, a vigorous rediscovery of the importance of the Bible in worship. In the Acts of the Apostles we get the most succinct description of the act of worship: 'They met constantly to hear the apostles teach, and to share the common life, to break bread and to pray' (Acts 2:42). I have a vivid recollection of attending a weekday prayer service of the Word of God Community in Ann Arbor, near Detroit, in the United States. This is a famous community whose influence deserves a careful analysis. On this occasion the service had many familiar ingredients, new and bright songs, choruses, intercession and prophecy. What struck me was the hour-long teaching on the difficult and important issue of spiritual dryness — *accidie* in classical terms. This episode is an example of one of the strongest contributions to contemporary worship, the Charismatic Movement's investment in teaching, exposition, explanation and preaching. For those who hold the ten minute sermonette in veneration there is a lesson to be learned. Christian proclamation, in a time when fewer and fewer people know even the vaguest outline of biblical history or the stories which were once made familiar in Sunday school and in religious education, becomes a matter of grave importance. Here the impact of the Charismatic Movement is worth taking into account.

There is another aspect of this. The first testimony I ever heard as a youth was by someone on a street corner with a small group of Salvation Army officers. A few of us loitered with a mixture of puzzlement and embarrassment. And later other testimonies seemed rather the same, a mixture of exaggerated awfulness and wonderful salvation. However, I suspect that the Charismatic Renewal has picked up this evidential style of witness and given it a new lease of life. Telling stories about experience with a kind of middle class patina is a fresh ingredient in the pattern of proclamation. I think it is important, especially when we learn from sociological analysis, such as the work of David Davies at Nottingham, that religious experience is more usual than the theologian might expect. The problem of how to help people discover their own religious experience of God is a critical pastoral issue, and explaining the notion of 'baptism in the Spirit' is clearly an essential part of this task. Enabling people to talk about their experience and give their testimony is undoubtedly an important rediscovery in worship.

Teaching, preaching, testimony and singing are ingredients in this task of proclamation. I want to look at music in another context but one cannot overlook here the significance of the words in the new songs, especially as they are very often the words of scripture. Psalms and familiar biblical texts inspire the charismatic-style song, and this is a vast improvement on some of the weaker poetry and strange sentimentality of many of the traditional hymn books.

Is this all good? Linked with the hunger for teaching is an easy neo-fundamentalism about scripture which is disconcerting. One way to illustrate this is to recall the way in which Pauline utterances about women, again from Corinthians, have become a base-line for some charismatic leaders. I think this kind of neo-fundamentalism about scripture reduces the quality of proclamation too easily; religious convictions can easily become bland conventions and then off-putting arrogance. From a liturgical point of view an objective, rational use of scripture is needed which, without diminishing its authority in any way, fosters a greater respect for the revelation of God in Christ. That is why Robert McAlister's keenness about the liturgical texts of the new lectionaries in 1980 was significant. Proclamation requires a serious consideration of the whole deposit of scripture, which is often uncomfortable.

Recovery of the Prophetic

Allied to the task of proclamation is perhaps an even more significant element of worship and one which had almost disappeared in conventional forms of worship, that is the prophetic. Clearly, the uncomfortable experience of taking the whole of scripture seriously must be directed at conventional religion as much as at the Charismatic Renewal. Paul, again in 1 Corinthians 14, spends much of his time on giving directions about prophecy. 'Of the prophets, two or three may speak, while the rest exercise judgement upon what is said . . . You can all prophesy, one at a time, so that the whole congregation may receive instruction and encouragement' (1 Cor. 14:29, 31).

The recovery of prophecy in worship is surely the greatest of pentecostal contributions in this century and the charismatic adoption of this has been enriching for many occasions of worship. It is still not a regular or easily accepted feature of worship, and perhaps it is more suited to the 'rally' style listed in the Church of England report. In my experience prophetic statements in worship have tended to be couched in biblical, often Old Testamental, style; to have made some generalisation on an appropriate theme; to have risked banality; to have become accepted as a kind of ceremonial sanction and sometimes to have been uttered in tongues. So quickly we are enmeshed in some of the most controversial issues of the Charismatic Renewal. It is important to note this prophetic element in worship itself and to examine three things.

First, at a general level I believe worship itself should as a whole have a prophetic character. That is to say its proclamation that Jesus is Lord is the most profound in prophecy. Worship should almost without exception express a kind of contradiction in the world — sometimes overtly, sometimes less so. Conventional religion has, of course, risked blurring this. Yet there are ways in which the most traditional style of service can respond to this prophetic stream. The salutary example in Britain was the Falklands Islands service in St Paul's Cathedral. Here worship came into its own as a contradiction to the expectation of some politicians and most of the media pundits. The difficulty is to know when the liturgy should stand by itself, as a proclamation of the Lordship of Christ, to contradict our own self-sufficiency, or when it needs to be elaborated and become explicit about a specific issue, as a sign of contradiction. The Canterbury Cathedral service involving Pope John Paul II and Archbishop Runcie had something of this latter character; Daniel Berrigan burning draft cards during the Vietnam War equally achieved this prophetic statement. Thus the prophetic can be incorporated into liturgy without being vulgarised by words.

Secondly, the prophetic tradition as adapted in charismatic circles raises one particular issue. The debate focuses on the nature of revelation and the nature of the Church. Here Roman Catholics in the Charismatic Renewal are perhaps most careful to distinguish between prophecy as a way of inspiration, animation and encouragement and prophecy as a direct and unmediated word from God. For them the Church is the proper authority for interpreting the revelation. They look askance at any claim to a direct revelation. So while the rediscovery of prophecy in worship has something to commend it for instruction and encouragement (1 Cor. 14:31) it ought not to be seen as some way in which anything new can be added to the revelation in Jesus Christ. This may seem obvious. However, it should be noted, so that the risk of aberration is understood, that in the Jesus Movement of the late sixties and early seventies, which had charismatic, Pentecostal characteristics, leaders emerged who overtly claimed prophetic authority of the direct and unmediated kind. The most notorious of these was David Berg, the 'Moses' of the Children of God. In these circumstances the solid understanding of the Church as the living and worshipping sign, the icon, of the Holy Spirit in the world today, as it is grasped by the Orthodox, is a hugely important ecumenical insight and contribution. The perception of the Church as the advocate for humanity before God while being, at the same time, the mercy-place of God's love and forgiveness to humanity, leads us directly to a third observation.

The rediscovery of prophecy in worship hints at a rather naïve sense of the prophetic. The risk that people may be looking for a kind of seer or Christian 'fortune-teller' or morality-giver quickly diminishes the quality of the prophetic as an announcement of God's action or irruption into the world. The latter has much more to do with prophetic action which transforms or transmutes the perils of our life; which offers a word to build up and encourage those ready to stand for the sovereignty of the Lord and against the new sovereignties of our nuclear age. This is the third factor. The churches have not been behindhand in this confrontation and contradiction. Indeed, the Charismatic Movement may invite people to simpler anodynes in a world which craves for grander prophecy. Yet it should not be a word of condemnation but a word of reconciliation. For worship has to be about the possibility of rediscovering, almost daily, one's utter acceptance by God even when one is almost daily repudiating the Lord.

The Touch of Healing

At the same time as I met Bishop Labbe in Chile I attended an annual service of the Iglesia Pentecostal de Chile when a number of pastors were ordained. While many exuberant things happened in the worship of these six to seven thousand people, including the characteristic dancing in the Holy Spirit of Chilean Pentecostalism, I was most impressed by what followed the ordination of the twelve pastors. This was not a eucharistic service. Yet after the presiding bishop and his associate leaders had consecrated the men their very first act as new presbyters of this church was to lay hands for healing on many who came forward. I was conscious that here was an affirmation of ministry that had withered in western churches. Here was an expectation about ministry which had almost shocking vitality.

The Charismatic Renewal has brought into focus in worship the significance of a healing ministry. But this leads me to argue that one of the most neglected elements in worship is a stance on healing. Not that this need necessarily be explicit, although for many years, almost in anticipation of the Charismatic Renewal, the churches' ministry of healing has had its special services and the laying on of hands. Indeed, this is one of the earliest new liturgical elements in conventional worship.

So it is not new. What is perhaps fresh is the incorporation of aspects of a healing ministry into major services. At Lincoln Cathedral in 1979 Colin Urquhart led the second service of Praise and Proclamation, involving many hundreds of people with a ministry of healing which was striking in its difference: not so much a physical touch but a reaching out in sensitivity and awareness. Other charismatic leaders have developed different skills, especially Francis MacNutt OP, who places a great emphasis on inner healing — the healing of the memory. Many people testify to physical healing and this has to be taken seriously in evaluating the renewal. But here we look at it as it pertains to worship.

There are three aspects to note. First, it is characteristic of any liturgical pattern that it reserves a place for an expression of repentance and forgiveness. However attenuated and formal this may become it is a residual element of the healing ministry, for healing means the restoration to wholeness, and this need to say sorry and to be forgiven is a crucial first step in seeking wholeness. The work of MacNutt, Ruth Carter Stapleton and others in the healing of memory reflects this awareness of how deep-seated physical disorder can be. The difficulty is to find how the prose and formality of the liturgical expression can be lifted into something more meaningful and more effective. There is a risk of imposing an overwhelming emotional burden. Nevertheless there are surely times when worship can risk carrying that weight. The Charismatic Renewal challenges the churches on this point. In 1977, at a small consultation in Rostrevor, Northern Ireland, a Roman Catholic participant transformed the urbanity usually associated with a form of confession and absolution in a liturgy into something profoundly deep and consciously therapeutic. He took on, in the extrapolation of the formal words, the greater weight of offence, church to church, of the Reformation and invited us to share in an act of solidarity in almost confessing our forgiveness which I remember vividly to this day. Such moments are perhaps rare but their very rarity should not discourage us from seeking to bring them into liturgy. There can be right occasions, proper moments, when repentance and forgiveness become a truly vivid reality.

Secondly, one of the more encouraging things to happen in recent years in many Sunday liturgies is an opening out of intercession. A happy mixture of the established formulae and local, personal and contemporary subjects for prayer brings to intercession a new dimension. Perhaps this is largely due to the growing need to identify the sick by name and to ask the whole congregation to consider and pray for those who are in need of healing. Whether or not this rather ordinary development in liturgy owes much or little to the Charismatic Renewal is hard to say, but it is certainly an important way in which the ministry of healing has begun to recover a place in worship.

Thirdly, there is a growing sensitivity about the need for more counselling in contemporary spirituality. This, I believe, grows out of the notion of healing in worship. And certainly it is an aspect of the Charismatic Renewal which has to be recognised. But it also leads into one of the most fraught areas of renewal, especially in the North American experience. During the seventies one of the major issues in the United States was over 'discipling'. The notion had its origins in the work of Juan Carlos Ortiz in Argentina. It became almost a rage in some parts of the States. Essentially it recognised the need for close counselling — and advocated a network of relationships based on groups of ten; each leader with ten disciples — each disciple with ten others. There is much sense in this. The crunch came when tithing also became a responsibility in 'discipling'. A threat to the lines of both pastoral and financial responsibility in the churches was too much. The crisis was more or less settled by 1976 though there are echoes in Britain today. The point about this experience is not its aberrant nature, but rather the insight about pastoral relationships and spiritual development. The average congregation is too large (yes, indeed, even with the cry about diminishing numbers of church-goers) for one pastor to be an adequate spiritual counsellor. This theory of multiplication has much to commend it, so long as it remains within the boundaries of pastoral care, that is to say within the context of the worshipping community.

Considering all that is involved in the idea of healing in worship is too large a task here. These points are made to illuminate just how wide the area is. It could, I think, yet be the most significant contribution of the Charismatic Renewal to worship.

The Diakonic Role

As most of the ingredients so far listed could well have been given a

Greek title from the New Testament (*koinonia, propheteia, kerygmatic, therapeutic*), we may as well use one now. *Diakonia* is a richer word than 'service' and it brings with it a fuller sense of what is involved. The tension between action and prayerful waiting in the Christian life-style has become a noticeable one in the last decades. Charismatics have been criticised as neo-pietists who dodge the critical edges of life by diving into prayer huddles. This seems a rough caricature. The first thing to afirm is that worship should have some element of this sense of *diakonia*.

Indeed, the obvious sign of this is in the collection, however self-serving this may have become with the high cost of maintaining buildings and ministry. Alms-giving has been an integral part of the congregation's responsibility since the earliest church; the distribution of resources being a particular function of the first deacons (Acts 6:1-6). The re-awakening of generosity in this matter has been a particular feature of the Charismatic Movement. Churches which have developed a charismatic style are quick to point out the upward leap in congregational giving. This rather elementary side-effect on worship ought to be recorded.

But more than this. The emphasis on prophecy and healing inevitably drives the Charismatic Renewal into the area of social engagement. At the Anglican charismatic conference in July 1978 the theme 'love in action, all over the world' led to the setting up of SOMA, Sharing of Ministries Abroad. Indeed, the Charismatic Movement has been criticised by conservative protestants for its worldliness and social commitment. From another point of view there are reservations about yet another sort of 'collection'. In Britain Christian Aid, the Tear Fund and CAFOD (the Catholic Fund for Overseas Development) surely offer enough opportunities. But this trespasses into other areas of criticism.

From the point of view of worship the most important thing is surely to recognise that worship should lead to service and give stability and courage to those who live in the thick of engagement. Whether or not the Charismatic Renewal takes sufficient notice of this ingredient in worship is an important matter. No doubt prayer is the essential way of focusing the potential for action. Here the Charismatic Renewal has given healthy insights into the possibilities for group and community prayer which not only communicates needs but also offers a chance to express solidarity with the poor, the unloved and those who lack care.

Worship which gives support to those engaged in service can quite

Rex Davis

often be worship which offers continuity and stability rather than excitement and distraction. There is a case to be made for this alternative to the glitter and turbulence of a charismatic assembly in full flight. Whether worship can be extended for long enough to contain all these elements is questionable. Perhaps with the rare and great rally a rhythm can be set. But most regular worship is shorter and occurs more frequently. The pace can therefore be disconcerting if it is always trying to meet expectations which are too high. Yet there is also an important contribution to be made by charismatically moved people and clergy to the quietly offered, unspectacular small act of devotion and worship: a weekday mass said with care in the context of mature charismatic development is a rewarding experience.

The hidden worship behind many who have taken the forefront in social action should not be disregarded. Whether the Charismatic Movement can offer insights to strengthen and develop that gentler pattern of stability, continuity and steadiness is doubtful.

Praise to the Holiest

The most commonly talked about issue among charismatics and perhaps the most controversial is the question of 'tongues'. I do not see it as a major matter, so it comes last deliberately. I recall, some years ago, being with a Jesus Commune in Holland for a few days. Attending their morning prayer times I observed that many in the group fell into praying in tongues with ease. They were young people, many brought into the group through a conversion experience. I asked them when they began to pray in tongues and listened with wry amusement to the puzzled question, 'Why, doesn't every Christian?' Reading St Paul's instructions on worship in 1 Corinthians 14 one again has a sense that this is such a commonplace that it needs to be disciplined if it is not to become a nuisance. At one great community church of a neo-Pentecostal kind the powerful pastor will not allow 'tongues' in public worship. They are an occasion for private piety. So there is a wide range of understanding. The Pentecostal tradition in North America has brought back into worship the possibility of praying in tongues; from a Chilean point of view we might even have dancing! Clearly one has to analyse this with some care.

On the whole the question of praise in worship is not well treated. There are great hymns, polyphonic anthems, marvellous fugues: we mostly concentrate the notion of praise in music. With the Charismatic Movement there comes too a wider range of bodily involvement, so that praying and singing in tongues, acclamations, raising of hands, waving of handkerchiefs, great processions can add to and enrich the quality of praise. There is great emotional investment as well. Perhaps, as Gordon Davies says, there is an element of playfulness or game in worship, a kind of discharge, which the stricter shape of liturgy keeps in rein. I think this is a better way to understand these phenomena: elements of play and even anarchy within the limitations of decency and order. Room for laughter, delight, the quick smile, the sense of fun needs to be found in liturgy. Perhaps this discovery may be one of the better contributions to worship the Charismatic Renewal will make.

Surprisingly I think its least satisfactory contribution, so far, has been in the quality of its music, which is usually considered one of the most characteristic parts of charismatic style worship. But when all is said about the new songs and lively jigs and easily remembered choruses there doesn't seem to be much there. The Word of God Community at Ann Arbor has been prolific in its publication and recording of music and songs for its own and wider use. Karen Lafferty's *Allelulia* and *Seek Ye First*, Daniel Iveson's *Spirit of the Living God*, the Spanish song *Alabaré* have become stock pieces. The two hymn books *Sound of Living Waters* and *Fresh Sounds* have become handbooks of the movement. But even with the recovery of musical instruments in worship, the easily remembered melodies and the familiarity of choruses, there is something thin about the musical tradition. Bishop Labbe's reaction to the music of Westminster Abbey comes to mind. There are vast riches in the musical tradition of the churches hardly known from one to another. The ecumenical strength of sharing these experiences is scarcely tried: indeed, there is yet another tradition of song and poetry which has hardly gripped the churches.

Perhaps the effort to praise God is not buoyant enough. The African Independent Churches with Pentecostal roots have gone so much further with drums and trumpets. The Kimbanguist Church of Zaire, with its curious Baptist/Catholic roots, has a Salvation Army style about it and a rumbustious music which sets the great congregation marching. Musical praise is also strong in the Latin American experience of Pentecostalism. The Charismatic Renewal has started on a significant track here, but will it yet leave a lasting mark?

Building the Church

Finally, is all of this building up the church? St Paul's criterion needs to be recalled when we try to assess the impact of the Charismatic Movement on Worship. Perhaps the severest criticism is that much of what happens, especially at a surface level, can trivialise worship. The longing for stability and steadiness is a genuine one and deserves respect. Immature charismatic styles of worship can greatly harm the integrity of worship. On the other hand a mature charismatic insight can assist very much in the opening out and enhancing of worship. But who is to judge levels of maturity? Perhaps this comes with insight and experience. I am pretty convinced, though, that many of the better things happening in the worship of local congregations owe more than people admit to the Charismatic Renewal, or, if the obvious is stated, to the Pentecostal revival.

The Charismatic Joy of
Liturgical Dance Movement

NELL CHALLINGSWORTH

Prayer has many forms, and dance, which is an extension of speech, is both a new and an old expression of love and communication between people, and between people and God. Language and age are transcended and whether one is a viewer or a dancer a wonderful bonding takes place in this gentle art form. The Charismatic Movement is a sweeping one, covering almost too vast a canvas, yet what a challenge and joy this interpretation of worship is! To offer one's talents to God is a form of worship and prayer, and whereas once rigidity in religion was taken for granted, the open world that we live in today permits and encourages us to surmount barriers that once were impassable.

Liturgical dance movement is an old, yet new, form of prayer, and it is accepted as world-wide Christian activity in modern times. There are many versions, but all are walking and dancing along the same broad path to the Lord. In the scriptures, references to dance and movement are mostly linked with praise and joy, as we read in Ps. 149:2-4:

> Let Israel rejoice in their Maker;
> Let the people of Zion be glad in their King,
> Let them praise His name with dancing
> And make music to Him with tambourine and harp,
> For the Lord takes delight in His people.

In all approaches to charismatic worship, discipline is vital — for a choir singing as loudly as possible or an organ being played at full volume does not make the singer or organist a more worshipful person. So in liturgical dance movement a knowledge of control and of light and shade is essential if this form of prayer is to be offered and understood. Perhaps we could say that dance is the Cinderella of the arts: the easiest to abuse, not written, not recorded, ephemeral, received by the eye, and even as it reaches the mind it is already away and gone. Yet sometimes the memory of beautiful movement does linger for a lifetime. Dance in worship presents a wonderful opportunity to express Christian thoughts and feelings, irrespective of our denominational differences.

No art falls like a mantle on our shoulders. The learning process, the discipline, the disappointments and the joys are all there in dance, just as they are in music, painting, sculpture and poetry. There is a yearning in us all to be better and this means applying ourselves to the utmost to any offering we may make. To work together in depth is very soul-warming, but if this is to be done at all, then it should be done to the very best of our abilities. Self-satisfaction is a danger to be avoided. It is so easy to dance our prayers to God, enjoying ourselves thoroughly whilst irritating and exasperating the watching congregation, just as if we were singing out of tune.

Wishing is not enough, there must be effort too. To my mind all dance and movement is Christian in its striving to perfect the body and soul given us by God. We all make our prayers in different mediums and in today's charismatic world drama and mime are frequently used, but if dance is chosen then much work must be done to achieve and maintain a good, consistent standard. Too often one hears, 'But the Lord led us to this easy, slack way of moving', or 'The Lord gave His Spirit to us to sit around and talk, but not to do.' This danger of neglecting the effort needed to meet a fresh challenge, has to be faced resolutely.

To be charismatic is to be positive. Polite disinterest is the attitude of many people towards religious movement prayer. This must be accepted and understood. Not all of us sing in choirs, not all of us serve the Lord in other ways, so why should the world stand still for those who wish to dance? A great disservice is done to sacred dance by the unintentional over-enthusiasm and forcefulness of the dance prayer where the participant seems to be saying, 'watch me dance, or else!'

All nations have dance formats, so all peoples have dance forms within their folk lore and culture to serve as a foundation for their offerings on movement. This door is opening wider and wider for everyone to use in one way or another. In Australia, the very vastness of the country presents difficulties for organised progress. The original Australians contribute richly with their dance and creative art forms. The purity of their talents is outstanding, and the Christian Dance Fellowship of Australia, a nationwide association, as well as other groups, feel most privileged to work with these artistic people.

In every way, inter-relationships are of the greatest importance nowadays. No blended charismatic activity should depend on just the dancers. There should also be the full collaboration of musicians, composers, designers, sound specialists and lighting experts. These need not necessarily be professional, but competent and willing to work and pray together over this art form.

To see the word 'charismatic' defined is revealing. Its primary meaning is: 'an extraordinary power (as of healing) given a Christian by the Holy Spirit, for the good of the Church'. But the word has also acquired the secondary meaning, 'a personal magic of leadership' and 'a special magnetic charm or appeal'.[1] These qualities all add up to the joy and happiness of this movement expressed through liturgical dance. The joy of contact through the meeting of the eyes, the touching of hands, and the special 'togetherness' of rhythmic movement not only bring people closer together but may well touch the hearts and spirits of those who are already Christians from hearing and reading the gospel but who have never tried to experiment in this entirely different, unusual art form.

There seems to me to be no need for argument concerning the various forms of dance worship. Whether structure is used, or whether creative movement is the basis of each offering, both are beautiful in their own way. The occasion and the clergy both provide guide-lines, and it is for the dance leader, whether professional or not, to be fully aware of the danger of over-exposure and take special care to understate a little. Within any religious service dances should silently materialise, causing no disturbance to the congregation, and then de-materialise. Dances should not take place weekly, but at rather longer intervals. They should be not a worry but rather a solace and an inspiration to those attending the service. I greatly applaud the suggestion put forward by Margaret Daniel, a reviewer for the English *Church Times*, that it must surely be only a matter of time before the first School of Church Dance is established to complement the School of Church Music. All arts emphatically can and do enrich worship.

Outdoor religious pageantry, re-enacting stories from the scriptures, was performed at the time of the Eucharistic Congress of 1973 in Melbourne. A choir of one hundred voices combined with two hundred parishioners from all age groups, both dancers and non-dancers, to portray scenes from the Bible. On another important occasion, dance was woven into the ecumenical service celebrating the Ascension, during the Australian week of prayer for Christian unity and the World Council of Churches' Conference on Mission and Evangelism. This took place at St Patrick's Cathedral, Melbourne, on Thursday, 15 May 1980. Fifty dancers, starting on the grounds outside, led the dignitaries into the cathedral. Liturgical dance movement was also part of the service for 'the procession of the Word', and also at the time of the 'gifts'. At 'the going forth' the dancers led the procession out to the organ music of the third section of Olivier Messiaen's *L'Ascension*, 'Transports de joie d'une ame devant La Gloire du Christ, qui est la sienne'. On this occasion the colours for the dancers' robes were taken from the stained glass windows, using ruby, gold, purple, sapphire and emerald. Illustrations of this event may be seen on the cover of my handbook, *Liturgical Dance Movement*.[2] Here was religious pageantry in its fullest form, with dance as an integral part of the worship. But even one or two dancers in the smallest chapel can equally express the overwhelming joy of liturgical dance movement as we know it today.

Notes

1 See 'charismatic' in Webster's dictionary.
2 Nell Challingsworth, *Liturgical Dance Movement* (Mowbray, Oxford, 1981).

The Spirit of Truth

MARTIN ISRAEL

However, when he comes who is the Spirit of truth, he will guide you into all truth, for he will not speak on his own authority, but he will tell you only what he hears; and he will make known to you the things that are coming. He will glorify me, for everything that he makes known to you he will draw from what is mine. All that the Father has is mine, and that is why I said, 'Everything that he makes known to you he will draw from what is mine.'

John 16:13-15

An essential property of the Spirit of God is that he is the messenger of truth. What he imparts leads us into the full liberation of the person from the shackles of superstition, ignorance and fear. He leads us into truth not so much by imparting mysterious, arcane information as by making us more open to the full thrust of God's love. This love sets us free from a self-centred way of life in which we are intent above all else on maintaining our own status and what we regard as our private identity. It liberates us from a driving regard for our own safety by opening us to the immense potentiality of life. As Jesus teaches, 'Whoever cares for his own safety is lost; but if a man will let himself be lost for my sake and for the Gospel, that man is safe' (Mark 8:35). The ultimate truth of the human condition is that all attachment to earthly things is vain, since they are by their very nature transient. Man has a nobler, higher destiny than this: he is to escape the corruption with which lust has infected the world, and come to share in the very being of God (2 Pet. 1:4). This visionary end of the human struggle, so often apparently consummated in the futility of a failed life — failed at least by human standards — will amuse the atheistic humanist by its naïve refusal to face basic facts of mortality. But it is nevertheless the stuff of spiritual aspiration, and has been attested, at least in some measure, by the saints of all the great religious traditions, and by none more fully than by Jesus Christ. In Jesus we see one who not only showed extreme charismatic powers but also identified himself completely with the human condition at its most tragic, dying in agony between two criminals. And by this death he showed that death itself can be a precursor to a resurrection of all mortal, corruptible elements. It is in this context that the belief in the resurrection of the body finds its most exalted substantiation.

What has the Charismatic Renewal Movement to say to us about these momentous themes? It is evident that throughout the history of the Christian Church and more particularly in fairly recent times believers of a considerable denominational range have been the recipients of an ecstatic religious experience. It has usually been sudden and not infrequently unpremeditated, but sometimes it has been transmitted in groups by the imposition of hands or the psychic transmission of enthusiasm in the emotional fervour of a religious meeting. The main feature of this ecstasy is an opening of the personality to the warmth of a universal relationship, so that a person who was previously shut up in himself, emotionally inhibited and unable to pray with real conviction because of stultifying intellectual agnosticism or personal pride, is now released to show himself to the world, even as a child. We are told by Jesus that whoever does not accept the kingdom of God like a child will never enter it (Mark 10:15). All at once the promises of the Christian faith cease to be either visionary illusions or primitive prescientific superstition, but become instead the very staple of reality. Above all, the gifts of the Holy Spirit, enumerated by St Paul in 1 Corinthians 12, become tangible, and the renewed person may experience at least some of them. The most typical, but not invariable, gift is a peculiarly rapt personal way of prayer described alternatively as speaking in tongues, glossolalia, or the gift of ecstatic utterance of different kinds. Other fairly common expressions of spiritual release of the personality are the gift of healing, effecting unusual phenomena, and a deep faith in God's providence as stated through the authority and promises of the Bible. Less common gifts are those of discernment, wisdom, interpretation and prophecy, at least in their more fully realised expression. It may be that these rather more profound manifestations of spiritual power require a radical cleansing of the personality.

It would seem that there is an opening of the personality to the renewing power of the Holy Spirit, who is both within the person and a universal transcendent presence that unites all who are available to his presence into a dedicated body of believers. This Spirit bears his own harvest of spiritual qualities, of which the three principal ones are love, joy and peace: others are patience, kindness, goodness, fidelity, gentleness and self-control (Gal. 5:22). As one becomes fully infused with the power of the Holy Spirit, so one can relinquish one's fears and insecurity to his care and start to become open to the challenge of life, especially to one's fellow men. In this openness there can be self-giving love that does not fear depletion, a peace that depends on God's inexhaustible providence, and a joy of being oneself as one was fashioned, without a single reservation or regret. It is in this frame of reference that there is a free exchange of psychic energy to those around one — this is an emanation of emotional power with strongly spiritual overtones that flows directly from the centre of the personality that is traditionally called the soul. It is this interchange of psychic energy that lies at the heart of a real relationship between two (or more) people. They are bound together by ties of mutual regard that transcend mere intellectual agreement or emotional dependence. All real living is meeting, in the words of Martin Buber. Meeting is sharing, giving, receiving and healing one another by the power of God's Spirit, who unites all believers committed to God's service into a single body. The result is that the focus of personal identity expands to include many other people, thus fulfilling the second great commandment of loving one's neighbour as oneself. Only when I am my neighbour in expanded consciousness can I regard him as myself; only when I am aware of God's love for me can I love myself. This self-love is an essential precondition for loving everyone else in like acceptance and with similar intensity. When the Holy Spirit has infused one's whole being to this extent, one is fully charismatic. Jesus Christ showed the power and extent of this charismatic gift in its fullest range and most exalted quality.

When these properties of the full spiritual awakening in a person are compared with the fruits, so far as I have seen them, of the Charismatic Renewal Movement, there is much positive evidence of enhanced spiritual awareness for which one can give unreserved thanks to God. At last prayer becomes a dynamic response to God's love, and His presence is the central focus of one's life. The charismatic praise of God for His presence and the thanksgiving for all that He has given us is a real acknowledgement of His saving power. In other words, the Renewal Movement has brought religious observance alive to many people who previously recited set prayers and offices in a detached way, more a ritual than a living communication with God and with their fellow Christians. It is a sad fact of human nature that we tend to move all too easily from one extreme to another. When a religion becomes established in the life of a people it settles all too easily into a fossilised ritual action devoid of living content. At the same time, the analytical intellectual faculty dissects its language and preconceptions until they appear to be merely relics of archaic thought processes. When religious faith tries to gratify the prince of this world by serving mammon as well as God, it often so dilutes its spiritual content that it is in danger of sacrificing its identity and nullifying its unique witness. Fortunately there is a recurrent tendency for spiritual enthusiasm to infuse the hearts of at least a few exceptional people, so that a deeper insight into reality is vouchsafed them than their more pliable contemporaries who identify the *status quo* with the height of wisdom.

But spiritual enthusiasm has its own dangers. The chief among them is a conviction of its own impeccable correctness that tends to brush aside, if not totally ignore, any other approach to truth. We all have deep within us a yearning for that absolute truth which will set our weary hearts at rest. Then we can at last surrender ourselves in complete trust to a tried way of life that will solve all our problems and elucidate all our difficulties. We are told by Jesus to love God with all our heart, soul, mind and strength, and to love our neighbour as ourself (Mark 12:29-30). This means that every aspect of the personality has to be included in the love of God, which is a precondition of both accepting ourselves and accepting others in the same open faith. Spiritual ecstasy can emphasise the emotional and intuitive side of the personality while laying too little stress on the demands of the body and ignoring the claims of reason altogether; in other words, God is loved with heart and soul, but the intellect and the social context of common life are by-passed. This is a danger of all spiritual movements, that they may move towards a type of gnosticism that pays too little regard for earthly reason and devotes too little attention to the social need in its vicinity. It can become elitist and other-worldly while being sincerely devoted to the service of God and the love of Christ. Therefore, the feeling of certainty that spiritual renewal imparts may be dangeorusly partisan; its one-sidedness may blind one to other aspects of truth, which are then either ignored or else assailed as the work of the dark, demonic forces that govern the material world.

If the Charismatic Renewal Movement is to be a real life-giving force to the Christian witness, it must, in the form of its master, Jesus Christ, assume the role of a servant. It must learn the greatest of all spiritual lessons, humility. The Son of God neither spurned the virgin's womb nor did he reject his final earthly situation, nailed to a cross between two criminals with whom he was inseparably identified. Indeed, one account of the Passion identifies one of these criminals as the first genuine Christian for he acknowledged the humiliated Christ, when all those below the cross remained bewildered (Luke 23:41-42). There can be no love without humility, for only the humble man can be unconditionally open to the love of God. Indeed, the power of the Holy Spirit can work to its full effect only in a person so cleansed of egoism and personal demands for assurance and recognition that he sets up no barrier to the Spirit's action in him and through him. This demand for inner purity becomes real to many of us only after the illusions of personal ownership and importance have been shattered by the vicissitudes of life. We, like the Prodigal Son, may have to come to our own destitution before we are able to hear the Spirit within us leading us to the Father. There is no easy way to spirituality, and yet the call of the Holy Spirit is one of child-like ease to the person who has left his ego behind in service to those around him. The Holy Spirit works most abundantly in the person who is aspiring to a knowledge of God by the practice of contemplative prayer and an assiduous service to his fellow men. A part of this service is faithful, unobtrusive membership of a worshipping community, for we do not exist as whole people except as members of a corporate body of believers, whether seen or unseen.

When the Holy Spirit awakens one to one's full humanity, he also leads one into the unconscious depths where one has to encounter the shadow side of one's personality. This was described symbolically in Jesus' journey into the wilderness to be tempted by the devil after he was baptised and the Holy Spirit descended fully upon him. Indeed, it

was the same Spirit that led him to a confrontation with the evil of
the world. Though himself without sin — which means a selfish concern
for his own well-being at the expense of other people's need — he
accepted the world's stain in order to cleanse it and rescue his fellow
men from the domination of the darkness of evil. The climax of his
ministry centred decisively on the assumption of evil in order to redeem
its victims, so that he ended his life as a figure of execration on the
cross. The great word in this process is not destruction but transfigura-
tion. The Holy Spirit heals all fallen elements — these, too, are part
of God's original creation — and brings them transformed to play their
unique part in God's kingdom. Until the full renewing thrust of the
Holy Spirit has made its mark on the personality so that perfect love
has overcome all fear, the religious devotee tends to see life in terms
of a dualism of good and evil. He looks with revulsion on his own past
life, that life which extended up to the momentous event of his second
birth in Christ, and that disapproval is visited on to all others who do
not share his present enthusiasm. Amongst those who especially evoke
this lack of charity are members of his own worshipping community
whom he regards as second-class Christians because they cannot accept
all his insights unconditionally. It follows that many congregations have
been split asunder by the force of an ill-digested Charismatic Renewal.
This does not necessarily mean that one faction has greater right on
its side than the other, but simply that forbearance and patience have
been in abeyance. And these two qualities are of the very essence of
love, which St Paul reminds us can face anything since there is no limit
to its faith, its hope and its endurance; indeed, love will never come
to an end (1 Cor. 13:7-8). To whom much has been given, much is
expected. Indeed, the one rich in spiritual gifts is the servant of all in
the likeness of Christ. There is no judgement in love, only outflowing
compassion that is consummated in practical help. If the help is rejected,
the love continues in prayer, and communion is not broken.

There can be little doubt that some members of the Renewal Movement are highly censorious of their fellows. This tendency to judge others
is not due simply to a strong conviction of their own spiritual rectitude
based on charismatic gifts of prayer or healing. It has a more dangeorus
component of claiming discernment of spirits, so that those not in the
fold are insidiously identified as agents of darkness. 'He who is not with

me is against me', is a characteristic expression of this attitude, and the results can be devastating in the lives of many people. It is in this very question of discernment that the most serious criticism of aspects of the Renewal Movement rests. The most immediate impact in any human relationship is motivated psychically — from soul to soul without rational content — so that a strong impression of good or evil, truth or falsehood, is indelibly communicated. What is imparted in this way must then be tested rationally before a final assessment can be made. The psychic sense and the intuition must always be subjected to critical intellectual analysis; on the other hand, it must retain its own authority despite intellectual criticism, for all truth has a non-rational, as well as a rational, component. Where psychic impressions and intuitive judgements are so liable to distortion is in the matter of unresolved emotional conflicts raging in the unconscious. This emotional instability leads one all too easily to accept what one wants to believe rather than what is necessarily true. The question of psychic sensitivity is complicated further by the possible intrusion of mischievous elements in the collective unconscious of the human racial mind. Some of this material derives from residual mental processes or memories (often called thought forms), and there is also the presence of the 'spirits' of people once living in this world and now deceased to be considered. That other presences, alternatively angelic or demonic, may also make their presence felt in this vast psychic realm seems probable, especially to those of us who are sensitive.

It is for this reason that meddling in the occult is very strongly condemned in all spiritual teaching, especially that of the Bible. Although the psychic realm is not as black as its antagonists paint it — it is somewhat similar in spiritual content to our own world, but being intangible, it is more subtle in its effects — it is certainly not a dimension to be glibly explored. Inasmuch as like attracts like on the spiritual plane, so the degree of spiritual awareness will determine the type of contact a casual investigator is likely to encounter. People of high spiritual calibre do not involve themselves in occult exploration, but as part of their healing work they may offer themselves to help all living forms in all dimensions of reality. This is their contribution to the resurrection of created forms to the immortal sphere. Prayers for the dead are one expression of this healing work, but there are more demanding ways of self-giving that may be revealed by the Holy Spirit. None of this, it should be added, is undertaken as an individualistic venture; it is shown to the charismatic person as his special work of discernment and deliverance according to the direction and inspiration of the Spirit of God. It is well-known that saintly people tend to manifest spiritual gifts as their sanctity develops. This is the right way of development of charismatic power: the spiritual precedes and informs the charismatic with its strongly psychical component. When there is a strong psychic power without spiritual direction, the person possessing and emanating the force is as likely to be an agent of destruction as one of healing to those who are attracted to him. This is why psychic healing power devoid of a spiritual concern for people and a devotion to God is not likely to be ultimately beneficial, no matter how impressive its immediate effects may appear to be. Members of the Charismatic Renewal Movement are especially aware of this danger, and in this respect they are to be commended.

But is the psychic sensitivity that may be a product of the Renewal Movement any more to be trusted than that of a naturally gifted person who has no strong religious faith or spiritual attitude to life? If the recipient of the spiritual grace is a person of deep spirituality, the answer lies in the affirmative. If, however, a person is new to the spiritual dimension of reality, and is full of emotional enthusiasm based on an ecstatic experience of release from past inhibitions and doubts, the degree of discernment is severely limited and not to be trusted. It is much more likely that such a person is simply jettisoning his newly-released unconscious complexes into the general psychic atmosphere, and especially on to anyone or any teaching of which he disapproves or whose impact he fears. This indiscriminate psychic rejection leads to a spirit of fanaticism that finds its apogee in the traditional witch-hunt of all who may threaten the warm certitude of the believer. As we have already noted, the first action of the Holy Spirit in the life of a believer is to bring him face to face with the truth of the less acceptable elements of his own unconscious. As these are accepted, so they are redeemed by the power of the Holy Spirit. And as we accept more and more our own divided self, so we can begin to accept a wider range of the people around us. This acceptance is not an impersonal permissiveness devoid of all moral content. It is a practical love that seeks, in the greatest humility, to lift those around it from the bondage of death to the freedom of a new type of life. When we are centred in ourselves we are bound to mortality, but when that centre extends to embrace our fellow creatures, we move from death to life. As St John puts it, 'We for our part have crossed over from death to life; this we know, because we love our brothers' (1 John 3:14). It is then that the psychic rapport between ourselves and others is quickened and also purified. There is neither self-seeking nor fear, only a love that brings all creatures into its orbit. 'There is no room for fear in love; perfect love banishes fear' (1 John 4:18). It is the two self-centred attitudes of acquisitiveness on the one hand and fear on the other that colour and distort the psychic sensitivity which lies at the heart of the gifts of the Holy Spirit. Only when the personality is attaining to some degree of purification of its aberrant elements, can the full work of the Spirit of God find its place there. Then discernment, which is frank, critical and unsentimental, is balanced by love with its full acceptance. The two work together towards the healing of all that was aberrant and maladjusted. In this way, justice and love work hand-in-hand towards the resurrection of life in eternity.

The Charismatic Renewal Movement is potentially one of the most important manifestations of spiritual life in the Christian world. It breaks down denominational barriers by 'making fast with bonds of peace the unity which the Spirit gives' (Eph. 4:3). It opens the rigid mind to the practical consequences of God's action in the common life, thus making prayer the most exalted work of the human spirit. But until it has effected a radical self-knowledge in the life of the believer, its wider effects are as likely to be distorted and aberrant as integrated and healing. An injudicious opening of the personality can let in various ill-informed influences from afar that can cause personal, as well as communal, havoc, especially as they can all masquerade as authentic manifestations of the Holy Spirit. The mind as well as the heart has to be renewed by the Holy Spirit. This means a sharpened critical faculty to dissect all specious spiritual claims, and also a keen regard for social issues confronting the world so clamantly at present.

Holiness involves all aspects of the person — body, mind, emotions and spiritual intuition. It also involves all members of society. It cannot tolerate injustice and exploitation under the guise of a religious *status quo*. When the Charismatic Movement shows a constructive understanding of psychic sensitivity, a proper respect for the critical function of the intellect and a deep concern for raging social issues in the world's midst, it will have fulfilled its central concept of renewal.

The Charismatic Ethic and the Spirit of Post-Industrialism

DOUGLAS DAVIES

While enough research has now been done to justify the view that glossolalia is a naturally occurring and acquirable phenomenon other findings record tongue-speakers saying that as it is a gift from God alone human efforts will never fully explain its true significance. These two dimensions provide the challenging setting for our exploration of charismatic religion. We look first at the more psychological aspects of speaking in tongues as it affects the individual, then at the sociological factors touching that individual in a group context, and finally we consider some theological issues which inevitably arise from these reflections. All of this discussion is seen as taking place within that broad shift from industrial to post-industrial society which we witness now in Britain and which we believe is not without important consequences for religious life and thought.

For the individual who has come to possess charismatic faith life has changed quite dramatically in a qualitative way. After a period of uncertainty and doubt and a suspicion that religion should be more rewarding than it seems to be, the person concerned is likely to become associated with those already holding a charismatic position. Those already within religious bodies, and they appear to be the largest constituency, often feel somewhat inferior to the charismatic Christian. This sensation of inferiority is fostered by the actual state of uncertainty and doubt common to many people at some time during their life, not least in the earlier stages of professional life, and by the living example of flourishing spirituality presented in the charismatic friend. The person feeling inferior then concedes religious rank to the charismatic, and sets out to gain that desired status which consists of a particular religious experience. [1] Very many kinds of religious conversion may begin with such a juxtaposition of felt need and identified source of satisfaction, and while in many religious groups it is possible for the newcomer to imitate the behaviour of established members in the course of emulation, this very thing is deemed impossible in the charismatic context precisely because it is God who confers the gift of the Spirit. The necessity of supernatural intervention further increases anxiety especially in people who are normally very competent in organising their own life and its vicissitudes. And this is likely to be the case since it is the middle-class domain which has been most influenced by the Charismatic Revival of religion, unlike the classical Pentecostalism of the early twentieth century which embraced many working class and industrially based members. Attendance at prayer meetings or other gatherings at church or in homes familiarises him with glossolalia and shows it to be a goal attainable by him even though it is of such a divine origin.

The breakthrough into his own speaking in tongues may come in several different ways or contexts, but it is very likely to involve a religious leader praying with him, over him, and for him in order that he should gain this heavenly gift. He may even be encouraged simply to open his mouth and make sounds for the Spirit to mould as He will. The initiate may speak there and then, first falteringly but with increasing fluency as time goes on, or he may find himself so speaking when alone. Whichever is the case the event will be a profound emotional and religious experience and will make him feel bolder, more self-assured and competent not only in his religious life but also in his work and married life. J. P. Kildahl's important psychological study shows that the sense of achievement accompanying the euphoria of initial glossolalia is linked with a submission to the authority figure of the charismatic group, one who acts as a focus for regression and a transfer of relationship for the new speaker. Furthermore approximately eighty five per cent of those entering this verbal state have experienced an anxiety state at the time of entry. [2] With the speech comes a relief and a sense of group member-ship which carried with it a subtle disrespect for those who do not speak in, or show an interest in, tongues. Those who cease to use this speech do so most frequently after disagreeing with or otherwise falling out with the leader. In fact the authoritarian leader is an important figure for the individual member of a charismatic group, and may have been overlooked under the widespread supposition that charismatic religiosity is spontaneously free and devoid of regulation. The masochistic element of submission to a strong leader is noteworthy for the linking of a leader with a source of divine power implies the existence of a spiritual leader, who is a fairly distinct type within the phenomenology of religion.

Peter Ball has shown that glossolalia is not as significant as might at first be thought in forming a sense of personal identity, though some caution is needed here because his attempt to liken glossolalia to the actual languages of ethnic minorities is suspect.[3] Perhaps a sense of identity is formed by several features which include glossolalia and submissive group membership.

One important factor is the conviction that this language is definitely not learnt but received as a gift, a feature which is all the more intriguing if it is indeed a learned behaviour. No single and conclusive reply can be made here but one potentially very interesting suggestion may be offered, arising from Ernst Cassirer's study of mythological thought. Cassirer associates mythological language with that intuitive mode of thought which seems to be one of the major kinds of thinking process of mankind, and he notes how the intuitive source of ideas often leads to the thinker perceiving his thoughts as something bestowed upon him.[4]

If the glossolalic act is itself a behaviour pattern which originates in a combination of the intuitive centres of thought and the speech centres, involving a lack of higher conscious control of proper verbal content, then it would perhaps be possible to see how it is perceived by the speaker to be a 'received' language. When we add to this the belief in its divine source we can well understand the power which attaches to it as a religious experience. Tongues thus enables the expression of emotion and sentiments of worship without the use of discursive language; the ineffable is spoken but in a language of mystery — of mystery even to the speaker. The transcendence of linguistic convention mirrors the transcendence of ordinary life as the intuitive mode of thought is given free rein in a medium usually restricted to rationally controlled messages. Unlike purely private religious thoughts or sentiments glossolalia is also a social sign marking a fellow-feeling and fellowship with similar speakers.

The role of the intuitive dimension of thought needs stressing when considering the tongue-speaker's certainty that baptism in the Spirit is the source of wholeness and fulfilment in life. Batson and Ventis have reported that profound conversion experiences seem to activate the non-logical mode of thought and response which seems to affect the individual in a creative and integrative manner.[5] While such experiences are a kind of regression they appear to be positive and beneficial for the individual. The important research of Felicitas Goodman which takes a cross-cultural perspective also hints at the neurological basis of the universal similarity of glossolalic utterances.[6] It may perhaps not be an accident that glossolalia has been described as musical sound, for the very capacity to sing may belong to those brain centres dealing with intuitive creativity.[7] It is certainly the case that the Charismatic Renewal has witnessed an extensive growth in hymnody and its ethos marks the communal nature of this spirituality. Moreover, the songs are noteworthy more for the repetitiveness of phrases than for discursive statements of a theological kind.[8] Even if the explicit power of assertion is lacking in charismatic hymns, as in glossolalia itself, both forms of expressed sentiment serve to focus and heighten commitment to the charismatic group. Though glossolalia may function as a personal and private ritual which touches those depths of human emotion of joy and sorrow which are normally expressed in laughter and weeping, as R. A. Hutch rather unconvincingly suggested, its undoubted strength lies in uniting speakers into a powerful group.[9] Indeed the psychological evidence that exists tends to show that glossolalia is relatively insignificant as a personality integrator when compared with the general influence of a group of like-minded people centred on a respected leader.[10]

It is within such a group that trust and surrender to the will of others emerges. While a degree of anxiety in life and with religion assists a newcomer to yield to group values and behaviour, too great an anxiety or too much depression or hostility probably prevents a person becoming glossolalic.[11] This now brings us to consider the importance of the group as a factor in charismatic religion. We have already stressed the significance of the leader; what we have not noted is the fact that the leader's 'tongue' is reflected in that of the group members. Although each person's 'tongue' alters slightly over time, there remains a recognisable pattern within it, and that pattern itself resembles the speech of the one who introduced the speaker to speaking in tongues.[12] While there is no doubt that the group helps to educate and stimulate the beginner, it is the case that a 'tongue' can emerge spontaneously without having been imitated.[13] But this is rare, and it is more common for the newcomer to be familiar with the sound of tongues before speaking himself. The breakthrough into speech may assist other changes taking place in life: tongues can act as a sign of breaking with past events and committing oneself to new friends and new use of leisure, as well as to church membership.

Glossolalia is not a 'language' in any strict sense of the word. I do not yet know of any authentic cases of people speaking a language they have never heard or learnt despite the fact that charismatics tell and retell stories of people who are supposed to have done such a thing. In the Christian tradition with its heavy emphasis upon the Word of God revealed through prophets and enshrined in scripture the notion of a communicative language holds high status; thus glossolalia has acquired the status of a language proper, though this cannot be accepted on linguistic grounds. It is interesting to note that even a theologian of Professor C. F. D. Moule's standing can let slip the aside that it sometimes appears 'that the ability to speak a known human language is bestowed on someone', but if any theological sense is to be made of glossolalia it behoves us to arrive unequivocally at a strict understanding of the phenomenon in question.[14] Here it is assumed that glossolalia is a naturally occurring human vocal behaviour, which serves different purposes in different contexts, only one of which I want to pursue here, namely that of middle class charismatic groups.

Before stating what I have called in the title of this chapter the charismatic ethic in relation to the Spirit of Post-industrialism, a task involving much generalisation, it will be useful to outline a more limited theory of glossolalia as a major element in the dynamics of charismatic groups. In effect I am outlining an argument I first advanced some years ago and which applies the concept of linguistic and social codes to glossolalia.[15] Professors Mary Douglas and Basil Bernstein have argued that different forms of social organisation found in, for example, working class and middle class families, generate different styles of language.[16] Bernstein denotes as a 'restricted code' that pattern of language use which reinforces social solidarity, and in which meaning is logically implicit but poorly differentiated. Such a 'public' language may be contrasted with a 'formal' language operating upon an 'elaborated code' base and which serves to communicate more highly conceptualised statements and which makes the speaker stand out as an individual with a point of view of his own. 'Baby-talk' may be taken as the polar type of restricted code language since its cognitive content is minimal and its affective and relational quality is of maximum importance. A philosophical dispute by contrast is reckoned to communicate a strict message with minimum personal involvement in the event. The restricted code user makes the form of the language express his relation to the hearer while the elaborated code user expects the content to serve that purpose. A further technical distinction has been drawn between those 'positional' groups in which concepts of hierarchy and status distinction underlie notions of power and inform all relationships taking place, and those 'personal' groups grounded in notions of equality. The first category stresses the status and role of individuals, while the latter emphasises the quality, mood, and sentiment of the individual himself. Our theoretical scheme is established once the positional form of social group is linked with the restricted code form of language and the personal form of social organisation with the elaborated code base.

My hypothesis is that very many charismatic converts have originated within the more elaborate code groups of a personal nature but in which the concerns of the individual have been rather coldly handled. Some have come from similar elaborate code contexts but with a more hierarchical form of power structure, for that arrangement of concepts is also possible, as in professional realms. People who have been very competent in using language as a tool of professional work have, nevertheless, been verbally inept in talking about themselves and their feelings. The stiff upper-lip has hindered fuller trust in others and emotional commitment to others. The gift of tongues has come to many such people as the key which has unlocked the emotional restraints of life so that they may freely use a 'language' without having to be careful about what they say. Emotion which cannot be put into words can now be put into sounds, which in turn prompt the support and encouragement of the group towards the new speaker. Such tongues function on a restricted code base, group relations are strengthened and fostered, the speaker is drawn closer to other speakers and does not seek to alienate himself by expressing any idiosyncratic theological or other opinion. The rise of house churches, small fellowship groups, and communal residences attests to this shift from individualism to corporateness. The feedback phrases of prayer and praise meetings exemplify such restricted code utterances: 'Praise the Lord', 'Thank you Jesus', 'Alleluia' etc.

In classical Pentecostalism another picture emerges which our code concept enables us to interpret without much difficulty. Largely arising within working class contexts, which generally operate on a restricted code base and which often involve a pre-existing close-knit community life, and sometimes found to be strong in, for example, West Indian groups, this kind of Pentecostalism sets a different scene for the drama of tongues. Malcolm Calley's study of West Indian movements suggests that speaking in tongues marks the status of the speaker over against other congregational members. Indeed he argues that tongues are used to 'impress the congregation with the holiness of the talker'; they are also employed as part of the power relations and competition for leadership.[17] Glossolalia as vocal behaviour can thus be said to serve an integrative function for charismatic groups but a competitive one for some other Pentecostal groups, though doubtless there is a great deal of mixing of these functions in the various practical contexts of each glossolalic group. Religious leaders themselves are not unaware of the potential negative use of tongues and warn against desiring glossolalia for use as a status-gift.[18] So the precise social context of a glossolalic group needs to be identified before the role of tongues can be determined; this further clarifies the status of glossolalia as a socially influenced phenomenon.

As far as the charismatic groups in English middle class settings are concerned it is likely that glossolalia does function as a restricted code communication serving to integrate individuals into a caring and sharing community. The very use of these adjectives indicates the power and attraction of the charismatic ethos in the nineteen sixties, seventies, and eighties, so perhaps it is opportune now to speak of the charismatic ethic in relation to that post-industrial society in which this form of Spirit-directed religion has emerged.

If Max Weber's Protestant ethic was grounded in worldly activism under the influence of predestination and the inscrutability of the divine will in a pragmatically and rationally organised world of a mechanistic type, then the contemporary charismatic ethic is rooted in a personal fulfilment in supporting relationships in this life within a potentially alienating and atomising world of partial personal relations within the service industries. An interest in personal salvation remains but its realisation has been brought forward from the hereafter to the here and now. Personal authenticity replaces certainty of an elected status in the eternal decrees of God. Tongues and fruitful group relationships replace economic success as a sign of the divine approval. Here sociological issues become inextricably bound up with theological ones, and we must look at the themes of mystery, secularisation, salvation, and concepts of God, all within a changing social world.

Acquaviva's interesting discussion on the decline of the sacred in industrial society ended with him enquiring what image of God was most appropriate for the post-industrial context.[19] I am inclined to agree with his assumption that the human and redemptive significance of religion changes with the shift in equilibrium of a society from agriculture to industry and from industry to services, but this assumption needs to be qualified in the light of Daniel Bell's critique of the secularisation hypothesis. Bell argues against a generalised notion of secularisation and prefers to deal with social entities under three heads; the political and institutional which embraces the ecclesiastical and in which equality and participation are predominant sentiments; the techno-economic where functional rationality has prevailed; and finally the cultural domain of family and private life where self-realisation and gratification has come into predominance.[20] While the first two areas may be said to manifest aspects of secularisation it is in the third that a real disenchantment has come about. The charismatic response is, I would argue, an act of re-enchantment of the individual domain involving family, leisure and corporate life outside politics though related to work in the service industries. Charismatic experience is interpreted as a divine approval of the person; it legitimates personalism, and does so not as a restricted individualism but within a group context. Authenticity is guaranteed by the Spirit of God which confers the seal of truth; here all cynicism is countered and a firm base for commitment to others is laid. Bryan Wilson's allusion to cynicism as an acquired art of survival is thus reversed in the charismatic ethic.[21] The slightly broader stress on being born again in the American context may hint at the same anxiety over duplicity in social life. When an American politician stresses his rebirth he is indirectly asserting his inability to live two lives, one in private and another in public. It is difficult to assess either the real influence of individual belief on public action, or the power of a re-enchanted cultural world in Daniel Bell's sense to change the wider technical realm, but we should not suppose too quickly that secularisation is an inevitable process working in one direction. [22] To what extent the Charismatic Movement is related to issues of a political nature involving nuclear war and moral purity it is hard to say at present, but the matter will have to be considered by historians in the future. [23]

Here we can focus more specifically on the doctrine of God which this form of religion has preferred, and I would argue that it is one which relates rather well to the models of man prevailing in post-industrial cultural contexts. For it is God the Holy Spirit who features most prominently and whose work is most appreciated in charismatic religion. Some care is needed here because the Christian doctrine of the Holy Trinity necessarily involves each divine person in the activity of the others, yet there is something of a pattern in the charismatic case. While the Holy Spirit has been much stressed as the one working among people in renewing them and uniting them into a group which becomes the body of Christ operative here and now, it is interesting to note that the great upsurge of new charismatic hymns has not to any significant extent emphasised the Spirit more than older hymns did. But it is more telling to observe that the concepts of sin, the Bible, heaven, grace and salvation are less frequently dealt with, whilst notions of love for fellow man have increased. [24] This accords with an earlier observation which I have made in seeing recent charismatic theology as operating upon a 'personal' form of conceptual code rather than a 'positional' or hierarchic model. [25] In terms of christology it means there are fewer substitutionary atonement motifs and that they are replaced with notions of Jesus as an intimate friend within the group context. The Holy Spirit has always been a difficult concept to handle as a hierarchical or positional model, unlike the Father and the Son whose social and anthropomorphic analogies come to mind more readily. But with the rise of models of man focused upon the self and its sensitivity in interpersonal relations there emerged the possibility of conceiving of the Spirit as a highly personal force dealing intimately with each individual believer. [26] So the notion of salvation becomes one of renewal and fulfilment of the self in deep mutual relations. The day of Pentecost comes to be a more powerful symbol of salvation than Good Friday. This fact can be seen at a general level in the recent liturgical reform of the Church of England whose rites have moved from the positional concepts of sin, repentance, grace and atonement, once for all accomplished by God the Son at Calvary, to a celebration of the contemporary presence of the Spirit animating members into the body of Christ. Salvation means wholeness and embraces integrity of self and healing of ailments; in these it is the power of the Spirit which is seen as vitally necessary. [27] Here some Christian ideas come particularly close to secular notions of well-being and there is the need to remember the importance of duty and ethics as the consequence of redemption.

This brings us to the final theological evaluation of charismatic religion. Here we do not speak from the privilege of some water-tight position of systematic theology, but from a view which admits both the evidence of traditional theological argument and that of social psychological research. Again any full treatment would need to specify the original religious context within which charismatic responses have emerged. It seems, for example, that evangelical traditions have 'digested' these developments more easily than Roman or Anglo-Catholic traditions. [28] It should be noted that the Bible has come to life for many charismatics, especially in Catholic contexts, and it is fascinating to see the way in which personal belief is now related to the source accounts of the Christian community. Many Christians have felt the need to explain why the events of the earliest years of Christianity have not remained common in subsequent generations. But for charismatics the miraculous moments of the Acts of the Apostles are experienced anew: for them the Holy Ghost of Acts is still the same. It is as though the cognitive dissonance between what was normal then and what is normal now is removed as the baptism of the Holy Spirit and contemporary events link the believer with the earliest events of Christianity. This produces a deep sense of the truthfulness of the Bible and of the genuine nature of charismatic experience, and these elements feed back upon each other. And this is where a critically important question of theology must be raised, for if it can be proved that glossolalia is merely human vocal behaviour, can it still be used to full effect by the charismatic?

Is the supernatural and divine source a necessary mystical element in the power of glossolalia? Cardinal Suenens believes that 'the importance of tongues is not minimised if we situate it on a natural plane'; indeed he compares the gift of tongues to the gift of tears in the Christian tradition, but is able to retain a Christian validation for its use by taking recourse to the Catholic notion of intention. [29] Karl Rahner tackles the issue more subtly by asserting the necessity of being open to 'the charismatic factor' yet in the full realisation that 'experience of the Spirit is not constituted by a particular operation "from without" working upon the human spirit.' [30] This kind of containment of spiritual power by relating it to the ordinariness of the created world and human consciousness may make good sense from his theological standpoint but it is unlikely to appeal to charismatic individuals for whom the dramatic intervention of the Holy Spirit is all important. It is interesting to find that people no longer find power and significance in things that have been explained: they feel reduced in stature once their rationale of action has been spelt out to them; and this is likely to be the case with glossolalia. Unlike the art of piano playing (which is learned and utilised for the service of God and one's neighbour) the gift of speaking in tongues will probably lose its appeal once it is also believed to be naturally occurring. Within a secularised environment this is just what might be expected, for if God is worshipped he is believed to be a supernatural and qualitatively distinct entity. G. W. H. Lampe's admirable study of the Holy Spirit could be useful here, for he regrets the tendency of modern Christians to suffer an attenuation of belief in God's continuous creativity in the world and in the lives of his free creatures with whom He 'enters into communion at the personal level'. [31] Too great a stress on ideas of divine 'breakthrough' leads away from the belief, which he wished to emphasise, that 'every charisma is a work of God and man in union', and (to use an ancient term) a 'theandric' operation. In one sense then the rise of charismatic religion with its sanctification of individuals through that potent symbol of vocalisation can be seen as a response both to an increasingly secular society and to a world in which the needs of persons are more central than ever before. The churches must not merely reflect or validate these motive forces, but consider them carefully to see whether or not they contribute positively to social processes at large. If my own suggestion is correct about the post-industrial clientele of charismatic religion then the churches must be all the more concerned because it is likely that the majority of congregation members as currently composed, certainly in the Anglican Church, belong to this broad group. [32]

A final element within the charismatic ethic, and one which is important in theological reflections, is the desire for authority. We mentioned earlier the important role of the leader within charismatic groups, as well as the pleasure gained from membership in and submission to such a group. We have also touched upon the renewed significance of the Bible and of the growth of special groups for worship and prayer. What we have not done is to issue the warning that the often repeated definition of charismatic groups, as Pentecostals who have remained within their parent denominations, may be either false or premature. It is still early days in this movement even though many speak of a post-charismatic era or look back on the nineteen seventies as a period of special blessing in the Spirit, so it is important to observe that some charismatics are seeking a more definite authority in teaching and pastoral guidance than is found in many of their parent churches. The growth of house churches of an independent kind is no meagre tendency in Britain, and it cannot be presupposed that the charismatic ethic will not follow that tendency in the future. Much depends upon the leadership within the larger parent bodies, on what they are prepared to validate for the sake of instant peace and congregational dynamism, on what theology they actually think tenable, and on their grasp of wider social currents. And this requires as full a knowledge of a phenomenon like glossolalia as it is possible to possess, because the spirit of an age need not always be the Spirit of God.

Notes

1 This is a psychological use of Martin Orans' concept of rank concession described sociologically in his book, *The Santal* (Wayne University Press, Detroit, 1965).
2 J. P. Kildahl, *The Psychology of Speaking in Tongues* (Hodder and Stoughton, London, 1973).
3 Peter Ball, 'Dimensions of Neopentecostal Identity in the Church of England', *European Journal of Social Psychology*, vol. 11 (1981), pp. 349-63.
4 Ernst Cassirer, *Language and Myth* (Dover, New York, 1953).
5 C. D. Batson and W. L. Ventis, *The Religious Experience* (OUP, Oxford, 1982), p. 91.
6 Felicitas D. Goodman, *Speaking in Tongues* (University of Chicago Press, Chicago, 1972).
7 Adams Lovekin and H. Newton Malony, 'Religious Glossolalia: A Longitudinal Study of Personality Changes', *Journal for the Scientific Study of Religion*, vol. 16 (1977).
8 Bill Hopkinson, 'Changes in the Emphases of Evangelical Belief 1970-1980: Evidence from

New Hymnody', *The Churchman*, vol. 95, no. 2 (1981). Cf. Claude Lévi-Strauss, *The Naked Man* (Cape, London, 1981), p. 646ff.

9 Richard A. Hutch, 'The Personal Ritual of Glossolalia', *Journal for the Scientific Study of Religion*, vol. 19 (1980).

10 J. T. Richardson, 'Psychological Interpretation of Glossolalia: A Re-examination of Research', *Journal for the Scientific Study of Religion*, vol. 12 (1973).

11 Lovekin and Malony, 'Religious Glossolalia', p. 392.

12 Goodman, *Speaking in Tongues*, p. 123.

13 Virginia H. Hine, 'Pentecostal Glossolalia: Towards a Functional Interpretation', *Journal for the Scientific Study of Religion*, vol. 8 (1969); William Samarin, *Tongues of Men and of Angels* (Macmillan, New York, 1972), p. 227.

14 C. F. D. Moule, *The Holy Spirit* (Mowbray, Oxford, 1978), p. 87.

15 D. J. Davies, 'Social Groups, Liturgy and Glossolalia', *The Churchman*, vol. 90, no. 3 (1976).

16 Basil Bernstein, *Class, Codes and Control* (Paladin, St Albans, 1971). Mary Douglas, *Purity and Danger* (Penguin, Harmondsworth, 1966) and *Natural Symbols* (Barrie and Jenkins, 1973).

17 Malcolm J. C. Calley, *God's People: West Indian Pentecostal Sects in England* (OUP, Oxford, 1965).

18 W. T. H. Richards, *The Charismatic Movement in the Historic Churches* (Marshall, Morgan and Scott distributors, 1972); Larry Christenson, *Speaking in Tongues: A Gift for the Body of Christ* (Fountain Trust, London, 1963).

19 S. S. Acquaviva, *The Decline of the Sacred in Industrial Society* (Blackwell, Oxford, 1979).

20 Daniel Bell, *Sociological Journeys: Essays 1960-1980* (Heinemann, London, 1980), ch. 17. Cf. Krishan Kumar, *Prophecy and Progress* (Penguin, Harmondsworth, 1978).

21 Bryan Wilson, *Contemporary Transformations of Religion* (OUP, Oxford, 1976), p. 108.

22 Bryan Wilson, *Religion in Sociological Perspective* (OUP, Oxford, 1982), p. 153. Wilson also seems to avoid mentioning the internal authoritarianism of charismatic groups, p. 141.

23 David Martin, *A General Theory of Secularisation* (Blackwell, Oxford, 1978), p. 64.

24 Hopkinson, 'Changes in the Emphases of Evangelical Belief', p. 134.

25 D. J. Davies, 'Theologies in Code', *Research Bulletin of the Birmingham University Institute for the Study of Worship and Religious Architecture* (1981).

26 Philip Rieff, *The Triumph of the Therapeutic* (Penguin, Oxford, 1973). Christopher Lasch, *The Culture of Narcissism* (Abacus, Tunbridge Wells, 1980). C. R. Badcock's interpretation of the Holy Spirit as a survival of otherwise unused supernatural concepts from the Old Testament and in a psychoanalytic way hardly deserves serious mention, *The Psychoanalysis of Culture* (Blackwell, Oxford, 1980), p. 172ff.

27 John P. Baker, *Salvation and Wholeness* (Fountain Trust, London, 1973).

28 Ball, 'Dimensions of Neopentecostal Identity', p. 360.

29 Leon Joseph Suenens, *A New Pentecost* (Darton, Longman and Todd, London, 1975).

30 Karl Rahner, *Theological Investigations* (Darton, Longman and Todd, London, 1979), vol. 16, p. 28. Cf. vol. 9, p. 255, for Christ in relation to full human development, and vol. 12, p. 84ff. for charismatic elements.

31 G. W. H. Lampe, *God as Spirit* (Clarendon Press, Oxford, 1977), p. 206ff.; F. D. Bruner, *A Theology of the Holy Spirit* (Hodder and Stoughton, London, 1970), affords a useful introduction to Pentecostal thinking. Morton T. Kelsey, *Tongue Speaking* (Hodder and Stoughton, London 1968), is a reasoned defence for tongues. Typical of hostile Catholic reaction is *Pentecostalism and Catholics*, by Leslie Rumble of the Anglo-Gaelic Civic Association (no date).

32 Benjamin Zablocki, *The Joyful Community* (Penguin, Harmondsworth, 1971). This discussion of the Bruderhof movement in America gives one of the few sociological comments available on post-industrial society and religion, p. 289. Christian Lalive d'Epinay, *Haven of the Masses*

(Lutterworth, Guildford, 1969), deals with the Pentecostal Movement in Chile and falls outside our interest in post-industrial contexts.

The Church's Healing Ministry
and Charismatic Renewal

JOHN RICHARDS

'There is one hard obstinate fact that the future historian will be unable to ignore when examining the Christian scene in the present century and that is the renewal . . .' The quotation went on '. . . of the Church's ministry of healing.' The church's ministry of healing and the current Renewal, or Charismatic Movement are aspects of church life today to be reckoned with. If you first met the Christian healing ministry through experiencing or reading about the Charismatic Movement it would be natural to assume that they are part of the same movement. There are many whose experience of healing within the Charismatic Movement has led them to assume that the practice of the healing ministry in the mainstream churches is twenty years old at the most. This is not so. The quotation with which I began was written by the Chairman of the Churches' Council of Health and Healing, a body founded in 1944 by Archbishop William Temple. Nor did the rediscovery of the healing ministry start with the foundation of this council. The Guild of Health was founded in 1904 to promote the healing ministry in the churches, and this was followed in 1915 by the formation of the Guild of St Raphael, specifically to serve the Anglican church. Each organisation seeks to promote within the churches a proper understanding of the healing ministry by leading and instructing ministers in the use of anointing and laying on of hands, and by encouraging groups for prayer and intercession.

Successive Lambeth Conferences considered the right expression and role of healing in the church. In 1930 they rejected the false three-fold division of man into spirit, mind and body as if these were separate entities, and urged the recognition of 'gifts of healing' in the church, not knowing that thirty years later a 'gift' movement would emerge in the churches — the 'charism' of charismatic meaning nothing more extraordinary than 'gift'. There are today two strands within the church's healing tradition, which might be labelled the 'sacramental' and 'charismatic'. To understand the 'charismatic' contribution it is necessary to understand the context of healing before the 1960s.

Healing homes had been founded; Crowhurst for example in 1928. The *Book of Common Prayer* had been revised in the same year and its theologically and pastorally inadequate service for the sick was improved, with provision for the laying on of hands. In 1935-6 services were authorised for not only the laying on of hands but for anointing with oil ('unction'). These developments were interrupted by the Second World War, after which there was a flurry of activity. The Churches' Council of Health and Healing (CCHH) included representatives from the Royal (medical) Colleges, the major denominations and the Guilds and Homes of Healing. The British Medical Association (BMA) turned its attention to the church's ministry and urged co-operation between doctors and clergy — a move which ultimately led in 1964 to the formation of the Institute of Religion and Medicine (IRM), a forum for interdisciplinary dialogue. This era saw a spate of books by notable writers, and the titles and names of the time are significant, e.g. Dr Leslie Weatherhead's *Psychology, Religion and Healing* (1951); Dr R. A. Lambourne's *Community, Church and Healing* (1963); and Dr Michael Wilson's *The Church is Healing* (1966).

The first fifty years were aptly marked by the Archbishops' Commission which reported in 1958. No understanding of the Church's healing ministry would be complete without reference to it. It asked (and answered) most if not all the questions usually raised in connection with this subject. It considered that the following opinions or beliefs were misconceptions: that suffering is always contrary to God's will; that healing inevitably follows faith; that God must heal; that death is a disaster; that sickness is directly due to the sin of the sufferer; that medicine has superseded the Church's ministry; that only the specially gifted can practise this ministry; that healing is separate from the Church's other work; that physical healing is all that matters; that anointing should be reserved for the dying. In addition, they rejected three terms in common usage to describe the Church's ministry: 'divine healing' because it might imply that God was not working within his creation and through medicine; 'spiritual healing' because of the possible confusion of the Church's work with those who contact spirits and who call themselves somewhat misleadingly 'spiritualists'; 'faith healing' because of misgivings about the teaching that healing must follow faith. The term they used to replace these was 'the Church's Ministry of Healing'. The Commission was wary of exorcism and healing services and gave guidelines for both.

The strengths of this sort of approach to healing, which I have labelled 'sacramental', include a strong theology of death, a theology of healing, and a grounding in learning and the study of the subject. Moreover, it is strongly priest or minister-centred and therefore strong in the sacramental tradition and in confidentiality; and it is well protected against excesses of teaching or practice. This 'sacramental' tradition found its focus in the rediscovery of the ministry of anointing the sick (based on Jas. 5:13ff.). This ministry was generally seen as belonging to the parish priest who, when summoned by a member of the Church, would — after adequate preparation and teaching — anoint them with oil in the name of the Lord. Professor Charles Gusmer wrote a detailed and scholarly book in 1974 in which he documented the developments which had led up to this.[1]

The Charismatic Tradition

This Renewal Movement burst onto the scene in the 1960s when many people — mainly Christians — saw and experienced healing for the first time, unaware that there was any history of the healing ministry to write about. 'It is difficult', a former director of the Fountain Trust once said, 'to be aflame and mature at the same time.' If maturity is generally associated with age, and fire with youth, the coming of the Renewal Movement seemed like a spontaneous combustion into 'flame' in a tradition that was characterised by a seemingly incombustible maturity! Given the half-century of development of the sacramental tradition, how was it that the average church-goer's experience of the healing Christ was limited to singing 'At even 'ere the sun was set . . .'?

The reason is the age-old one about strengths being also weaknesses, and the strengths of the sacramental tradition undoubtedly had their corresponding weaknesses. The priestly emphasis led to a general failure to see and to work out the 'corporate' nature of the ministry indicated by the term 'The Church's Ministry of Healing'. The desire not to upgrade healing or to publicise it meant that society around the church was usually unaware that it even had a healing ministry. This reticence meant that even many of the 'faithful' (to whom the ministry was generally restricted) were unaware of their minister's healing work. The strong confidentiality meant that the local vicar did not write a paperback book of testimony to what he believed the Lord has done in peoples' lives. So, often, they simply did not know; and a fear of anything unseemly or unpredictable led to a reserve which hindered the development of the ministry.

After the 1960s (which has sometimes been called the 'God is Dead' era) came the realisation by the Charismatic Movement that God is very much alive and that his life can be experienced. David Edwards had bemoaned our 'theological enthusiasm for the death of God, the suicide of the Church, the unknowability of Jesus, the impossibility of preaching, and the uncanny ability of so much contemporary church life to avoid mentioning matters such as God . . .'[2] Such is human nature that this absurd abnormality existed with apparently few misgivings, but when the pendulum swung (as it had to if the church was to survive) misgivings and panic abounded as Christians celebrated the fact that 'He Reigns', and raised their hands in the air in the traditional (and natural) gesture of the early Church.

Such a movement was young, and maturity would have been strange at its outset. While, in the Anglican tradition, bishops at confirmation pray that the confirmation candidates should 'daily increase in the Holy Spirit more and more' they do not very often leap forward to guide, nurture and teach about that increase in the Spirit which may be personally experienced by the individual. The movement therefore had to look elsewhere for guidance and interpretation of what was happening. A very small body, the Fountain Trust, was set up and served the movement for fifteen years; and, while it did much to guide the Renewal and to enable it to blossom within the denominations, the movement initially turned to the Pentecostalist tradition and American neo-Pentecostalism for interpretation of the new experiences and the terminology with which to describe them.

Styles of ministry and theology exerted their influence. The Pentecostalist weaknesses in their doctrines about healing were sometimes inherited. These included the failure to give due place to medicine; an over-awareness of spiritual warfare, leading to an inflated demonology; and a 'triumphalism' which focused exclusively on experiencing Christ's victory now and which was not 'earthed' in the real suffering of humanity or the cross of Christ. Because the term 'charismatic' is so heterogeneous it is not surprising that these weaknesses are still encountered. But despite many weaknesses and distortions — and a preoccupation with healing for its own sake can itself become a form of sickness — the Charismatic Movement has brought to the healing scene a considerable enrichment in a number of ways, not least in the rediscovery of the 'corporate' nature of the healing ministry. This emerges in the typically 'charismatic' prayer group in which members experience the power of the Lord's presence to heal in a way which they had not so far come across in church meetings and services. 'Every member ministry' was soon a catch-phrase of the movement and church members grappled with the practical working out of the 'body' concept. This synchronised in medicine and elsewhere with a more corporate sense both of sickness and of pastoral care. 'Every member ministry' did not mean that every lay person should minister as one ordained, but it did mean that each person had a contribution to make and was needed in God's economy for the Church's existence and work.

To say that the Charismatic Movement 'rediscovered' prayer would be misleading and would seem to imply that those outside knew nothing about it. But it would be true to say that their rediscovery that God is not dead but truly alive puts back into prayer and worship a vitality which had not always been apparent. If the charismatics verged sometimes on almost heretical views about the 'power' of prayer, it was because of their rediscovery that prayer is part of a living relationship with God — a God who is actively calling for our co-operation in his saving work among all people.

Although 'gifts of healing' are in fact only incidental in the Church's healing ministry, the Charismatic Movement re-established that the Church was God-built, God-founded and designed to be God-empowered and God-directed. This meant that the quality of the Church did not rest on human abilities and the professional qualifications of its members, but on God-given 'gifts' (charisms) given by God to each person for the building-up of the body of Christ. The church had not altogether ignored charisms; indeed the charism of organisation (1 Cor. 12:28) seems to be demanded of Christian leaders more than all else. The Renewal Movement's message was to say that God has given, and gives, a wider range of charisms to his Church than we generally assume. Interestingly the gift of organising (or administration) occurs in the same verse as gifts of healing and gifts of tongues.

Another contribution of the Charismatic Renewal is an advance towards a 'total' Christian response to God. So often in the past either an intellectual response was required to right doctrine about God, or a response of the will to acknowledge that Jesus is Lord. Such responses were merely facets of a total personal response. The renewal began to experience and realise the essential unity of man, so that bodies and hearts were expected to respond, not merely minds and wills. Liturgical movement (sometimes called 'dance') and the gift of tears are sometimes in themselves healing to the individual concerned but in a wider sense they reflect a more integrated and therefore more healed view of man. While emotionalism is to be abhorred, responses in which by conditioned reflex emotion is forbidden may bring a superficial good-ordering, but they lack authenticity, reality and truth.

One of the most obvious contributions of the Charismatic Renewal to the healing scene has been the upsurge of literature written by those in or close to the charismatic tradition. Much of this is termed 'testimony literature', and it has its positive uses in teaching, building faith and encouragement as well as answering weaknesses at the levels of medical analysis and theology. Testimony literature should certainly not be our sole spiritual diet but frequently it is used by God to 'turn the switch' in a person's life, and set him or her along some new and better road.

Healing services remain something of a question for all Church members. The Charismatic Renewal brought a new urge to move healing out from the closed confidentiality of the vicarage study to be part of a public proclamation of the gospel. As the movement has matured so there has been a very considerable move away from explicit healing actions like the laying on of hands and away from special services. This move has taken place because of the growing conviction that the essential places of healing are those central occasions in the life of the Church family when all are gathered together in worship. Increasingly the eucharist is regarded as the occasion of healing, as healing takes its rightful place as one facet at the centre of Church life and is no longer considered to be a fringe activity undertaken by an extraordinary group at an extraordinary time.

The Pentecostalist churches had traditionally run large healing missions and rallies in which evangelism and healing went hand-in-hand. By contrast most evangelism in Britain emerged from an Evangelicalism which, in spite of its claim to be biblical, generally relegated healing and everything associated with it to the first century of the Christian era. Although their numbers are not great, the movement has some evangelists whose ministry reflects God's desire to touch and transform whole persons, not merely to free them from sin or demand the allegiance of their wills. To lay hands on the sick and have them recover was one of the promises given at the end of Mark's gospel — it was one of the 'signs following'.

'Inner healing' is a somewhat technical and restrictive term used in the Charismatic Renewal to indicate a specifically prayer-based Christ-centred spiritual ministry for the healing of the deep inner areas of our lives. I find the term confusing since confession and absolution (forgiveness of one's sins) is so clearly 'inner healing', as is the activity of any good psychiatrist or psychotherapist. But the term has come to stay. In this ministry the role of laity and the caring group is important and, when linked to a healthy sacramentalism and respect for medicine, it is one of the most wonderful things to emerge in recent Christianity. The rediscovery of 'inner healing' simply testifies to the fact that the good news of the gospel is good news for mankind in its totality, and that Christ came, and comes, to bind up the broken-hearted and to set at liberty those who are oppressed.

The Charismatic Movement has brought a broadening of the ministry of exorcism. This can be illustrated by the titles of the two major reports. The first consisted of the findings of the Bishop of Exeter's Commission on Exorcism and was entitled simply *Exorcism* and was published in 1974.[3] The second report of the Archbishop of York's working party was entitled *The Christian Ministry of Deliverance and Healing*. It is interesting that a movement, which is assumed by the media to be equated with a strong demonology, has contributed so significantly in recent years to our acknowledging that within the ordinary and traditional items of Christian spirituality, worship and devotion, God is at work to heal and to deliver us from all that imprisons us. As Wesley wrote:

My chains fell off, My heart was free,
I rose, went forth, And followed thee.

I have labelled the two main streams of healing 'sacramental' and 'charismatic', and their use must not be taken to imply that the former is without the Spirit or the latter without sacrament. The two belong together. It is possible to be mature and aflame at the same time, and this is most apparent when in healing and in other areas these traditions merge and order is not threatened by flexibility; when sacramental graces are enriched by charisms; and when the riches of one are married to the riches of the other. For it is surely no coincidence that each tradition is at its weakest where the other is at its strongest. When the church's healing ministry is truly sacramental and truly charismatic then it will itself be the more healed and a better instrument for the healing which has been entrusted to it by the risen Lord.

Notes

1 C. Gusmer, *The Ministry of Healing in the Church of England: An Ecumenical Liturgical Study* (Mayhew-McCrimmon, Great Wakering, 1974).
2 Quoted in J. Richards, *But Deliver Us from Evil* (Darton, Longman and Todd, London, 1974).
3 Dom Robert Petitpierre, OSB, ed., *Exorcism* (SPCK, London, 1974).

The Instinct of the Herd

RONALD NOAKES

There is an old book by R. A. Tassey entitled *How to Promote and Conduct a Successful Revival*. Amongst other advice, the author states that:

> Revival preaching to be effective must be positive . . . A revival is a revolution in many important respects, and revolutions are never brought about by timid, fearful or deprecatory addresses. They are awakened by men who are cocksure of their ground, and who speak with authority . . . Revival preaching must be directed towards the heart and not the head . . . Get hold of the heart and the head yields easily![1]

The preaching of the late Dr Spurgeon, William Booth, Billy Graham and others who have concentrated on the affective element in religion, is of such a nature. It is true that an understanding heart is an essential component of the Christian religion, but with these preachers there is a conscious or unconscious dismissal of the rational element in religious belief. M. Le Bon in his book *The Crowd* attributes the exclusion of the rational element in religion to what he calls 'crowd psychology'.[2] By a crowd, M. Le Bon means a group of persons united together by some common purpose or interest. It can be a religious meeting, a political gathering or a football match. There is in every crowd a ready response to emotion, as is clearly seen at a football match when the throng sings with such gusto 'Abide with Me': Tears stream down many faces and some sob openly. Again, when people gather together in large numbers to listen to a speaker there is inevitably a vigorous response to oratory, which would leave its members cold if it were addressed to them as individuals. Cicero, Pericles and Hitler understood this perfectly; so does Dr Billy Graham.

Everyone who forms part of a crowd to hear a speaker is actually acted upon by a form of herd-suggestion, and this comes about by the impact of all who are being influenced by the orator. By singing or by shouting or merely by clapping, a crowd is often worked up into an emotional and almost hypnotic state into which suggestions are easily implanted. If, on such occasions, there is affirmation — such as shouts of 'Here, Here', 'Hallelujah' or 'Go on, Sir' — then suggestion is heightened considerably and beliefs may be changed. Doubtless on Palm Sunday, when the Jewish mob shouted the old Messianic cry 'Hosanna to the Son of David' as Jesus rode his donkey to Jerusalem, Pilate grew fearful and doubled the guard, and later on when he heard the repeated shout 'Crucify Him', he decided to wash his hands of the issue. Whatever his personal thoughts, he was undoubtedly influenced by the crowd.

A classic example of herd-suggestion is the well-known funeral oration of Mark Antony in Shakespeare's play *Julius Caesar*. At first, the mob is hostile towards Mark Antony. The people are for Brutus and not for the dead Caesar whom they had regarded as a menace to the Republic of Rome. 'T'were best he speak no harm of Brutus here', says one of the crowd. Another says 'This Caesar was a Tyrant!' In a subtle speech Antony extols the merits of the late Julius Caesar but pauses from time to time to say 'Yet Brutus is an honorable man!' Gradually, the gathering is worked up into a sort of hypnotic state and then, almost imperceptibly, the suggestion is implanted that Brutus is not an honorable man and that Caesar was a paragon of virtue. The mind of the horde is changed at once and the cry goes up 'We'll mutiny. We'll burn the house of Brutus.' The opinion of the crowd has been ingeniously reversed.

Within the last century, there have been several examples of herd-suggestion within the sphere of religion. There have been the campaigns of Billy Graham and other somewhat flamboyant evangelists. Then there was the Oxford Group of some fifty or so years ago — a movement which attracted Beverly Nichols and many other society lions from both sides of the Atlantic, with the adherents meeting in groups to confess their sins, openly and to each other. This resulted in an exaggerated sense of sin which, in an odd way, became fashionable. It was very much a middle-class crusade and did little by way of evangelism. There were even those who 'cashed in' on it like:

The man from Pretoria
Whose sins grew goryer and goryer
But by fasting and prayer
And some *savoir-faire*
He now lives at the Waldorf Astoria.

They also had their 'quiet times'. They sat in small groups and each wrote down what they thought God had directed them to do. Often this was the projection of their own wishes. And now, perhaps because the church is so preoccupied with such things as liturgical reform, synodical government, ecumenism and revival we have the Charismatic Movement with its exuberant togetherness and kissing in the aisle, its dancing in the sanctuary and its convivial penitence in the cosy 'house groups'. The late George Addleshaw, Dean of Chester, with his great love for the ethos of Anglicanism would, one feels, have been most disturbed.

The worship of the Charismatic Movement has a great number of hymns, each with a strongly emotional content. Choruses are repeated again and again until the congregation is in a slightly emotional state. Sometimes this state clearly resembles attacks of hysteria. Glossolalia, or the so-called 'speaking with tongues', is, one feels, an abnormal manifestation which does nothing to build up the Church, as it is merely a stream of meaningless syllables sometimes mixed with a few real words, which are poured out under the influence of intense emotion. The herd-instinct is clearly manifested in the Charismatic Movement and it is difficult not to be moved. One cannot deny that the charismatics have been instrumental in bringing many people back to the church or that the movement has done much to counteract the apathy and materialism of this present age, but one must guard against its dangers. The preoccupation with sickness, evil spirits and demon possession is surely undesirable and could lead, in certain cases, to mental instability so that, so to speak, the 'last state of that man is worse than the first'. A proper respect for the traditional values of the Anglican Church could well be 'revived' as an antidote to revival.

Notes

1 R. A. Tassey, *How to Promote and Conduct a Successful Revival* (Melrose, London 1901).
2 G. Le Bon, *The Crowd* (Unwin, London 1896).

The Orthodox Church and the Charismatic Movement

ANDREW WALKER

The Marginality of the Charismatic Movement
to Eastern Orthodoxy

Perhaps the most interesting and significant feature of the modern Charismatic Movement is the extent to which it has taken root in the historic churches. While 'enthusiasms' of many kinds have existed in these churches, the advent of a Pentecostalist revivalism under the less threatening title of 'Charismatic Renewal' was not altogether to be expected. The effect of this renewal, growing and flourishing in the traditional soils of Roman Catholicism, Lutheranism and Anglicanism appears to be grafting the sectarian offshoots back upon the original stemmata.

The seeds of renewal, however, have not been so successful when sown into the ground of Eastern Orthodoxy. As far as the peoples of Eastern Europe, Greece, and the middle East are concerned the seeds of charismatic revival are a Protestant and western phenomena that do not directly concern them. Orthodox communities in the traditional heartlands are barely aware of the western crop of neo-Pentecostalism. There are rumours of charismatic plantings in Rumania and the student population of the Lebanon, but gossip hardly constitutes evidence. It would seem, for the moment, that Orthodox soil is either too sterile (or, perhaps, too rich) for charismatic spores to fructify, or else the renewal has simply not yet reached the east with any germinating power. The new Pentecostalism has sprung up in the Third World in Protestant and Catholic countries; in no sense, therefore, should the renewal be seen as a purely western phenomena (as some Orthodox erroneously think).

In the west, where the Orthodox *diaspora* exists in a pluralistic Christendom, charismata have made a showing. Individual members of Orthodox churches have participated in charismatic meetings, and some have laid claim to the experience which is still usually called 'the baptism of the Holy Spirit'. Archbishop Paul of Finland, in *The Faith We Hold*,[1] has warned of the superficialities and sentimentality of charismatic experiences, whilst Metropolitan Anthony of Sourozh in England prefers to judge each case on its merits rather than openly endorse the whole Charismatic Movement, or condemn it out of hand. A Serbian priest (who has recently become a bishop in the Orthodox Church of America) was involved in the Renewal Movement for some years. He supported it, on the whole, whilst worrying about the lack of discipline. Cryptically, he used to say 'When you open the window to let in the fresh air, you also invite bad smells.'

The Greek Orthodox Church in America is the only major Orthodox community in the west that has seen the Charismatic Movement flourish on its home ground. Influenced by Protestant and Catholic renewalists, an Orthodox journal, *Logos* was the focal point for the movement. There followed considerable controversy, personality clashes, and the eventual official curtailment of one of the leading charismatics, Fr Stephanou. In the last few years, the movement has become more muted, and the new charismatic journal, *Theosis* with its whole editorial staff, are notably less 'protestant' than the earlier leaders. Indeed, the movement has dropped the word 'charismatic' for the more Orthodox phrase, 'Spiritual Renewal'.

The Charismatic Movement in America has challenged the nominal commitment of many Orthodox Christians, and a number of priests and lay people have welcomed the emphasis (seen as Orthodox) on repentance and a strong personal commitment to Christ. However, even amongst those Orthodox who see much of positive worth in the Renewal Movement (the late Fr Lev Gillet, for example) there are aspects which genuinely concern them. Other Orthodox writers such as Hiermonk Seraphim Rose, have seen the rise of the new Pentecostalism as demonic,[2] whilst some Orthodox priests, at the World Council of Churches consultation on the Charismatic Movement in 1980, tended to see the whole thing as the final twitchings and convulsions of a dying western Christendom.

Western Christians often have a view of Orthodoxy that has very little grounding in reality: they sometimes tend to see it as a monolithic, unchanging religion dominated by men with long beards and funny hats; in short, an antiquated and antiquarian corner of eastern Christendom where the people are convinced that they are right on all matters doctrinal and spiritual, and the west is simply wrong. Such a caricature (not without some merit) fails to see the quarrelsomeness of Orthodoxy within its own ranks, and the extraordinary freedom of beliefs and practices that surround the commonly held dogmatic position (which is primarily the insistence on the original Nicene creed as being the most consonant with the biblical good news). For most Orthodox, many of the questions and issues of what has become known as the Charismatic Movement are issues of private opinion, pious opinion (views of a non-dogmatic nature by fathers of the church), and theological opinion (*theologuomena*). This being so, it is not the case that the Orthodox Church — in whatever ethnic guise — is likely to pronounce on the phenomenon with any great authority. Pronouncements, pontifications, and the 'correct line' are not popular nor traditional ways of defending the faith. The rest of this paper will attempt to outline Orthodox opinions concerning neo-Pentecostalism, and raise one crucial dogmatic issue concerning charismatics' understanding of the Holy Trinity.

Orthodox Responses to the Charismatic Movement

Whilst it remains true that the Charismatic Movement remains marginal to world Orthodoxy, Orthodox Christians living in the west have nevertheless had to face the issues of neo-Pentecostalism as a matter of ecumenical imperative. As already remarked, some Orthodox have made their views known in print or by word, but on the whole the approach has been investigative. An abiding memory of many of the delegates to the World Council of Churches consultation on the renewal in 1980, was of the Greek Metropolitan, who attended nearly every charismatic prayer meeting because he simply wanted to know what it was all about.

This sense of curiosity and the investigative stance that follows from it has led a number of Orthodox Christians to be convinced that the Charismatic Renewal is primarily a mutation from classical Pentecostalism.

To ask an Orthodox Christian what he thinks of the Charismatic Movement is really to ask him what he thinks of Pentecostalism. There are really no new questions thrown up by the Renewal that are not already raised by its sectarian parent: questions concerning the so-called 'baptism'; questions concerning the nature of tongues and the gifts of the Holy Spirit as outlined by St Paul in 1 Corinthians 12; and questions concerning the nature of Pentecostalist spirituality and liturgy.

The phrase, 'baptism in the Holy Spirit' is in fact known to the Orthodox east. It was much used by St Symeon the New Theologian, who clearly believed not so much in a second (or third) blessing, but in a continual infusion of the holiness of God the Holy Spirit. This insistence on the holiness of God, the necessity of repentance and the subjective reality of knowing God's presence, was for him objectified by a sign — or seal — from God. Unlike Pentecostalists, however, he did not see glossolalia as the outward sign, but tears. Tears remain in Orthodoxy as a spiritual gift, but it distinguishes the tears of ascesis and prayer from the normal outflow of human emotion. St Symeon is one of the great mystics and poets of the Orthodox east, but his experiences and explanations of the 'baptism of fire' would not be the only, or primary, rebuttal of the Pentecostal experience as a distinctive phenomenon. The Orthodox, like Roman Catholics and some Anglicans, would want to know what would be the sacramental status of a Pentecostal baptism, and whether it was truly biblical.

Concerning the issue of glossolalia *per se*, many Orthodox would be prepared to argue the matter. Certainly, it is the case that the phenomenon is not unknown in the private prayer of individuals. As to whether this phenomenon is indeed the biblical speaking in tongues is disputed, in the same way as it is within the evangelical constituency. (It is interesting to compare Packer's reflections,[3] many of which would be endorsed by Orthodox opinion.) What is not in dispute, however, is the confusion of glossolalia with xenolalia in so many Pentecostalist circles. The distinction between tongues of ecstasy and the ability to speak in a foreign language is recognised by charismatics, but the distinctive Pentecostal experience was not one of glossolalia, but mighty rushing wind, tongues of fire, and speaking recognisable foreign languages. To index the 'baptism of the Holy Spirit' — with its distinguishing feature of glossolalia — as Pentecostal is in fact a misnomer. (Some Pentecostalists, to be accurate, do not insist on tongues accompanying the Spirit baptism; the Elim Movement does not, for example.)

Orthodox Christians would never deny God's ability to heal the sick. Charismatic leaders are often unaware that praying for the sick to recover physically is not only a regular practice within the Orthodox church, but that it has been recognised that some men and women have the gift of healing. Such a gift, however, is not a licence to set up practice either outside the Church or against its teachings and sacramental practices. The question of healings, miracles, visions, prophecies etc. within the Charismatic Movements throughout the world is a question for most Orthodox of discerning the hand of God, or the machinations of psychological and psychosomatic processes from the work of the Devil. It follows, therefore, that a watchful Gamalielism in a spirit of sobriety is the hallmark of a truly Orthodox approach. A simple rule of thumb is to measure rigorously the spiritual gifts outlined by Paul in Corinthians by the spiritual fruits spelled out by the same Apostle in the letter to the Romans. A more elaborate approach would be to see how charismatic experiences are consonant with the Word of God and the teachings of the Church. As we shall soon note, there are issues here which are not only issues of opinion (*in dubiis libertas*), but of the fundamentals of the faith (*in necessitatibus unitas*).

The nature of spirituality in charismatic circles is a puzzle for the Orthodox Christian. Enthusiasm is not, of course, a peculiar feature of Pentecostalism. Neither is it unknown in Orthodoxy. In Russia, for example, Fr John of Kronsdat was not only a famous healer, but in some respects spirituality under his direction had a strong emotional appeal to the peasants and the new working classes of the late nineteenth century. His famous book, *My Life in Christ* would not seem out of place in the latter stages of the 'Great Awakening' of American evangelicalism. However, in no way did he radically restructure the Divine Liturgy (with the possible exception of mass public confessions). Charismatic worship, on the other hand, seems to most Orthodox to include practices that belong more to Protestant sub-cultures than to a truly biblical or traditional understanding of spirituality.

Hence, Orthodox observers of the renewal note that at the very moment that charismatics claim to have rediscovered forgotten biblical truths, and the supernatural power of God's kingdom, they also adopt practices which seem to militate against those truths. Why, the Orthodox ask, does the charismatic experience seem to lead to free-wheeling liturgies and the adoption of secular music (often of a wildly enthusiastic nature with rock, march, waltz or ragged timing)? Dancing and drums and shrieks and shouting seem to an Orthodox ear to be outward signs of emotionalism, subjective individualism and exhibiting a lack of self control. At Bossey in Switzerland, the site of the World Council of Churches' 1980 consultation on the Renewal, both the Orthodox delegation and some of the Africans saw the white Protestant (and Catholic) usage of shaking, mumbling and ritualistic raising of hands as a manifestation of Renewal that they would rather do without. They saw in it an unconscious cultural imperialism. Paradoxically, many Orthodox do not object to the wild enthusiasm of many black Pentecostals. This is not simply because it looks more natural than the rather stilted copying of secular practices within the western white churches, but also because the black emphasis appears more liturgical to Orthodox eyes: clapping God in worship as a congregational body — without the emphasis on solo singer, or individualist expression — seems to capture the spirit, although not the resonance, of Orthodox worship. Admittedly, it is the case that black Pentecostal worship does not have the liturgical shape of say slave music in the antebellum period of American history. It is true, also, that many charismatic services are more restrained than some of the classical Pentecostal counterparts. What they all seem to share in common, however, is a deep-rooted sentimen-tality that the church fathers always saw as the enemy of a mature spirituality. Not that Orthodox can afford to be triumphalist in this matter: many Greek, Coptic and Russian icons bear the very marks of sentimentalism that Orthodox see as the hallmark of western spirituality and in particular Protestant pietism. (Many Orthodox see the renewal — even in its Catholic setting — as essentially pietistic.)

Orthodox believers can see the personal response to God, and the concomitant repentance, as a positive feature of the Charismatic Movement. Rejoicing at this, however, is tempered by a concern that the sheer noise and chatter of Pentecostalism, which seems to be so often accompanied by a marked self-consciousness, will stifle the quiet still voice of the Holy Spirit. Charismata are always gifts from God, who in His sovereignty responds to the faith of His children. Such faith, which is itself God's gift, is not an invitation to laziness or a denial of ascesis: charismatic power without self-control is the 'cheap-thrill' response to God's action; and power without responsibility is dangerous in any situation. When Michael Harper, in *Charismatic Crisis*,[4] pointed out that fun and wholeness need to give way to holiness and discipleship in order that the renewal should move onto a new maturity, he was at least speaking a language which Orthodox understand.

Not that central features of charismatic spirituality are that clear to interested Orthodox. Why are so many 'prophecies' and the interpretation of tongues, which are presumably understood as coming directly from God, taken so lightly and casually? Why is it that so many charismatic believers forget so easily God's messages?[5] The messages themselves seem to be so often banal, or the sort of homilies that a good priest or preacher comes up with every Sunday. Does the omnipotent Holy Trinity speak in this way? Individual practices (not shared by many sections of the Pentecostal world) seem particularly strange. 'Slaying in the Spirit' whereby the charismatic leader touches a 'prayer line' seeker (usually on the forehead), who subsequently swoons to the ground in an apparent faint or trance, seems an odd New Testament methodology. Or again, the 'word of knowledge' whereby the person with this 'gift' claims to diagnose some sickness or sin appears more like a method of mediumship rather than a Christian response to the prompting of God the Holy Spirit. Clearly St Paul in 1 Corinthians 12 distinguishes word of wisdom (*sophia*) from word of knowledge (*gnosis*), but how does this relate to modern day charismatic practices?[6] If these are issues on which Orthodox are seeking elucidation in order to ground a Christian critical response (*in omnibus caritas*), there is an issue of a dogmatic nature that is of far greater importance.

Is the Charismatic Movement Trinitarian?

Since the beginning of classical Pentecostalism there has been a dispute concerning the formula to use for water baptism. The 'Jesus only' faction claimed that the New Testament does not record a trinitarian formula. Even to this day, some black Pentecostals and some branches of the House Church Movement continue to baptise in the name of Jesus only. But

whilst it is the case that most classical Pentecostals and renewalists have
rejected this formula, it is by no means clear that, in practice, charismatics
adhere to a biblical doctrine of the Holy Trinity.

Although Orthodoxy is often seen as a mystical religion, it is firmly
committed to the God of revelation, and in that commitment it sees
the essential mystery of the Godhead as trinitarian. The belief that western
Christianity has been essentially binitarian (with the person of the Holy
Spirit being relegated to a function of Christ) or even unitarian is not
a peculiarly Orthodox notion. Theologians in the Presbyterian Reformed
tradition have said as much for years (Professors Tom and James Torrance,
for example). In some senses the Charismatic Movement sees itself as
rediscovering the lost person of the Trinity. Professor Nissiotis has
claimed, in *Orthodox Ethos*,[7] that enthusiasm and charismatic revival
are nostalgia for the God who is lost. To rediscover God the Holy Spirit,
the Lord and Giver of Life, can only be truly Christian if that discovery
is rooted in the trinitarian Godhead. To see this as a fundamental issue
of faith, grounded in the scriptures and the Nicene creed, seems often
to be of no interest to the charismatics aflame with the immediate religious
experience: who needs creeds, one might argue when the Holy Spirit,
Deus Absconditus has been persuaded to tarry for a while?

Without a balanced trinitarian doctrine, in which all the Persons of
the Godhead are worshipped and honoured, and without a recognition
of the unique function of each Person (Hypostasis) within the one nature
of God, an unhealthy and lopsided Christianity develops. And yet we
find in so many charismatic circles, not an upraising of the Paraclete
to a position of glory, but an understanding of the Holy Spirit as 'power
for living', or a kind of spiritual energy emanating from Christ. In short,
a christocentric theology emerges where the lordship of the Spirit
somehow loses his holiness, and the creative role of the Spirit in creation
and incarnation is lost.

At least a christocentric theology preserves the Lordship of Christ
(but for many Orthodox, western theology has over concentrated on
the centrality of the atonement at the expense of incarnation). Whilst
this is not as preferable as a consistent trinitarian faith, it is less dangerous
than that other imbalance within Pentecostalism, 'pneumatomonism'.
When God the Spirit usurps the unique position of the Father (*monarchia*)
in charismatic theology, then the risk is run of despotic charismatic

leadership that is more dangerous and oppressive than any clericalism. At its worst, this can become the hell of the Jones cult, or give rise to the false prophet of David Moses of the Children of God sect. At its best, it bears the hallmarks of discerption, schism, anti-institutionalism and 'triumphalism'. The triumphalism of some charismatic movements is characterised by the barely controlled smugness that God is only really alive and working in their own fellowships and churches.

But, of course, triumphalism is not a feature of Pentecostalism *per se*. What westerner could doubt that Eastern Orthodoxy is not without its fair share? In order to avoid any misunderstanding, I would like to stress that Orthodox responses to the Charismatic Movement and perhaps even more so to the classical Pentecostals, are responses of friendship. The above remarks may seem like a strange form of friendship, but politeness and western good manners are not really a feature of Eastern Orthodoxy: rudeness is a sign that friendship has a cutting edge as well as the ability to agree to differ. For the Orthodox living in the west, the charismatics are in many ways natural allies standing as they do for the fundamentals of the gospel, and against modernism in theology. 'Speaking the truth in love' is a much overworked phrase: love has to be demonstrated, and the truth defined and defended, but speaking comes first as a sign that interaction has begun. In that sense, this paper is an attempt to begin dialogue, not to dismiss Pentecostals as unworthy of attention, devoid of any truth or insignificant.

Notes

1 *The Faith We Hold* (Mowbray, Oxford, 1978).
2 Hiermonk Seraphim Rose, *Orthodoxy and the Religion of the Future* (St Herman Press, 1979).
3 J. I. Packer, 'Theological Reflections on the Charismatic Movement', 2 parts, *The Churchman*, vol. 94 (1980).
4 M. Harper, *Charismatic Crisis* (Hownslow Publishers, 1980).
5 cf. A. Walker, and J. Atherton, *Sociological Review*, August 1971.
6 cf. Colin Urquhart, *Faith for the Future* (Hodder and Stoughton, London, 1982).
7 'The Importance of the Doctrine of the Trinity for Church Life and Theology', in A. J. Philippon (ed.), *The Orthodox Ethos* (Faith Press, Leighton Buzzard, 1964).

Roots and Fruits of the Charismatic Renewal in the Third World

W. J. HOLLENWEGER

Songs and stories, prayer for the sick, pilgrimages, exorcism and glossolalia, in short all the expressions of 'oral' theology, function as a system for passing on theological and social values and information in oral societies in a way which can be likened to a modern computer, because the individual memories can be linked together in such a way that, although no one person communicates the whole tradition, in principle everybody has access to the total body of information. This communication system is vital for pre- and post-literary cultures. As these cultures are becoming increasingly important, it becomes imperative for western theologians to tune into these socio-psychological information systems and to communicate with the theologians and the Christians of these cultures. If mission is not only the geographical growth of our own culturally-determined form of the church, but also the cultural and theological growth which makes a global and ecumenical learning process possible, then we have to explore the intercultural theological exchange between different forms of the church in such a way that the cultural diversities of the church become an expression of its theological unity. This is important for the sake of both a deeper understanding of the gospel and a contribution to world peace.[1]

There is no reliable survey of the Charismatic Renewal in the Third World. Generally speaking we know that it is strong in Brazil, Mexico, Trinidad, Argentina, Indonesia, Korea and South Africa. As to its strength in other countries, opinions vary. Problems of establishing the extent and character of the Charismatic Renewal are almost insurmountable, first because the scene is changing all the time, secondly because there is no accepted definition of the Charismatic Renewal and thirdly because it is almost impossible to get accurate statistics and descriptions.

The question of definition is not only a semantic, but also a theological one. I mention only a few of the problems. Should the Spiritual Baptists in Trinidad, who are in no way more enthusiastic than the Catholic Pentecostals on the same island, be included in the Charismatic Renewal? Should the Kimbanguists in Zaïre, who by now are a well-established, hierarchical African church, be included in a survey of the Charismatic Renewal? (This question becomes all the more poignant as only ten or twenty years ago they were not even counted among the Christian churches.) Similar questions have to be asked about the indigenous Indian Pentecostal churches in Mexico, the revivals in Indonesia, the Christian gurus in India, the black churches in England, the Jamaa Movement in East Africa, and the many, powerful African churches in West Africa. Finally it is becoming increasingly evident that there is a growing and important charismatic renewal under way in eastern Europe (showing features that are similar to the Third World charismatic groups and churches) which, for obvious political reasons, must remain firmly within the traditional churches.

However, in his *World Christian Encyclopedia*,[2] David S. Barrett has produced statistics which are so far the best available, although one might want to question some of his extrapolations for the year 2000. These extrapolations are nevertheless valuable because they show certain trends which are already evident nowadays. The most important trends are not so much the growth of the Charismatic Movements in the traditional churches, nor of the classical Pentecostal denominations but much more the emergence and growth of a new type of charismatic church, namely what Barrett calls 'non-white indigenous churches' (see table 1).

The Roots

Two roots can be identified: first American neo-Pentecostalism and secondly, something which I would like to call 'oral theology' and which

TABLE 1
Charismatic and Pentecostal Movements in the World

	1980	2000
Catholic charismatics		
Africa	106,660	935,000
East Asia	123,000	800,000
Europe	932,800	3,926,000
Latin America	1,197,900	10,914,800
Northern America	2,110,000	4,930,000
South Asia	260,030	1,390,300
Oceania	41,000	205,000
	4,771,390	23,101,100
Protestant charismatics		
Africa	101,000	450,000
East Asia	1,505,000	3,020,000
Europe	622,000	2,100,000
Latin America	446,000	1,230,000
Northern America	1,445,000	3,150,000
South Asia	119,800	633,000
Oceania	48,000	235,000
	4,286,800	10,818,000
Orthodox Charismatics		
Europe	32,000	150,000
USSR	100,000	400,000
Northern America	23,000	120,000
Oceania	2,000	10,000
	157,000	680,000
Anglican Charismatics		
Africa	170,600	715,400
Europe	601,000	1,205,000
Northern America	205,000	425,000
South Asia	3,600	6,800
Oceania	110,000	310,000
	1,090,200	2,662,200
Black Charismatics (USA)	700,000	1,600,000
Total charismatics worldwide	11,005,390	38,861,300
Non-white indigenous		
Africa	24,457,970	54,355,960
East Asia	6,302,660	11,983,400
Europe	105,310	175,000
Latin America	12,556,250	27,542,940
Northern America	21,420,380	25,050,940
South Asia	17,233,650	34,861,700
Oceania	104,850	170,500
	82,181,070	154,140,440
Pentecostal denominations (worldwide)	21,909,778	no figures available perhaps 50,000,000

All figures represent adherents/members and are based on Barrett's *World Christian Encyclopedia*.

owes its existence to the encounter between the gospel as preached by western missionaries and various Third World cultural and political situations.

American neo-Pentecostalism

American neo-Pentecostalism is present in all main-line American denominations. It owes its existence to American Pentecostal spirituality and doctrine, which has infiltrated all the American churches through the Full Gospel Business Men's Fellowship International, the ministry of David Du Plessis and the Oral Roberts University. (One should never forget that Oral Roberts was accepted as a Methodist minister without having been asked to change either his theology or his practice; if a Pentecostal is rich and influential, American church authorities no longer insist on doctrinal investigations!) It is understandable that not only had the Vatican to make a thorough study of its relationship to Pentecostalism, but that the World Council of Churches had also to set up a programme to study questions of the Charismatic Renewal.

This is not the place to reiterate the story of American Pentecostalism. Only one point is important, namely that it emerged in the encounter of the Holiness Movement with black spirituality in Los Angeles in 1906. As important features of Roman Catholic spirituality have been integrated in the Holiness Movement, one could — in a somewhat simplified way — say that Pentecostalism is partly the result of an encounter between Catholic and black spirituality on American soil. Hence the fierce resistance of all strictly evangelical Christians both to Pentecostalism and to the Charismatic Renewal. In spite of some common ground, they rightly sense the difference between Pentecostal charismatic spirituality and their own. Only when Pentecostalism loosens its roots in Catholic and black spirituality, does it become acceptable to evangelicalism.

But it is precisely the link between Catholic and black spirituality which accounts for the growth of neo-Pentecostalism in the Third World. The Charismatic Renewal is likely to be successful in Latin America on account of its oral liturgies and its capacity to overcome the century-old Protestant antagonism towards the Roman Catholic Church. For the first time since the Reformation, protestants who are not particularly keen on any *Una Sancta syrenes* enjoy ecumenical eucharists with Catholics (unprompted by the World Council of Churches). The emphasis on healing through prayer, the importance of songs and speaking in tongues and the ministry of exorcism, all ring true to many African Christians who hitherto had been told by their sterner protestant teachers that all this was sub-Christian baggage from the past. A charismatic leader as the focus of the church makes it possible to link Christianity with the tradition of the guru in India. All that is highly risky and contains promises both for disaster and for healthy mission which will be discussed later.

Oral theology

Western Christianity and Judaism are of course religions with written records of their past. It is strange for us to learn that there are unwritten ways of recording and passing on the values of the past. They can be found amongst many Third World churches, and — perhaps surprising to some — in the Bible. As form criticism taught before structuralism became a fashion, the hymns and stories of the Old and New Testament were passed on for a considerable time through oral tradition. The theologies of the Bible shaped the values of old Israel and articulated the hope of the emerging church long before they were written down, just as the hymns, prayers, dances and liturgies of the non-white indigenous churches in Africa, of the black churches in the United States, and the Pentecostal churches in Latin America conditioned their theological communication. In these pre-literate, semi-literate or post-literate cultures the medium of communication is — just as in biblical times — not the definition but the description, not the statement but the story, not the doctrine but the testimony, not the book but the parable, not a systematic theology but a song, not the treatise but the TV programme, not the articulation of concepts but the celebration of banquets. Desmond Tutu comments, 'Why should we feel embarrassed if our theology is too dramatic for verbalisation but can be expressed only adequately in the joyous song and the scintillating movement of Africa's dance in the liturgy?'

Why should Africans feel embarrassed? The answer is simple. Because we theologians of the west, in particular evangelical theologians, do not consider such communication to be of the same academic standard as that which is expressed through our own cultural media. How little we have studied the form as well as the content of biblical communication! And modern 'progressive' theologians completely ignore the visions of hope and freedom which are expressed in a moving way in the songs and stories of these Third World churches. 'Such silence is inexcusable', says James H. Cone, a black theologian from the United States, in an analysis of the spirituals. 'It is hard', he continues, 'not to conclude that they (namely these theologians) are enslaved by their own identity with the culture and history of white slave-masters.' Even if one makes allowances for such a sweeping statement, the fact is obvious that our debates on development policy, political witness of the churches, 'church and society', 'theology of revolution', or whatever the slogans may be, ignore some of these highly effective ways of spreading and celebrating the gospel practised by the Kimbanguists in Zaïre and other African churches, and the Latin American indigenous Pentecostal churches.

In order to clarify the functions of oral culture I now re-tell the story of Antônio José dos Santos in his own words:

I was born in the state of Alagoas in the city of União des Palmares. The names of my parents were José Filípe dos Santos and Joana Maria da Conceição. At the age of six months I was taken to the state of Pernambuco where I was reared. At the age of twenty-one I was married. I married abiding by the laws of the Catholic church and only now have married legally. At the age of thirty-six I accepted the Word of Christ's Gospel. It happened in the município of Pôrto do Calvo at the Engenho Sao João. There already existed an assembleia in that place and that is where the Lord used me. And I went into the desert to pray for a period of ten months, then I started preaching the Gospel to the people.

Antônio José dos Santos then describes in detail how he received the baptism in the Spirit and how he was called by visions to the ministry. He earned his livelihood as a farm worker and preached when he had earned enough to support himself and his family. But he had a troubled life, never being permitted to stay more than a few months in any one place:

Once more I had to move on, so I returned to Sergipe and Campo Nôvo where my wife and children were, and preached the Gospel there. The owner of the farm and his entire family were converted and I started a small congregation. After eight days the people from Santa Brigida who had been converted began moving in over the thirty kilometers of trail between the two places. These people fled from Santa Brigida by night because of fear of the Captain of Police, José Rufino, and other people in the town. They came in groups of twenty-five at a time and within a few days there were about thirty families at Campo Nôvo, which amounted to about one hundred and fifty persons. We stayed there together for four years and eight months . . .

Now the owner of Campo Nôvo farm who had been converted had a son who had been absent for some years in the city of São Paulo. One day he came home and found all of those crentes (believers) farming on his father's property and he began immediately to agitate to have his father send us away upon the pretext we would eventually take the land entirely away from his father and the heirs. Really, though, what he wanted was the improvements we had put on the land in those years of hard work: thirteen good houses, five acudas (reservoirs for water) and a large number of tarefas (unit of land measure, equal to three-fourths of an acre) in Sergipe, of rice, beans, and cotton. His father finally agreed to his demands and I went to the authorities of the município asking them to try and intercede for us for at least some sort of partial payment for all we had to leave behind. On 27 May 1958 sixty crentes followed me leaving behind everything and we all travelled forty-five kilometers to another fazenda named Belo Horizonte. The wife of the farmer of Campo Nôvo turned against him when he treated the crentes in this manner, and came with us. Today she lives with us here on the Fazenda Belo Horizonte and has brought a suit against her husband for her share of the property of Campo Nôvo.

The fazendeiro of Belo Horizonte was named Agostinho Barbaso dos Anjos and he took all of us in, offering us land. He told us he would sell the land to us so we would never be chased again. But we did not have any money with which to pay. He said that it did not matter. I was to stay and work with the people and pay him as we could. After nine months at Belo Horizonte he gave us a written title by means of which I and all the people became registered owners of 2.300 tarefas. We had to work three years more in order to pay for it in full but after this we were free to move onto the property and build our homes on it. This is the settlement we have built, and are still building, and we call it Fazenda Nova Vida (New Life Farm). To the thirty families who moved here with me I appointed a piece of ground, all that they were able to work, and gave them a property document for it. Each family received land according to its size and the number of hands it was able to put to work. The church we have built we call the Evangelho da Paz. The public authorities of the município of Poco Redondo, in which Belo Horizonte was located at the time we came, refused to have anything to do with us up to and including this very day. On 24 September 1963, our church joined the Assembly of God igreja-mãe of Arcajú.

Donald Edward Curry, to whose anthropological research I owe this story, describes Antônio in the categories of a Brazilian messiah.[3] This is 'taken to mean a person believing himself to be divinely called, as a result of a dream or a series of visions, to lead a group of people from some catastrophic set of conditions into a more perfect state of affairs'. I would have preferred the term shaman for the same phenomenon. However, it seems to me that his conclusions — quoting Maria Isaura Pereira de Queiroz — are significant for our study:

> The . . . primary function (of the Brazilian messianic movements) is to transform the profane society . . . The second function is that of renewing the local political frameworks, by substituting for the tradi-tional chiefs — who no longer merit confidence — someone who is their superior — the messiah . . . The Brazilian messiahs thus owe the greatest part of their prestige to their skills in resolving the practical problems of daily life. Salvation in the hereafter is completely secondary in comparison to the importance of profane goals.

This is of course contrary to all that is usually said about Pentecostals and it might well be that Curry goes to the other extreme. But the structure of this oral culture and theology is clear. It is embodied in descriptive categories: the story, the witness and the vision.

This mood of theologising makes it independent of western experts, skills and capital. The tradition of their stories functions like an oral 'book'. Very few people can learn a whole book by heart, but it is easy to repeat accurately a song, one of Christ's parables, an Old Testament story or the story of Antônio. Each of these single pieces of information can be linked together so that the whole body of wisdom and theology is available to the whole community as long as it stays together. Not everybody knows everything, but in principle everybody has access to the whole tradition — which is exactly the function of a modern communication system, only in the case of an oral culture it functions without electronic gadgets.

That is why Charismatic Movements in the Third World not only have access to the literary tradition of the west, but also the collective wisdom of their own cultural situation, both Christian and pre-Christian. Obviously one would expect new forms of Christianity to emerge, just as the encounter of the Hebrew-Christian form of Christianity with the Hellenistic culture produced a different form of Christianity. The moral standards, the christological categories, the liturgical formulas and the eschatological expectations of the Hebrew Christians differed widely from those of the Hellenistic Christians. The infusion of the Charismatic Movement into the different oral cultures of Third World countries produces different types of movement. This is the reason for both its missionary efficiency and its possible theological deviations. If, however, external controls from Europe and America are imposed on Third World Charismatic Movements in order to enforce conformity to the European or American pattern, then the missionary outreach of the Charismatic Movement will be seriously hindered. When Antônio joined the Assemblies of God in Brazil he was not choosing a certain type of theology, namely the Pentecostal, but rather a type of Christianity within which he could operate without having to give up his own oral tradition.

The Fruits

In so far as the Charismatic Movement becomes part of the culture of the Third World, the following features will be recognised: a non-conceptual medium for theologising: song and story; an alternative or a complement to western medicine: prayer for the sick; an exploration into the dark side of the soul: exorcism; and a 'cathedral' of sounds: singing and speaking in tongues.

As I have already dealt with the first category I shall now consider the second, namely prayer for the sick.

Prayer for the sick

Prayer for the sick is especially important in the African and Latin-American churches. The treatment of illness as practised by Europeans is scarcely acceptable to many of them, even if they cannot explain in our terms what prevents them from accepting it. European medicine seems to them to be a new and worse magic which claims to be able to overcome the tragedy of sickness but which in fact isolates the body from the soul with the tools of modern science. In these circumstances a responsible integration of academic medicine (including psychiatry) and the African practice of hypnotherapy (healing by hypnosis) with healing through prayer is an urgent necessity. An example of such an integration is the Etodome Nyanyuie-Presbiteria Hame Gbedoda Kple Doyo-Habobo (The Prayer and Healing Group of the Evangelical Presbyterian Church at Etodome in Ghana). This prayer group was founded by the bricklayer Frank Kwadzo Do, a faithful member of the Presbyterian Church in Etodome. With the permission of the church authorities he began to hold Presbyterian services because the nearest Presbyterian Church was too far away. Since those who came to these services did not know any Protestant hymns he held special hymn practices for them. A dying child was brought to one of these practices and was healed by the prayers of the assembled congregation. At the same time Do received visions and the gift of speaking in tongues. This prayer and healing group in Etodome which grew up round Do worked within the Presbyterian Church, with the permission of the church authorities, although the speaking in tongues and other peculiarities caused a great deal of tension with neighbouring congregations. Its healing services are quite different from American healing services. They consist of friendly pastoral care for individual patients, with confession of sins, and advice for combating disease, the difficulties of pregnancy, miscarriages and still-birth, together with help in preparing expectant mothers for the task of bringing up their children. In addition, all the greater and lesser difficulties of marriage and the up-bringing of children which occur in daily life, are dealt with in a sympathetic, good-humoured, but never frivolous way, in what amounts to an unselfconscious form of group therapy.

Another example is from Latin America. Dr Binder, who is a disciple

of Albert Schweitzer, provides a model for the integration of South
American Indian medicine with scientific European medical treatment.
He does not fight the Indian medicine men but accepts them as equal
colleagues. Whilst learning from them, he passes on to them important
elements of European medicine and hygiene. Binder's dealings with the
medicine men therefore represent a dialogue between equals for both
the European doctor and the Indian medicine man are pupil and teacher
simultaneously.

I am inclined to think that in twenty or fifty years time our children
and grandchildren may be puzzled by the very expense and complication
of our medical techniques, and may well ask us, 'Why these complicated
X-ray machines? There are simpler ways of examining the inside of man.
Why these complicated operations? There are more human and less costly
methods of adjusting bones and of removing foreign bodies and growths
than cutting open the human body. Why these complicated anaesthetics?
There are simpler and less harmful methods of making the human body
insensible to pain.' These are not silly questions. The World Health
Organisation and the Christian Medical Commission (an agency sponsored
by the Division of World Mission and Evangelism of the World Council
of Churches) are conscious that a health service does not consist mainly
in the maintenance or even in the erection of traditional hospitals.
Hospitals, especially in the Third World, are becoming increasingly
expensive and ineffective in raising the general level of health of the
population, because they are 'bed-centred' and 'care-centred', instead
of being 'person-centred' and 'health-centred'. What is the use of treating
infectious diseases when the water they drink and the air they breathe
becomes more and more polluted? What is the use of treating heart
ailments when our modern way of life (even in the churches) imposes
an excessive burden on the heart? The most important question which
an African patient asks must not be side-tracked. This question is not,
'What is my disease (appendicitis or hernia)?' It is, 'What is wrong
with me, why am I ill (evil spirits or offences against the community)?'
In short, the African wants to see treatment for what he regards as the
root of the disease and not merely treatment of its symptoms. Thus
a decisive factor in the work of healing in Africa is co-operation with
Africans who have not had medical training but who are familiar with
the African approach to health.

Over the last ten years this insight has also spread amongst European medical researchers. In a provocative sermon on Mark 5:1-43, Walter Vogt, a Swiss general practitioner, said: 'Medicine has developed an unsuspected skill in restoring health without healing . . . The encounter with mental illness for example is avoided. Society avoids confrontation with what cannot be healed, because it has itself become unhealthy.' In other words, healing cannot really take place because the human machine must be repaired at all costs, even at the cost of hindering true healing. A man is seen as a combination of bio- and electro-chemical systems to be replaced and repaired. But if man is 'healed' like this, he falls to pieces. Hans Schaefer, a German professor of medicine, has investigated the underlying principles and effects of present-day medicine. He does not believe that an increase in technological medicine will bring us that health for which we are longing. Similar questions are raised in the English-speaking world. The English doctor, Michael Wilson, describes present-day medical practice as 'violence'. I do not advocate that we should replace European medicine with the practice of the African non-white indigenous churches or the prayer for the sick of the Latin American Pentecostals, but I would suggest that their experiences point to realities and potentials which we have neglected. Such neglect could be to our cost. And who would be better placed to take up this challenge than the members of the Charismatic Movement all over the world?

Exorcism

There was a time when the very mention of possession by ancestral spirits or demons would have been considered morbid or shocking or ridiculous. Consequently all phenomena of possession in Third World churches were considered part of the superstition of the uneducated. Today the pendulum is gradually swinging to the other extreme and we are faced in Europe with a growing wave of occultism, satan worship and demon possession. In spite of this the whole subject of demonic influence is insufficiently understood and the criteria for diagnosing demon possession are not clear (which is not the same as saying that demon possession does not exist).

The question of the presence of ancestral spirits is crucially important to African Christians, both in the main-line churches and in the newly

emerging independent churches. Gabriel Setiloane complained bitterly
how disappointed he was when the section on the presence of ancestors
was deleted from a publication which he wrote for the World Council
of Churches. Ancestors are present everywhere in Africa, not only for
the poorly educated but even for 'a Christian minister, born and raised
in a manse', and trained in European theology. Simon Barrington-Ward,
the well-known general secretary of the evangelical Church Missionary
Society in Great Britain, and Michael Singleton, see the belief in ancestral
spirits not just as a remnant of the African past, but as a way of dealing
with a complex technological and pluralistic situation, a way of repairing
a shattered world and making a bridge between Europe and Africa —
an idea already put forward by the great French sociologist Roger Bastide
in his studies on the Afro-Brazilian religions. The whole problem of
handling ancestor-worship in Africa needs a great deal of study by
theologians.

However, my topic here is not specifically ancestral worship but
exorcism. Since writing *The Pentecostals*[4] I have not come across a better
documented and analysed case than that of the exorcism in Southern
Germany of Gottliebin Dittus by Christoph Blumhardt. I therefore use
the material again. It is identical to experiences in Third World churches
which are unfortunately not so well documented. Amongst other things
it shows that the cultural barriers between Europe and Africa are not
insurmountable if we Europeans take serious note of those parts of our
history which are out of keeping with our view of Europe as entirely
rational and enlightened.

This is the story as reported by Blumhardt, a well-known pietist.
According to him the devil had magically introduced nails, frogs and
other substances into Gottliebin Dittus, who was finally set free in front
of witnesses as the result of months of prayer. I am not able to judge
whether there were parapsychological phenomena at work, or whether
it was a case of therapeutic practice which can be interpreted in terms
of modern psychiatry. A Swiss psychiatrist, G. Benedetti, says:

> A modern psychiatrist who, in treating a psychosis, allowed himself to
> become as infected as Blumhardt did, would be bound to cause us serious
> concern for his mental health. For the 'reality' in which we live today
> has much less room for the possibility of such experiences than did the

world view that existed a hundred years ago. Nowadays the occurrence of such experiences implies a far greater departure from the outlook and mode of experience of the healthy social environment in which they take place. In Blumhardt's time the world was much more open to many of the experiences of psychotic people. And I wonder whether this may not be the reason why patterns of symptoms like those of Gottliebin Dittus hardly ever occur in the present day. In our age suffering of this kind is a rarity. Extreme mental distress is expressed in different forms today. We observe it more in the autistic loneliness of schizophrenia or depression than in the colourful images of a spreading and contagious hysteria, occasional occurrences of which were still being studied at the beginning of this century by the early psychoanalysts. Consequently I think that to diagnose hysteria in the modern sense in the case of Gottliebin Dittus would be to fail to give a full account of the nature of her affliction. Hysteria in the present day is something different from what Blumhardt describes.

In bringing the demons 'face to face' with himself, Blumhardt became in part subject to them. This is the meaning which we can perceive in Blumhardt's 'mythological' narrative. Hallucinatory experiences which he shared with his patient show us how far he himself was affected by the stimulus of the psychotic situation. But the effect was unlike that upon people who completely shut themselves off from the affliction of the mentally ill person as a defence against it and yet who themselves fall victim to it in the very act of rejection. The cruelty of the persecution of witches was an expression of the fact that the persecutors had *succumbed* in this way. *By entering into the situation of the psychosis, Blumhardt finally overcame it.*

I think a 'critical reception' of African healing prctices and of African ancestral beliefs would have to proceed along these lines.

A theologian, Joachim Scharfenberg, has also studied the case of Gottliebin Dittus in detail. He agrees with Benedetti in regarding Blumhardt's relationship with the sick girl as a realisation of and a pointer towards 'the classical pattern of psychotherapeutic dialogue'. According to Scharfenberg the healing took place because in his pastoral care Blumhardt abandoned the atttitude of instruction and consolation and entered into an open dialogue with the girl, setting the faculties of experience free to receive a new experience. It is the area of consciousness which is enlarged in this way which is able to exercise a healing effect, both on the mental situations and on the situations of social conflict in which his son, the younger Blumhardt, tried to carry forward the line of development begun by his father.

It is therefore not surprising that, in the revival movement sparked off by Blumhardt, the sermon was replaced by an activity in which 'as far as possible all members were involved in dialogue with each other' — a description of the very essence of a charismatic renewal, in accordance with Paul's instructions for the relationship of the different organs within the body of Christ. In these meetings,

> the fateful division between the profane and the sacred is really broken down, here . . . a style of life is realised in which dialogue can develop, in which all who take part both give and receive. Here Blumhardt also learned to leave behind his former 'sharp' style of preaching and there was even a visible replacement of pastoral concern for the individual by this group dialogue. The effect of these impulses and promptings will spread far and wide, without setting up a situation of sectarian dependency upon them. Here people find liberation and — as Blumhardt set out as his aim — consciousness and 'knowledge of themselves'.

All this is another important bridging-function of the Charismatic Renewal between the cultures of the Third World and the north Atlantic.

Over twenty years ago W. Schulte, a doctor, gave a similar reply to the question, 'What can a doctor say to Johann Christoph Blumhardt about illness and possession?' According to Schulte, 'it is not possible to give a diagnosis which distinguishes between sickness and possession . . . They represent two possible aspects of the same event.' From this Schulte concludes: 'No discerning doctor will deny that the healing of a disease can only come about with the help of God. But this should not mean abandoning all medical activity in the sphere of psychological and mental illness and looking for the help from a miracle of prayer.'

All that seems to emerge from this medical evidence is that most phenomena of possession can perhaps be explained (although not understood!) within the framework of modern psychiatric knowledge, even if the possessed cannot be healed by psychiatry. Even so, there is an 'inexplicable remnant', which indicates that our methods of diagnosing sickness are relatively accurate only in those areas where the methods are appropriate. This is also the conclusion of a very revealing book on witchcraft in the west of France written by the French psychoanalyst, Jeanne Favret-Saada. She rejects the simplistic 'explanations' of traditional psychology and sociology and leaves the enigma open for the time being — probably the only honest conclusion for empirical research.

Furthermore we observe, that in certain cases in the Third World and in Europe, exorcism brings about healing where psychiatric treatment does not. It may be that this healing has to do with the willingness of the pastor or doctor 'to enter into the situation of the psychosis' (Benedetti). But if that is a condition for healing, the experiences of those Third World prophets, pastors, healers and 'exorcists' in the Charismatic Renewal are all the more important for us. How do they manage to enter into that psychotic situation without becoming psychotic themselves? Here is another important topic for intercultural study.

Glossolalia

Speaking in tongues is the usual, accepted habit in most Latin American Pentecostal churches, in many non-white indigenous churches and in all charismatic prayer groups. It is however not commoner amongst Mexican Pentecostals for example than amongst Catholic charismatic groups in the USA. The literature on glossolalia is of course vast. I will confine myself here to the analysis by a linguist William J. Samarin, himself not a glossolalic. On the basis of tape-recordings, visits to charismatic meetings, questionnaires and a good knowledge of the international literature, Samarin comes to the conclusion that glossolalia is a normal phenomenon, not aberrant but abnormal in certain cultural contexts, not pathological and having nothing to do with trance or schizophrenia. Glossolalia is not fraud or pious deceit; it is also not xenoglossy or speaking in unknown foreign languages, as some charismatics believe; nor does it necessarily happen in a loud or particularly emotional voice; it is also not supernatural; in fact it is not a language in the sense that the sounds have a systematic relation to meaning. Simply stating that it is either 'the voice of God or schizophrenic babbling' is establishing wrong alternatives. It is a 'façade of language', but there is more than phonetics and linguistics to glossolalia. 'It is impossible to translate into a series of consonants and vowels the totality of events that gives glossolalia its significance.'

What is its significance? Here Samarin knows Paul better than many scholarly New Testament commentators and antagonists of Pentecostalism. 'The individual and social benefits of this existential, "be yourself" religion have not been fully appreciated by observers in spite of the value that it places on just this kind of self-assertiveness.' 'Glossolalia is therefore not aberrant behaviour, only anomalous. It is anomalous, because it departs from run-of-the-mill speech, not because tongue speakers are in any way abnormal.' But society has 'judged glossolalic behaviour abnormal because of the belief by certain Christians that this comes from God. Society has therefore judged a *belief*, not behaviour or people. Yet both the speakers and the speech are condemned.' Both those who believe that glossolalia is from God and those who believe that it is pathological, are in error, and according to Samarin the latter error is the greater. Samarin then offers this interesting sacramental interpretation of glossolalia: bread in tl eucharist, he says, is bread but in the eucharist it becomes something that transcends ordinary bread, and it has a function which is entirely different from everyday bread. When a person speaks in tongues there is nothing supernatural about this, but

> he is saying that he is involved in something — at a given moment in time or as part of a pattern of life — that transcends the ordinary. In short, glossolalia is a linguistic symbol of the sacred . . . Glossolalia *says*, 'God is here', just as a Gothic cathedral says, 'Behold, God is majestic' . . . Viewed in this way glossolalia is symbolic in the very way that the eucharist is symbolic.

A cathedral is built of ordinary stones and yet its whole purpose is extraordinary and sacred. Here are people without a gothic cathedral or — in the case of the American Charismatic Renewal — who have left their gothic cathedral. Their symbol of the sacred, their liturgical space, their scenario is not set in stones and architectural design but in a design of another kind of language. It is a socio-acoustic sanctuary.

I am not advocating that we should imitate the songs, the stories the treatment of the sick, the exorcism and the glossolalia of Third World charismatics. I only want to free these phenomena from their aura of exoticism or absurdity and point out the opportunities for sound liturgical and missionary communication. I am convinced that at least some of these customs draw our attention to realities and methods of dealing with them which our forefathers knew but which we have forgotten. This could be a serious disadvantage for western theology because it hinders a truly intercultural approach to theology. Furthermore that process of repression and 'forgetting' could become extremely harmful when the 'demons of the past' break into our cultures (as can be seen already in the emergence of uncontrolled and sensational occultism) and we find ourselves completely at a loss to know how to exterminate these evils in a responsible way. For this coming confrontation, the charismata of the poor of the Third World will prove to be very much more than poor charismata.

Implications for Mission

If mission means more than exporting our own culturally-determinied attitude to the gospel to other cultures, and is truly that process by which the gospel passes from Jerusalem to Caesarea, then mission is not only concerned with the geographical growth of the church but also with its cultural and theological growth. The gospel which reached Caesarea differed from the one dispatched from Jerusalem. The Hellenistic Church was different (and necessarily so) from the Hebrew Christian Church. The same is true of the transition of the gospel from the Hellenistic culture to the Roman culture, and later to the Germanic and Anglo-Saxon cultures. And it is to the credit of the modern missionary movement that this same process is becoming visible in the transition of the gospel from the north Atlantic culture to the Third World cultures. This of course raises the question of the plurality of Christian worship, liturgy and ethics within the unity of the Christian community, a question which evangelical missionary strategists can no longer simply hand over to the World Council of Churches and other 'liberal organisations'. At least since the Conference on Evangelism in Lausanne in 1974, it is clear that there is an equally plural approach emerging in the evangelical community. This makes imperative an intercultural theological approach, for which I submit a number of theses.

The church is theologically a transcultural and sociologically an intercultural body. But as soon as the church speaks it uses cultural language because all human language is embedded in a cultural tradition. How does theology, which wants to mirror this intercultural entity and point to its transcultural reality, operate if theological language is by definition culturally-biased language and if this is unavoidable?

The first step for such intercultural theology would be to acknowledge its limits. Intercultural theology is that academic discipline which operates in a given culture without absolutising this culture. In that sense it only does what theology would do anyhow; in other words, it reflects or mirrors theologically the body of Christ. If theology is not just a rationalisation of our own cultural attitudes (i.e. a sectarian theology or worse a theologically-defended cultural imperialism) then it must attempt to be open to this universal and sacramental dimension of the Christian faith.

The methods by which this is achieved have to be chosen for their suitability. The north Atlantic tradition cannot *a priori* be ruled out as one of the possibilities but it should not be taken for granted that it is the only, or even the most important one, unless one has arguments which disqualify the great stories of the Bible, including the parables of Christ, as theology! In this 'body of Christ'-approach, theology has to hold its ground against all pagan and sectarian schools in the world of learniong (and in the churches). It cannot conform to the *stoicheia tou kosmou*.

Intercultural theology is not a form of 'pop-theology', and it does not make our task easier but harder. It does not mean that we abandon our critical scholarship, but rather that we apply it not only to the content of our discipline but to the whole process of communication. Intercultural theology is not only concerned with the dominant cultures but also — following the example of the early theologians of our tradition — with 'oral cultures' and 'oral theology', which is not necessarily 'unwritten theology' but which follows other patterns of thought and communication than the 'literary cultures'. This is all the more important if we take seriously modern exegetical insights and the findings of the Second Vatican Council, which concur in not leaving theological reflection exclusively in the hands of professional theologians but which expect the people of God to make a contribution to theology.

If, however, theology is that process which reflects critically on its own tradition within the cultural contexts of the people of God then we need bridge-building theologians who participate in that essential dialogue between 'oral' and 'literary', 'female' and 'male', 'black' and 'white'. The differences between these cultures should not only be seen in strictly marxist terminology (which in itself is a western thought pattern) but also in the idioms of different cultures which cannot be explained away within the marxist interpretation of history. If the church succeeds in organising an intercultural dialogue, then, for the first time in world history, a global communication would emerge without giving a privileged position to any one culture of our globe. This would be the translation of the theological concept of conciliarity into cultural categories, and it could release potentials and insights both in the 'old' and in the 'new' cultures.

Notes

1 A fully footnoted and documented version of this essay appeared in *Theological Renewal*, Feb.1980, and in *International Bulletin of Missionary Research*, vol.4/2 (1980). (An example of intercultural theology is W. J. Hollenweger, *Conflict in Corinth, Memoirs of an Old Man* (Paulist Press, New York, 1982). It uses modern critical historical exegesis fully. Not only theologians but also non-theologians and in fact non-academics can appreciate its intercultural function.)

2 D. S. Barrett, *World Christian Encylopedia* (Nairobi, 1982).

3 Donald Edward Curry, *Journal of Inter-American Studies and World Affairs*, July 1970.

4 W. J. Hollenweger, *The Pentecostals* (SCM, London, 1972).

Pentecostal Theology and the Charismatic Movement

JULIAN WARD

Introduction

At the united conference of Assemblies of God and Elim ministers entitled 'The Pentecostal Movement in the Eighties' (14-16th November, 1979), Alfred Missen, until recently the General Secretary of the Assemblies of God, spoke of the relationship of the Pentecostal movement to the Charismatic Movement in the historical denominations. He explained that he had attended the Fountain Trust International Conference at Guildford in 1971, but had left on the second day, being unable to feel at one with other participants. However, when attending the National Evangelical Anglican Conference at Nottingham in 1977, he was deeply impressed by the charismatic nature of the worship at the communion service and recognised a genuine spiritual reality in the singing of 'He is Lord' and 'Jesus is Lord'. This made him revise his attitude, and in his address he advocated an openness to what God is doing in the Charismatic Movement and an involvement in it where possible. For some, with their strong evangelical convictions, this was a hard saying. For others, this was a timely address with which they concurred. I wish to address myself to this tension between the Pentecostal and Charismatic Movements. Firstly, I would like to make a few comments on the title of this paper.[1] The term 'Pentecostal theology' appears to assume a thorough and scientific exposition of the revelation of God as known to Pentecostals, with a careful examination of presuppositions and an extended exposition of doctrines. I know of none. E. S. Williams of the American Assemblies of God produced a *Systematic Theology* (1953) but it lacks an adequate theological prolegomena and discussion of the relationship of Pentecostal theology to other more traditional Protestant and Catholic theologies. P. S. Brewster, the previous Secretary-General of the Elim Movement, edited *Pentecostal Doctrine* (1976), which is an exposition at a popular level of some of the doctrines held by Pentecostals.

However, inasmuch that theology is 'God-talk', that is, speaking of God in his acts of creation, redemption and revelation, we can identify a popular Pentecostal theology. My concern is with the Pentecostal doctrines that would constitute the consensus of beliefs held by ministers of the two largest Pentecostal denominations in this country. However, we should note that there is a divergence of attitudes to the Charismatic Movement within these bodies. We should also note that the term 'Charismatic Movement' encompasses the historic denominations and the house fellowships. What I have to say concerns mainly the former as it relates to the Protestant denominations, but I shall touch on the latter.

I wish to raise and try to answer the following questions:

What are the reasons for the divergent attitudes of Pentecostals towards the Charismatic Movement? The answer can be found by examining the beliefs and values of Pentecostals.

What attitude to the Charismatic Movement is consistent with Pentecostal theology? The application of a Pentecostal understanding of biblical teaching is relevant here.

What can be the contribution of the Pentecostal movement to the Charismatic Movement in the current situation? The relevance of Pentecostal spirituality can be considered in this context.

What can Pentecostals learn from the Charismatic Movement? To be true to their principles Pentecostals must be prepared to listen to what the Spirit is saying to and through Christians of other traditions.

To what extent can Pentecostals and charismatics work together? The spiritual decline and moral degradation of our country are all too evident. It seems desirable for professing Christians to work together as far as possible in evangelisation and social action.

What are the Reasons for the Divergent Attitudes of
Pentecostals towards the Charismatic Movement?

Pentecostals should be regarded as Protestant evangelicals who have had vivid experiences of God and who, until recently, have been rejected by other denominations because of these experiences. Such experiences of the divine and of rejection produced new doctrines and a new Christian sub-culture. This is nothing new in church history, and similar antecedents are found amongst the Anabaptists of the sixteenth century and the early Methodists of the eighteenth century. Pentecostals regard their roots as being in the Reformation tradition (although the Anabaptist and Arminian traditions may be more correct), the evangelical and holiness movements in the nineteenth century, and the spiritual awakenings in Europe and America from 1900 to 1914.[2] Pentecostal denominations were formed as a result of the ministries of charismatic and individualistic personalities, such as George Jeffreys and Smith Wigglesworth, and because of rejection of the Pentecostal doctrine and/or experiences by prominent denominational leaders and Bible teachers, as well as local ministers.

For the Pentecostal the supreme authority is the Bible, the inspired, infallible and inerrant Word of God to which all else must be subject. Gone are the days of regarding prophecies and interpretations as being of equal authority. The Bible is to be understood in a straightforward and fairly literal way, although typology is often applied.

From his vivid religious experience the Pentecostal knows that God is supernatural, beyond time and space, and not to be equated in a panentheistic way with the depths of our own existence or the ground of our being. He is deeply committed to the mystery of Trinitarianism. (Sabellianism or 'oneness' doctrine was once a threat to certain parts of the Pentecostal movement and it is still active in some Pentecostal sects today.) His experience of Jesus as the baptiser in the Holy Spirit assures him of the truth of the biblical teaching on the absolute deity of Christ. Any attempt to minimise or deny the ontological reality of this is to be regarded as being of demonic inspiration.

Pentecostal soteriology (or doctrine of salvation) is founded upon the entire sufficiency of Christ's death as a vicarious penal substitution. Man is justified by faith alone and any attempt to add to the one work of the one mediator as part of the way of salvation must be regarded as coming under the anathema of Paul in Gal. 1:8-9.

Christian initiation is in a three-fold form: born again of the Spirit, then baptised in water by immersion as a believer, and then baptised in the Holy Spirit, although the order of this pattern may vary in practice. The ordinances of baptism and the Lord's supper are no more than symbols of Christ's redemptive activity.

Pentecostals believe that they must seek to return to the standards of the New Testament church. Doctrine must be demonstrated from the Bible and not derived from spiritual gifts. Preaching of the Word of God from the Bible must have priority over testimonies and description of experiences, and it is felt that the Charismatic Movement has overemphasised the latter at the expense of the former. Further, it is thought that the house fellowship movement has exaggerated the authority of spiritual leaders and the consequent submission of adherents to the detriment of biblical authority and the priesthood of all believers.

Pentecostals strongly emphasise freedom in worship, individual participation in it, and the operation of the gifts of the Spirit. The common accusations of disorder or an obsession with tongues or the work of the Holy Spirit are not often valid today. However, Pentecostal worship does sometimes give the impression that spirituality is to be measured by the volume and emotion of worship, rather than by the degree of obedience to the divine will. Pentecostals are sometimes not aware of the stereotyping and traditionalism in their worship, and of the value of liturgy and other types of spirituality appreciated by Christians in other traditions.

From the biblical teaching on the final separation of the human race at the Last Judgement and from their awareness of the baptism in the Spirit as the divine empowerment needed for carrying out the great commission, Pentecostals have given priority to aggressive evangelism. They are critical of charismatic groups that become introverted or concerned for spiritual growth at the expense of active evangelism. For them, this is abnegation of Christian responsibility. Evangelism is usually regarded as the conducting of crusades, open-air work, door-to-door visitation and witness by miraculous signs, rather than the exhibition of a loving community or involvement in social action as with some other Christian groups.

Converts are taught the importance of living a godly life according to biblical standards and of separation from worldly standards and behaviour. Such practices as divorce, abortion and homosexuality are opposed as contrary to scriptural teaching. The abrogation of traditional evangelical taboos, such as the drinking of alcohol, by some charismatic groups, is disapproved of as moral compromise and bad Christian witness. Traditionally, Pentecostals have not been involved to any great extent in social reform as they have been busy with evangelism, expectation of an imminent parousia, and fear of the social gospel. More recently, there has been a developing awareness of social responsibility.

The Pentecostals experienced a generation of ostracism, criticism, ridicule and contempt. Even today, every Pentecostal minister is aware of a patronising and superior attitude in some fellow ministers in other denominations. To outsiders Pentecostals can sometimes appear to be insensitive, intolerant, naïve and over-emotional. Pentecostal theology can sometimes appear to be simplistic, unimaginative, rigid and narrow, and based on an unwarranted literalistic interpretation of scripture. It must be admitted that a sophisticated and comprehensive Pentecostal theology that can face the challenges of other theologies is lacking. But it must be remembered that doctrine must primarily apply to human life lived before God, and only secondarily to academic questions. The practical Pentecostal theology has been able to face and resist the onslaught of secularism, materialism and moral relativism. Doctrine is regarded as important by Pentecostals and fellowship based only on experience of the Spirit is regarded as quite inadequate and prone to doctrinal deviation. Considerable improvement in academic standards at Pentecostal Bible Colleges will bring about a more sophisticated understanding of biblical interpretation, theology and ethics. But it should be noted that it is usually activists rather than intellectuals who are attracted to the Pentecostal ministry.

The Pentecostal is concerned to avoid anything that would seem to undermine the evangelical gospel. He is thus opposed to an ecumenism that seems to involve any compromise of biblical authority or evangelical soteriology. For him the mainline denominations have allowed the absorption of an unscriptural liberalism and modernism, with a corresponding loss of spiritual power. By indiscriminate infant baptism millions have been misled into thinking that they are Christians and heading for heaven if they lead a respectable life, whereas in fact they are lost. The World Council of Churches is to be opposed as producing a false ecumenism and the true nature of this organisation is to be seen in its financial support for revolutionary groups, regarded as terrorists, in some parts of the world.

With these beliefs and attitudes it becomes easy to see why many Pentecostals are wary of the Charismatic Movement in both the historical denominations and the House Fellowship Movement. Commitment to the evangelical position makes many feel that it would be wrong to embrace non-evangelicals, for the truths of the saving gospel must be maintained at all cost. They are suspicious of the Roman Catholic Charismatic Movement, feeling that, as the Spirit is the Spirit of truth, if Roman Catholics have had a real experience of the Spirit, then they will be led to see the scriptural errors of Rome and so leave the Church of Rome. Moreover, they think that Roman Catholics are intent on persuading their 'separated brethren' to return to the Roman fold.

However, there are also many Pentecostals who take a much more positive approach. They recognise that God is at work in the historical denominations and they rejoice over that. They are perhaps perplexed as to why it does not lead to a greater commitment to evangelical theology, but they can recognise the genuineness of the worship and spiritual gifts experienced in the Charismatic Movement in the historical denominations. Other Pentecostals feel drawn to the style of the house fellowships, and their churches operate in a similar way. However, some Pentecostal churches have seceded from their denominations in order to gain the 'freedom' of the house fellowships. Consequently, the anti-denominationalism of this movement is viewed with suspicion by many Pentecostals.

Thus we see a divergence of views amongst the Pentecostals regarding both areas of the Charismatic Movement. Those who emphasise the evangelical theology or simply adhere to the traditional separation tend to be reserved; those who recognise the activity of God in the Charismatic Movement and those who emphasise the importance of the activity of the Spirit as defining the bounds of the Church are more responsive and increasingly open to this movement.

What Attitude to the Charismatic Movement
is Consistent with Pentecostal Theology?

Pentecostals are evangelical Protestants with a distinctive view of the
work of the Spirit. They are totally committed to the following relevant
doctrines, as well as certain others: the infallibility and final authority
of the Bible in an evangelical sense; the traditional doctrines of the Trinity
and the person of Christ; the accomplishment of man's redemption solely
and entirely through Christ's death on the Cross which was a vicarious
penal atonement; justification by faith alone — sacraments cannot add
to man's salvation; the validity of no other form of baptism but the
believer's baptism; and the doctrine that the baptism in the Spirit is
subsequent to regeneration and is a divine empowerment primarily for
the service of God.

It is the variation of views on authority, salvation and ecumenism
in the Charismatic Movement that constitute a particular problem for
the conscience of Pentecostals. This difficulty may be reinforced by the
anti-ecumenical stance of non-Pentecostal evangelicals, particularly in
the reformed tradition, who may accuse any involved with the
Charismatic Movement of engaging in theological compromise.

Some Pentecostals, often those who have had little or no first-hand
contact with charismatics, cast doubts upon the genuineness of the
spirituality of the Charismatic Movement. Whilst it must be admitted
that there has been the occasional spurious case and also that experiences
of the new birth and/or rededications are sometimes misunderstood as
being Pentecostal experiences, all the true signs of grace may be there
such as deepened involvement in Bible study, more intense prayer,
liberation in worship, greater devotion to Christ, practice of the spiritual
gifts, more effective evangelism and evidence of divine healing. To the
objection that the Charismatic Movement has led to unscriptural practices,
such as strong emphasis upon a leader's authority, anti-denominationalism
or deepened devotion to the Virgin Mary, it may be replied that the
baptism in the Spirit has a liberating effect on the emotions, with the
psychological result that previous beliefs or practices may receive a
psychological reinforcement.

Some Pentecostals cast doubt upon the validity of the Charismatic

Movement by arguing that the Holy Spirit is the Spirit of truth, and that if the Spirit of truth is received then one will be led to give up unscriptural practices. It may be replied that some born-again evangelicals hold certain doctrines, such as infant baptism, which are considered contrary to the truth revealed by the Holy Spirit, according to Pentecostals. Moreover, Pentecostals are unable to agree amongst themselves in other areas, such as eschatology. Further, it is the work of the Holy Spirit to lead us into holiness as well as truth, and most Pentecostals would not claim to have arrived at perfect holiness. Moreover, it is only by a gradual process that we appropriate divinely revealed truths, and that process will be delayed if one holds a sophisticated theology that seems to interpret biblical revelation adequately. Indeed, one may be preoccupied with more urgent tasks in the Renewal Movement and have little time for lengthy theological reflection.

Pentecostals sometimes object that charismatics are not led by the Spirit out of denominations which adhere to unscriptural doctrines or practices, but this viewpoint may be ignorant of certain important factors. For instance, charismatics have often been brought up in a church and so have a natural love for it, and having experienced spiritual renewal themselves, they desire to see it extended within their own denomination. They can also relate their own charismatic experience to certain strands in their denominational theology, especially those aspects which stress grace, faith, the work of the Holy Spirit and miracles. In addition, denominational attachment involves the subconscious adoption of cultural attitudes with respect to worship, behaviour and attitudes to other groups. Cultural attitudes are not easily changed. Moreover, certain forms in the denominational sub-culture may take on new meaning. For instance, those brought up in the liturgical tradition may find their liturgy conveys a deeper spirituality in worship, especially if it is combined with charismatic songs, choruses, spontaneous prayer, spiritual gifts. Charismatics may possibly be aware of unattractive features in evangelical or Pentecostal groups. They may well question what good would be achieved by leaving their own denomination and thereby losing contact with friends and colleagues. Furthermore, many charismatics in the historical denominations feel that it is God's strategy at this present time to renew the spiritual life of their denomination. This is therefore no time for schism and for leaving the place where God has placed them. To create new denominations would be a grave mistake.

Due account must be taken of the complexity and flexibility of theologies within the historical denominations, so that the question of leaving one's denomination does not appear to be as real or as clear cut as it does to the Pentecostal.

On the other hand, does the evangelical and denominational commitment of the Pentecostal preclude his involvement in the Charismatic Movement? We must apply the biblical teaching to this question. First, from the Pentecostal viewpoint, we may distinguish three groups of people: born-again believers who are evangelical; born-again believers who are non-evangelical due to lack of teaching or due to considered rejection of certain evangelical doctrines — one is not saved on the basis of holding a right theology but by a commitment to the Lordship of the resurrected Jesus (cf. Rom. 10:9); and those under the regenerating influence of the Holy Spirit, but not yet born again. Included in this group are professing Christians who have not yet made that inner dedication and self-commitment to the Lordship of Christ, although they may genuinely acknowledge His Lordship. I myself was in that situation for some ten years. (The sacramentalist is not likely to approve of this classification, but we are seeking to see what is consistent with Pentecostal theology.)

These three groups are likely to be found in most local churches, and they are also to be found within denominations. The Pentecostal can therefore regard the Charismatic Movement in the historic churches as God's way of bringing salvation to nominal Christians, biblical truth to non-evangelicals, and the power of the Spirit to those who, under the gracious activity of the Spirit, are hungry to know a deeper divine reality in their lives and Christian service. This interpretation calls the Pentecostal to positive openness towards the Charismatic Movement in the historic churches and a willingness to relate himself to the strategy and activities of God. When the Apostle Peter was rebuked for having abrogated traditional practices, his reply was, 'If then God gave the same gift to them as he gave to us when we believed in the Lord Jesus Christ, who was I that I could withstand God?' (Acts 11:17). (The non-evangelical will probably hold a different interpretation of God's purposes in the Charismatic Movement, but again we are concerned with the Pentecostal viewpoint.)

The Pentecostal may object further, however, that the New Testament repeatedly warns against association with those holding doctrinal deviations, e.g. Gal. 1:8-9; Titus 3:10; 2 John 10. It therefore follows that Pentecostals should not be involved in a doctrinally mixed movement. To this the following replies may be made.

Those associated with the Charismatic Movement are in general committed to traditional doctrines of the Trinity, and the person of Christ. Warnings in the New Testament against the syncretisation of Christianity with Jewish-pagan gnosticism, as in the Colossian heresy (Col. 2:8, 11, 16, 18; 3:11) and elsewhere (2 Cor. 11:3-6, 13, 22; 12:11; 1 Tim. 1:3,7; 6:20) and with Hellenistic-pagan gnosticism, as in the Johannine churches and elsewhere (1 Tim. 4:1-3; 2 Tim. 2:17-18; 3:4-5, 8-9; 4:4; 2 Pet. 1:16; 2:1-22; 1 John 2:19, 22; 4:1-3; 2 John 7; Jude 4-23), are applicable to modern theologies that deny the ontological reality of the Trinity or the deity of Christ.

The warnings against Judaising Christians in Galatians (Gal. 1:6-9, 12; 3:1; 4:9-11; 5:2-4, 7-12; 6:12), Hebrews and elsewhere (Phil. 3:2-3; Titus 1:10-16; 3:9) would be applicable to a rigid sacramentalism that abrogated the principle of justification by faith.

It should be noted that all official theologies of the historic Protestant churches have a significantly vital place for the prevenience of grace, regarded as totally unmerited, and justification by faith. Public exposition and popular practice may not always have corresponded to such aspects of official theology. Other aspects of these theologies may perhaps be inconsistent with these teachings. However, those involved in the Charismatic Movement tend to have a strong emphasis on grace and faith and to revise perspectives on other aspects in their denominational theology.

The fact that the experience of the Spirit does not automatically result in entirely evangelical beliefs is shown by those Jews who were converted to faith in Christ and yet still continued to observe the rites of Judaism (Acts 2:46; 15:5; 21:20-4). Peter and other Jewish Christians were slow to realise that the gospel removed the divisions between Jews and Gentiles (Acts 10:15, 28, 34; 11:2, 17, 18). Paul even rebuked Peter for relapsing into the practice of avoiding table fellowship with Gentile Christians (Gal. 2:11-14). The Council of Jerusalem required Gentile Christians to maintain Jewish food regulations for the sake of fellowship

(Acts 15:28-9). Christians at Corinth, Galatia and Colossae adopted some doctrinal deviations, but Paul sought to maintain positive relationships with them (1 Cor. 1:10; 4:14; 9:1-2; 11:2; 16:24; 2 Cor. 1:24; 2:4; 6:11; 7:2-4, 13-16; 13:9, 11; Gal. 4:19-20; Col. 1:3, 4, 9; 2:1, 5).

Despite Paul's anathema upon the Galatian Judaisers, he was still prepared to circumcise Timothy (Acts 16:3) and to undertake a Nazirite vow (Acts 21:20-6) in order to maintain contact with Jews and fellowship with the original Jewish church. He was prepared to become like a Jew and live as one under the law in order to win Jews to Christ (1 Cor. 9:20).

The New Testament calls upon all born again of the Spirit to recognise the essential unity that they have in the body of Christ (cf. John 17:21, 23; 1 Cor. 11:18, 29; 12:12-26; Eph. 2:14; 3:6). It is significant that growth towards the unity of the faith in Eph. 4:13 is a product of maintaining the unity of the Spirit described in Eph. 4:3. Christians are called upon to have a positive and loving attitude to one another (John 13:34; 1 Cor. 13:7; 1 John 3:14, 16; 17, 20-1).

In the New Testament the basis of fellowship between Christians is the common sharing of fellowship with Jesus Christ (1 Cor. 1:9; 1 John 1:3, 6, 7), participation in the Spirit (2 Cor. 13:14; Phil. 2:1) and fellowship in the Gospel Phil. 1:5, 7; Philem. 6). Because of this common participation Christians can give others 'the right hand of fellowship' (Gal. 2:9) and share in the apostles' fellowship (Acts 2:42).

Scripture also teaches that one should maintain standards of truth. Pentecostals must therefore maintain their evangelical commitment amongst those with whom they have fellowship. This also means that joint evangelism with charismatics is not possible unless the latter are committed to the evangelical gospel.

To sum up, Pentecostals should be open to fellowship with and ministry within the Charismatic Movement. They should also be sensitive to divergent views on this in their own ranks. As to whether they should actually be involved in a given situation must be a matter of prayer, discernment, wisdom, reflection and a desire to follow the leading of the Holy Spirit and biblical teaching that all believers are one in Christ.

What Can be the Contribution of the Pentecostal Movement
to the Charismatic Movement in the Current Situation?

The principal contribution of the Pentecostals to the Charismatic Movement is undoubtedly the reality of the Pentecostal experience, i.e. the baptism in the Holy Spirit, as a gateway into the supernatural dimension in Christian experience. Expectation of the reception of the power of the Spirit is the response of faith to the ascended lordship and Messianic rule of Jesus Christ (cf. John 7:37-9). The reception of the Pentecostal experience is the recognition and manifestation of the fact that Jesus has all power on earth as well as in heaven. The reality of the Pentecostal experience is the cutting edge of the Charismatic Movement, just as it has been for the Pentecostal movement over the last seventy years. Charismatic theologies that fail to label the Pentecostal experience as the baptism in the Spirit have the danger of losing this cutting edge, so that the Charismatic Movement becomes no more than hearty hymn singing and new forms of church life, but lacking the supernatural and the miraculous.

A second contribution is lively worship that engenders recognition of spiritual priorities and promotes godly living, Spirit-given enthusiasm, a healthy optimism and a holy zeal for righteousness and truth. After two generations Pentecostal worship is still able to evoke these New Testament characteristics in very ordinary men and women today. It is commonly commented that relatively few congregations in the historic denominations are affected as a whole by the Charismatic Movement.

A third contribution is the unshakeable conviction that the supernatural gifts of the Spirit are the norm for Christian church life, worship and service. They are not to be restricted to the mid-week prayer meeting of the charismatic clique.

The healthy church is the one that gives priority to evangelism. It is much easier to plan programmes of evangelism and to teach methods of evangelism than to actually evangelise. Evangelism in Pentecostal churches is inspired by worship, prayer and the preaching of the Word of God, rather than by programmes.

A vital contribution is the certainty that divine healing is the biblical sign that the gospel saves. Although malpractice may have been far too common, Pentecostals have maintained and manifested this New Testament principle. Moreover, practical and vivid preaching makes the Word of God relevant to the everyday lives of Christians.

A further contribution is an emphasis upon eschatology and the Second Coming of Christ. Biblical eschatology and apocalyptic reveals the good and evil spiritual forces at work behind history and human governments and authorities. From such a perspective the Church should speak prophetically to the existing events in the world so that society can understand to some extent what God is doing in tumultuous times. An emphasis on the Second Coming adds urgency to the evangelistic task, clarifies the ultimate issues of life and death, and calls believers to get their priorities right.

Furthermore, Pentecostalism is able to communicate the gospel to the working classes and to have a greater attraction than worldly entertainments. It is commonly commented that the historic denominations are predominantly middle-class.

Finally, many Pentecostals believe that charismatics should be willing to learn from their past mistakes, such as telling a person to empty his mind in order to receive the baptism in the Spirit, failure to discern false prophecy, over-emotional worship, misuse of biblical texts and schism and division.

What Can Pentecostals Learn from the Charismatic Movement?

I would suggest that Pentecostals are able to learn a number of valuable things from the Charismatic Movement, such as

A greater sensitivity to the voice of God, hearing it not only in the wind and fire of the deep experiences but also in the still small voice of the holy dove from heaven, in inner leading, contemplation, reflection and creativity;

A more sophisticated and more correct handling of biblical texts that is truly spiritual and truly intellectual and therefore allows the written Word of God to speak to modern practical situations, e.g. those not healed when prayed for, amongst many other examples;

A correspondingly more sophisticated theology of the Holy Spirit
that listens to the great (and divinely inspired) theologians of the
past and yet handles the Bible creatively in the context of modern
experiences of the divine activity in salvation, healing, exorcism,
counselling, community life, evangelism and social care;

A sensitivity to the workings of Spirit in worship, community life,
counselling and healing, particularly of psychosomatic and mental
disorders, and varieties of spiritual gifts and ministries beyond those
traditionally identified by Pentecostals.

In addition, Pentecostals can learn more about the meanings of the
church as the community of God, as the body of Christ, as the incarnation of divine love and as a historical continuity as the Israel of God.
There are so many lessons to be learned here that space forbids the
enumeration of them. The interaction of biblical teaching with charismatic
experience will expound these lessons for us. The priestly, prophetic
and kingly roles of the Church will become evident. Traditional types
of spirituality and the care of spiritual lives could also be studied.
Pentecostals do not always realise that they sing some Anglo-Catholic
and Roman Catholic hymns and that much spiritual wisdom of the
centuries is unknown to them.

Furthermore, it must be admitted that the social aspects of salvation,
Christian responsibility to society and Christian ethics are areas in which
charismatics appear to have given more thought than Pentecostals. A
system of Pentecostal Christian ethics that will give answers to the
perplexing questions of modern life, such as medical questions, industrial
strife, revolution and nuclear warfare has yet to be produced.

To What Extent Can Pentecostals and Charismatics Work Together

I would like to suggest that Pentecostals and charismatics could work
together over social action and protest. They can make common cause
in protests against social evils, such as poverty, exploitation, bad housing,
racism, abortion, euthanasia, pornography or the abolition of religious
education in schools. They can join in social care and rehabilitation

projects. They could combine for co-operative and planned action within the realms of politics, education, trades unions and social welfare.

Pentecostals and charismatics could join together in a number of other ways, especially in fellowship expressing Christian love and unity in the Spirit; in dialogue that repents of spiritual pride and recognises that God wishes to speak to us through each other; in Christian witness and presence on state and local occasions, such as the coronation of the monarch, Remembrance Sunday and local civic events; in evangelism if, and only if, there is complete agreement on what constitutes the Christian gospel; and finally in mutual co-operation in pastoral care if, and only if, there is complete agreement on the spiritual function of the Church.

I believe that the Pentecostal and Charismatic Movements have an important prophetic function in the years that lie ahead. This they will fulfil if they follow God's revealed will in His written Word on how they are to relate to one another. As prophetic to a lukewarm Christendom and to a secular society, they are to hear the Word of God, then to be the embodiment of the Word of God and then to reveal that Word of God to all sections of British society by their lives, their words and their actions. As I envisage Britain in the eighties I cannot imagine a more important function.[3]

Notes

1 This paper was presented to the Fountain Trust Consultative Council in December 1979 and to the European Pentecostal Theological Association in February 1981. Parts of it were incorporated in my paper, 'The Basis of Fellowship' presented to the Elim Ministerial Conference in Southport in 1981. The paper has been slightly revised for publication.

2 See Vinson Synan, ed., *Aspects of Pentecostal-Charismatic Origins* (Logos, 1975).

3 Discussion of some of the above issues may be found in the following: A. Skevington Wood, 'Unity and Schism', 2 parts, *TSF Bulletin*, nos. 67 and 68 (Autumn 1973 and Spring 1974); I. Howard Marshall, 'Orthodoxy and Heresy in Earlier Christianity', *Themelios*, vol. 2, no. 2 (September 1976) pp. 5-14; Geoffrey W. Grogan, 'The Theological Limits of Evangelical Co-operation', *Scottish Tyndale Bulletin* (1977); David Lillie, *Beyond Charisma* (Paternoster Press, Exeter, 1981); Charles Farah, 'Towards a Theology of Ecumenicity or Doctrinal Disagreements and Christian Fellowship', *Theological Renewal*, no. 19 (October 1981); Martin Conway, 'Growing into the Unity Christ Makes Available — the Promise of Pilgrimage in Councils of Churches' (a paper presented to the 1982 Venice Consultation between the Roman Catholic Church and the World Council of Churches).

On Evangelicals and the Ecumenical Movement: Martin Conway, 'One Man's Attempt towards a Survey' and David Gregg, 'How the Ecumenical Movement Looks to the Evangelical Constituency' (Working Papers from the Division of Ecumenical Affairs presented at the 80th Meeting of the Council held at the Sixteenth Assembly of the British Council of Churches, Spring 1982); papers on 'The Basis of Fellowship' by L. Bowring, D. A. Lambelle, P. Smith and J. W. Ward presented to the Elim Ministerial Conference of the Elim Pentecostal Church, Southport, 6-8th October, 1981.

On WCC Sub-unit on Renewal and Congregational Life: *Report of the Consultation on the Charismatic Renewal for the Churches* (report on the Conference at Bossey, Switzerland, 8-13th March, 1980).

The Theology of
the 'Restoration' House Churches

ANDREW WALKER

*Introduction: The House Church Movement as
a Charismatic Phenomenon Outside the Mainstream Churches*

During the late 1970s, when the Charismatic Renewal was at its zenith
in Great Britain, leading figures in the movement became increasingly
aware of another strand of Pentecostalism, the House Church Movement.
In 1979, the British Council of Churches in association with the Fountain
Trust, held a consultation with senior British churchmen to discuss the
significance of the Charismatic Renewal.[1] The consultation included
Michael Harper, David Watson and Tom Smail (who with Colin
Urquhart were probably the best known leaders of the renewal in Britain
during the 1970s). It was Tom Smail who first introduced, to many
of the denominational leaders present, the House Church Movement
as a distinctive brand of neo-Pentecostalism.

Since that time the Fountain Trust has collapsed, and the denominational version of Charismatic Renewal has entered decline. The House
Church Movement, on the other hand, has become Britain's fastest rising
religious phenomenon (as evidenced by BBC Radio 4's documentary
on March 23rd 1984). In 1979, even though Tom Smail made it quite
clear that the new movement was sectarian in nature, a number of church
leaders at the BCC consultation still tended to identify House Churches
with the Charismatic Renewal *per se*.

The belief that the House Church Movement seems to have risen to
sudden prominence by clinging to the coat-tails of the Renewal
Movement, is an illusion. In reality, the so-called House Churches have

their roots outside mainstream Christianity; they are firmly planted in Protestant sectarianism. Although it is true that members of the new movement include disaffected renewal supporters, both the leadership and the theology are essentially sectarian. (This is not to belittle it in any way, or an attempt to downgrade it significance: it is merely an attempt to place it in its historical context.)

Almost nothing has been written about the new movement so far. The pioneer work is the MA dissertation of Joyce Thurman, which is now published under the title *New Wineskins*.[2]

By drawing on her work augmented by my own research (over the past two years), we can safely draw the following conclusions concerning the nature and form of the House Churches. First, it must emphatically be said that the phrase House Church Movement is a hopeless misnomer. Whilst it is true that both the idea and reality of the church in the house plays an important part in the new movement, what has really emerged are not house churches, but simply churches. Secondly, the notion of the House Church Movement masks the fact that there are in fact different movements. Of these, the South Chard group and Pastor North's churches are perhaps the most important historically, but if they are not yet a spent force, they have certainly been overshadowed by two other groups. The first of these are the 'Restoration' churches which are a group of churches linked together not only by common ideology, but by personal commitment under a rubric of 'apostolic' teams. These churches do have house groups, which are essential to the movement, but these are part of the overall structure. To demonstrate that it is churches which are the centre of life one need only note that in Bradford under the apostolic team of Bryn Jones a congregation of 600 regularly meet, whilst in Hove under the apostleship of Terry Virgo 500 regularly meet. There are many other churches where attendance is much larger than the average Baptist and classical Pentecostal gatherings.

'Restoration' is not the official title of these churches (leaders still, on the whole, eschew the notion of denomination or sect) but Restoration is the most commonly used word, and it is the name of their magazine. Terry Virgo dislikes labels, but feels that if there has to be one, 'Restoration' is the best.

The second large group is a more disparate, less structured collection of churches (or fellowships) which are offshoots or splinter groups from

Restoration. Their theology is basically the same as Restoration, but they tend to be less conservative than the parent body. Although they are organisationally separate, there tends to be a mutual recognition of ministry. As there is virtually no difference concerning the fundamentals of the faith between these two groups, I usually refer to both movements as Restoration 1, and Restoration 2 respectively (or R1 and R2 for short). In addition to these major groupings, there are numerous independent fellowships, such as the large community at Basingstoke, and the Ewell fellowship (featured on BBC Everyman's 'Unearthly Powers' in 1982). As the Restoration churches (particularly R1) are the largest and fastest growing of the 'House Churches' (and Restoration leaders would not be unahppy if I suggested that we now bury that name once and for all), the rest of this paper will concentrate on some central theological beliefs of Restorationism showing, where possible, their sectarian origins.

The Theology of Restorationism

The true significance of the Charismatic Renewal is that it made inroads into Catholic and sacramental Christianity as well as traditional evangelicalism; members included theological liberals as well as conservatives. Restoration, on the other hand, is clearly a Protestant evangelical expression of Pentecostalism. In many ways its central theological tenets are those of the classical Pentecostal sects: a belief in the 'born again' experience as the initiation into the church (an invisible body of Christ), a belief in believers' baptism, and a commitment to the 'baptism of the Holy Spirit' as the means whereby God initiates believers into Pentecostal power. This power, as most Pentecostalist sects believe, opens up the possibility of the supernatural charismata as demonstrated in the Acts of the Apostles, and outlined by St Paul in 1 Corinthians 12. As with other Pentecostalist and evangelical groups they understand sacramental worship as mere signs and symbols of the faith. They are strongly adventist, and like so many Pentecostalists they believe that they are living in 'the end time days'. Although their leaders do not like the term 'fundamentalist' (because of its negative overtones) many of their attitudes are fundamentalist; such as, for example, a commitment to creationism and a repudiation of the evolutionary theory. (I do not think this is a dogmatic ruling; it is a tendency I have observed.) Given the similarity with classical Pentecostalism it may seem surprising to some that they are forming yet another strata of Pentecostalist life. Professor Walter Hollenweger has sensibly pointed out that theological similarity does not, in itself, promote unity.[3]

Restorationists place a great deal of emphasis on healing, and the reality and dangers of demonic powers. In this, as with their lively liturgical style, they are very little different from the older classical Pentecostalists. They do have, however, a number of doctrines which are not typical of say Elim and Assemblies of God in Britain, or the Church of God and Assemblies of God in America. These more unusual doctrines were sometimes in evidence in the earlier stages of some classical Pentecostal sects. Other doctrines, as we shall note, belonged to other sectarian theologies. It is misleading to suggest that Restoration leaders think that they are original (though I believe that many of them do not see their sectarian ancestry); they would rather say that they are involved in a new movement of the Holy Spirit.

Restoration stands for a radical anti-denominationalism. Leaders proclaim that denominations are not in the plan of God. In the New Testament, they point out with some accuracy that there is simply 'the church'. They see the church universal as the congregation of 'born-again' believers, and the local church as a fellowship that 'breaks bread' and follows the apostles' teaching. How close this is to the vision of John Nelson Darby (1800-82). This Northern Ireland clergyman who became the leader of the Exclusive Brethren sect, originally envisaged a world-wide church where brethren would meet without clericalism, denominational structures and ritualistic liturgies choking the simplicity (as he saw it) of New Testament apostolic doctrine. (Curiously, and only time will tell how significantly, I have heard a number of people from Restoration 2 jokingly refer to R1 and R2 as the 'Exclusive' and 'Open' Brethren.)

The question of what God intends the church to be, and how it should be ordered is the fundamental ecclesiological issue which makes Restoration so distinctive. For them the matter is clearly set out in the Epistle to the Ephesians, chapter 4, verses 8 to 12. Verses 11 and 12 (NEB) are the key: 'And these were his gifts: some to be apostles, some prophets, some evangelists, some pastors and teachers, to equip God's

people for work in his service, to the building up of the body of Christ.'
What emerges from this is a clearly delineated hierarchical structure.
At the top are the apostles. These men are not elected, but are believed
to be divinely appointed. Apostleship is something that has to be
demonstrated to members of Restoration, so that leadership conforms
to the pattern of Max Weber's charismatic leadership as well as a strictly
theological view. Restoration teaching on this matter contrasts the
democratic election of Saul to kingship (seen as against God's will) with
the divine appointment of king David. This is then used, typologically,
to explain the system of apostleship as outlined in the Ephesians' epistle.

Chronologically, prophecy preceded apostleship. After apostleship
became established the apostles then initiated and established prophets,
pastors and other leaders. In practice, an eldership system has emerged
whereby an apostle heads a team of men (who may or may not be pastors;
they are often house group leaders). Recently, Restoration has started
a greater evangelical 'outreach' under the apostleship, but it is hoped
that evangelists *per se* will emerge. Certainly there are prophets: Arthur
Wallis as the elder statesman of Restorationism is not an apostle, but
his prophetic role is widely acknowledged.

Allied to this ecclesiology (which is also an organisational principal)
is what has become known as discipleship, 'relatedness', or more brutally
— from outsiders — submission. Although many people within Restorationism tend to play it down, this doctrine is quite different from the
usual practice of discipleship as understood in most Pentecostal churches.
There, discipleship is usually seen as a personal response to God's
prompting — no doubt under the watchful eye of the pastor but with
little organisational control over believers. Most classical Pentecostals
simply do not have a mechanism within the local congregation — or
the larger church — to operate such a system of control.

In the Restoration Movement, however, discipleship is a serious affair
that covers every area of believers' lives: children submit to parents,
wives to husbands, all to elders, who submit to apostles, who in turn
(in collegiate fashion) submit to each other. Subjects for direction do
not only include what are usually understood as spiritual matters; they
include the financial, social and sexual matters of life. The whole system
is seen as one of personal relationships: things are worked out and talked
out together. Apostles and elders do not give orders, and it is clear that

elders take their responsibilities very seriously and conscientiously.

Strictly speaking the discipleship issue (or 'relatedness' as some still call it) is not derived from a theological position at all. Although the scriptural canon is replete with stories and homilies on what could be called 'discipleship', there is no evidence that the early church operated a system such as that in operation in the Restoration churches. Such a system is open to abuse, especially in lay communities where the strictness of, say, a monastic rule cannot apply. Such strictness has had its historical counterpart in Protestant history. One thinks of the Puritan Covenants of the seventeenth century, and perhaps more so of the Shakers during the eighteenth century expansion of the American frontier. As Joyce Thurman points out in her book, the churches we have been examining offer alternative societies: God's kingdom is not of this world. In that sense, discipleship is understood by this charismatic movement as an eschatological imperative; a restored kingdom needs restored believers — soldiers of the church militant.

Whilst discipleship, and ecclesiology may seem marginal theological concerns, it is precisely these concerns that mark Restoration off from its classical Pentecostal counterparts. If on the level of churchmanship and attitudes to women we can detect echoes of the Brethren Movement (and a number of apostles and elders are ex-Brethren members), the ecclesiology is a modern version of older Pentecostalism.

The precursor of modern Pentecostalism is the Catholic Apostolic Church. This nineteenth century charismatic movement, like the Restoration churches, included many professional and middle-class adherents. Nicknamed the Irvingites (after Edward Irving) they organised their churches according to a novel interpretation of Ephesians 4. The hierarchy included not only apostles and prophets, but also angels! Irving, however, was not only a charismatic; he was a traditionalist. In this he was in marked contrast to the holiness sects that were to be the crucible of twentieth century classical Pentecostalism. The modern successors of Irving are not, therefore, Restoration despite the similarities of interpretation of the Ephesians' epistle. (The Irvingites' successors are the so-called Orthodox Church of Great Britain; their chosen see is Glastonbury.)[4]

The direct roots of Restoration's ecclesiology are to be found in the Apostolic Church founded towards the end of the great revivals

of Glamorgan in South Wales before the Great War. Bryn Jones, the
most well known of Restoration's apostles (and an outstandingly gifted
preacher) was born in Aberdare; this is the heart of revival country.
For a time, in Wales, Bryn Jones was a member of the Assemblies of
God church. Almost certainly he would have come across the Apostolic
Church. Not to be confused with the British Israelite United Apostolic
Church of Faith, this sect is dominated by Wales. It lacked Bryn Jones'
world-wide vision of the restored church, but it nevertheless set up
churches organised according to the principles that Restoration leaders
find in Ephesians 4. The Apostolic Church may have been founded before
the Great War, but it never really emerged as a powerful denomination
nor was it able to rival Elim and the Assemblies of God.[5]

Having attended a number of Welsh Apostolic meetings in the 1960s
and Restoration services in the 1980s, I would say that of the two the
Apostolic churches are the most insular: their hearts are still in the singing
revivals of mining Wales, and their tongues and voices are more Welsh
hwyl than glossolalia. However, the Apostolic Church is the natural
precursor of Restoration's ecclesiology though without the discipleship
structure interwoven with its apostleship network.

Conclusion: Will Restoration Restore The Kingdom?

The fact that many of the theological tenets of Restorationism are the
same as mainstream evangelicalism should not blind us to the fact that
this is true of all forms of classical Pentecostalism. I have attempted to
show briefly that those aspects of Restoration teaching which mark them
off from other charismatic groups have their roots in Protestant sectarianism. There is one other distinctive feature of Restoration theology
(though, I believe, 'religious teachings' is a more accurate term than
the over-extended use of the term 'theology') which is noteworthy,
and that is 'kingdom theology'. In his highly entertaining book, *What
on Earth is this Kingdom?*,[6] Gerald Coates points out that Jesus Christ
did not come to set up a church, but to establish a kingdom. We have
already noted the anti-denominationalism of this new movement, and
the idea of establishing the kingdom, or restoring the purity of the early
Church, is a dominant theme.

The Lord Jesus is the king who has divinely appointed his apostles to establish the kingdom in enemy territory: the territory is the world, and its prince is Satan. As the Jewish zealots have taken Zionist communities into the Arab-held West Bank, so Restorationists are reclaiming territory for God in the form of fellowships, churches and communities. Restoration does not wish to become merely another denomination: it wants to establish the kingdom. Although this is clearly reminiscent of Millennial sects, such as the seventeenth century Levellers, there is nothing political implied here. The kingdom of God is within, and yet also where his people reside. Restoration begins with restoring relationships with God, then with other 'born again' subjects of the king. When the kingdom is ready — when the church is charismatically restored — The Lord Jesus will return to earth in power and glory.

David Tomlinson, an apostle now in Restoration 2, has a strong commitment to a social gospel as well as the evangelical good news. He is afraid that Restoration will delude itself into thinking that it is claiming territory for the king, when it is in reality standing on the sidelines as a Godless world slips inexorably into hell. It is difficult to believe that you are on the sidelines when, as Restoration 1 shows, they can organise 10,000 people at the Dales Bible Week, and experience excitement and revivalistic fervour wherever they go. But as Os Guinness has pointed out in *The Gravedigger File*,[7] such groups fail to realise that the forces of secularisation have removed them to the periphery of our modern culture: pietistic and revivalist Christianity has become a consumer option in a pluralistic society. To restore the kingdom is to reclaim that part of culture that has gone over to the adversary: the political, industrial and scientific infrastructure of modern societies that even mainstream Christianity has retreated from without hope of recapture.

Notes

1 The Fountain Trust was an independent organisation that promoted Renewal within the mainstream denominations; it was charismatic rather than revivalistic.

2 Joyce Thurman, New Wineskins (Verlag Peter Lang, 1982).

3 W. J. Hollenweger, 'The House Church Movement in Great Britain', *The Expository Times*, Nov. 1980.

4 This is a sociological observation. Theologically, I think the Irvingites far superior.
5 Nevertheless, they have had great success in Africa and more recently South America.
6 G. Coates, *What on Earth is this Kingdom* (Kingsway, Eastbourne, 1983).
7 O. Guinness, *The Gravedigger File* (Hodder & Stoughton, London, 1983).

The Charismatic Movement in African Israel Church Nineveh (Kenya)

HENRY ASIGE AJEGA

The African Israel Church Nineveh was formed on the principles of the Charismatic Movement.[1] When the Word of God was brought across the ocean from Europe the idea of the working of the Holy Spirit remained a mystery to the church. In 1921 the Spirit of the Lord was revealed at Kaimosi in Western Kenya. This was a new and different experience for the church in Kenya and many people wondered what had happened. Some said that this new experience was madness and others said that it was a group of poor confused people. The saved group, as they were referred to, found themselves rejected by the Church. They could not mix freely with other members of the congregation. This led to the formation of the so-called Kenya Independent Churches and they are considered as representing the Charismatic Renewal.

In 1932 the founder of African Israel Church Nineveh, the late M. P. D. Kwuti, who also used to despise the work of the Holy Spirit, received this power. This is the description of his conversion, in his own words, as quoted by F. B. Welbourn:

> On 12th February I received the Spirit. As I was singing in my house something lifted me and threw me to the ground. Everything became dark and I was temporarily blind. That night I began to speak in tongues like the apostles of the New Testament. The whole house was filled with light. For the next seventeen days I was blind and I heard a voice as of thunder. For twelve days I could eat nothing, and during this period God commanded me not to shave my beard, and to take the name of Paul. Then I stayed in my house, praying, night and day.

When I recovered I had lost interest in my professional job (teaching). I wanted to preach the Word of God. So I began going from village to village, singing and converting people. The power of God filled me. I began praying for the sick and they were healed. I also prayed for barren women and they got children. People began to come to my house, so that I might pray for them. Usually they would come on Thursday evening and I prayed with them till morning when we held a big meeting. The Kellers (white missionaries) supported me, but many members of the Pentecostal church disliked me because I urged them to confess their sins. They wouldn't let me preach in their churches.

From this example we can see that once you have received the power of the Holy Spirit you are completely changed and you become a new person. Your old friends wonder and keep away from you and think you are confused and emotional, if not mad. It becomes extremely difficult to understand the new changes in yourself.

You cannot receive the power of the Holy Spirit if you do not repent sincerely. You have first to accept that Jesus Christ is the Son of God and that he came to the world to redeem us from our sins. You have to see and feel spiritually the suffering of Jesus Christ on the cross. You have to be truly grateful for his precious blood which was shed on the cross for our sins.

Charismatic renewal is not something which can be imposed. It is the will and work of God. It is a complete change. Paul said in his letters, 'you have to put off the old man in order to become a Christian.' We believe and have experienced that the Holy Spirit works in you as long as you keep to the commands of the Lord. People see a new change in you as the gifts of the Spirit are manifested.

The members of this church have come to believe and discover that once you have the Holy Spirit the Lord can use you in many ways. The church has expanded all over the country through these supernatural powers of the Holy Spirit. These are some of our experiences of the work of the Holy Spirit:

The healing of the sick.

Through prayer water came out of a dry stone at Givavei hill during a drought and people were able to drink.

Rain has fallen as a result of prayer and meditation.

Members of the church can move and dance spiritually without getting tired.

Many prophecies have come true.

Many tribes have been united, regardless of tribe, race, language, colour or strength.

The love of God has been manifested amongst the members.

People have learnt how to share what they have and help the needy or those in trouble.

We have got a deeper knowledge and understanding of God and his purpose to mankind through Jesus Christ.

We have managed to minister to other churches which did not know or understand the work of the Holy Spirit and we have been able to spread the Charismatic Renewal to them.

I am very pleased that the Lord has made it possible for us to talk and discuss the Charismatic Renewal and united us in the Spirit at such an international meeting. I am very happy because the prophecy has come true and all mankind is now seeking to be renewed in the Spirit. It makes me very proud here to see the work of the Lord being accomplished. It is my prayer and hope that we all get renewed and united in the Spirit at this consultation, so as to manifest the work of the Holy Spirit and the reality of God. We are nevertheless bound to witness to others our new discovery of the Holy Spirit after this consultation. May God bless you and give you a deeper understanding of the Charismatic movement as much more than just a theological or sociological issue.

Notes

1 This paper was presented to the Sub-unit on Renewal and Congregational Life, at the Consultation of the Charismatic Renewal for the churches, during the Conference of the World Council of Churches in Switzerland in March 1980.

Speaking in Tongues:
a Philosophical Comment

BRIAN DAVIES OP

Catholics with some biblical knowledge will clearly be familiar with the expression 'speaking in tongues'.[1] Those who have encountered what is known as 'Catholic Pentecostalism' or the 'Charismatic Renewal' will be even more familiar with it. For within this, though not always considered essential, it certainly is regarded by many as a topic of considerable importance.[2] Up to the present, however, there has been little of a philosophical nature said on the subject and the purpose of what follows is to go some way towards remedying the deficiency. My comments will be necessarily curtailed for the sake of space, but, hopefully, something of interest will emerge.

What is Speaking in Tongues?

Advocates of speaking in tongues undoubtedly have a biblical basis for introducing the topic. According to Acts, on the day of Pentecost the apostles were 'filled with the Holy Spirit and began to speak in other tongues' (Acts 2:3 RSV; cf. Acts 19:6-7; 10-66). In 1 Corinthians 14, although he has some harsh things to say on the subject, St Paul declares: 'I thank God that I speak in tongues more than you all', and he makes it clear that speaking in tongues is a gift from God. The New Testament witness is not, however, a great deal of help in deciding what exactly speaking in tongues amounts to. It is not even clear whether the biblical authors regard the phenomenon as speaking in unknown but genuine languages.[3] St Paul's contribution is meagre enough and could hardly be called a fully worked-out analysis. He alludes to speaking in tongues only to make the negative point that this should not detract from Christian edification. Only when stating what he considers to be edifying does be begin to expand.

Modern writers are less reserved. To the question, 'What does it mean to speak in tongues?' there is a fairly orthodox reply. According to this speaking in tongues is first and foremost a gift of the Holy Spirit. More precisely, it is uttering sounds that do not manifestly correspond to items of natural languages. At the same time, it is to speak or to use language and, indeed, to pray. This is made clear by Kilian McDonnell,[4] and Simon Tugwell explains that speaking in tongues 'appears to mean the production of genuinely linguistic phenomena, which may or may not be identified by someone present as some definite language, but which does not convey any ordinary semantic significance to the speaker himself'.[5] In *Did You Receive the Spirit?* Tugwell explains that 'It is that one speaks words which do not mean anything in any language known to himself.' This says Tugwell, is 'God's action' in us, 'the working of the Holy Spirit', a 'manifestation' of the Holy Spirit. According to Tugwell, 'someone speaking in tongues may turn out to be talking in some known language; even where this is not the case there is generally some linguistic pattern.' 'You do the speaking, the Lord chooses the words.' 'In speaking with other tongues we surrender one little limb to God's control.' 'It is a prayer of praise, a prayer of peace.'[6] According to a standard work on Catholic Pentecostalism, speaking in tongues is 'praying . . . it is the child's delight, the glee that greets the fireworks display on the Fourth of July, not the display itself.'[7]

Pentecostals may be expected to differ among themselves but we can conclude then that, according to many of its supporters, speaking in tongues may be considered first as using a language, and secondly as God using language through us in order to assist our prayers. Since we find it said that one who speaks in tongues may also be interpreted we can perhaps add as a third point, that speaking in tongues can be an aid to a Christian group. This seems to follow, for if speaking in tongues comes from God and is God using language, then interpreting what God says is, presumably, making clear the word of God. So the chief questions that arise with regard to speaking in tongues are 'Can we indeed regard speaking in tongues as a use of language?' and 'Can speaking in tongues be viewed as a use of language where the user is regarded as God?' Neither question can be answered until we have some idea of the necessary conditions of an utterance being the use of language.

When is an Utterance a Use of Language?

The nature of language forms an important debating point in contemporary philosophy. Much that has been said on the subject is complex and a really adequate commentary on the issues at stake is not possible here. Normally, however, it would be agreed that if L is a genuine language at least the following conditions must be satisfied:

(1) L must consist of utterances involving regularity of sound;
(2) L must be capable of analysis in terms of grammar and syntax;
(3) L must have rules for the correct application of its elements.

To these specifications some would add:

(4) The utterances of L must employ terms the meaning of which is understood by more than one person;
(5) L must be rich, i.e., capable of sustaining communication over a wide range of human activities and interests.

Are there any reasons for accepting (1)-(5) as stating necessary conditions for L being a language? We can, I think, take it for granted that if L is a language then condition (1) is satisfied. Language is a means of communication. As any natural scientist will agree, not all communication involves sound but, even where there is no acoustic signal, regularity of some sort is required for communication. If A is a communicative factor, e.g., a gesture or facial expression, it must be somehow constant on different occasions if it is to remain A. And if A is a sound the same applies. In the case of language, however, must this regularity extend to matters of grammar and syntax? Here there is room for disagreement. We sometimes refer to the language of music and we frequently interpret a piece of music as if it were an effort in communication. It is natural to say that a given musical example expresses, say, hope and confidence and that 'There are grounds for hope and confidence' is the message of the example. Wittgenstein says 'Understanding a sentence is much more akin to understanding a theme in music than one may think . . . understanding a sentence lies nearer than one thinks to what is ordinarily called understanding a musical theme.'[8] If we can say this then we appear to allow for a piece of music the substitution of a sentence which is clearly intended as an assertion. From this it is no long step to regarding the music as a novel form of language or a substitute of one form of language for another.

On the other hand, can one say that a piece of music really can constitute a message unless there are some conventions correlating, even in the broadest sense, the composition of notes and a proposition? There must, in fact, be a 'key' for the interpretation of music in terms of assertion if the music is to be understood in this way at all. Furthermore, the key here relates music to a linguistic unit (whether written or spoken it does not matter). Independently of this key the music does not *mean* at all and neither is it language. But this implies that mere regularity of sound does not make for language. Whether or not such regularity can be understood as a language, as may be the case with music, depends on the contingent fact of its relation to language itself, and where X is only L contingently, depending on its possible association with L, it is not L itself. Music itself is not therefore an example of language. Rather, it may be considered to stand proxy for a use of language where the use is itself capable of identification independently of the music itself. Language itself presupposes grammar and syntax.

Proceeding to the idea that rules are important in language we can begin by noting that some people would deny that any language must have rules for the correct application of its elements. A unit of language, it is sometimes said, need not be rule-bound, which implies that words need not be regarded as conforming to any kind of convention. This seems to be Kierkegaard's position in works like *Concluding Unscientific Postscript*. According to Kierkegaard, it is possible to speak in the language of theology while admitting that the way one uses words conforms to no criteria for intelligibility posed from outside. He maintains that within theological discourse a word may take on a life of its own so that knowledge of its function in secular discourse is of no concern to anybody wishing to use it theologically. Accordingly, Kierkegaard can offer us the following perplexing occurrence of the word 'truth': 'An objective uncertainty held fast in an appropriation-process of the most passionate kind is the truth.'

In response to such a viewpoint, however, there is an important point to be made. In conversation with Humpty Dumpty, Alice says: 'The question is . . . whether you *can* make words mean so many different things'; our answer to this should be: 'You cannot unless there is some connection between two terms used in different contexts'. Language is a highly conventional phneomenon and a word whose use bears no relationship to some of its other uses is free from rules and independent of conventions but it is also unintelligible. The rules, we may say, need not be stipulatable or hard and fast, for we frequently find ourselves unable to provide a list of rules for the use of terms. This is hardly surprising since we are constantly applying old words in new situations. But to some extent, as the work of Wittgenstein has surely made clear, rules must be present. 'To understand a sentence means to understand a language. To understand a language means to be master of a technique' — which means that language is itself a technique. As one commentator on Kierkegaard justly declares: 'You do not make a false or doubtful proposition true by calling it true any more than you make socks into shoes by calling them shoes.'[9] And if what is implied by this is true, something of consequence follows regarding the fourth criterion of language noted above. For if we can challenge an individual's use of a word it must also be true that to be part of language an utterance must conform to public rules with reference to which the whole idea of understanding and meaning must arise in the first place. (4) is therefore true; if L is a language L must employ terms the meaning of which is understood by more than one person. Thus we are left with the problem posed by (5).

An interesting passage relevant to this occurs in the early part of Wittgenstein's *Philosophical Investigations*:

> A is building with building stones: there are blocks, pillars, slabs, and beams. B has to pass the stones, and that in the order in which A needs them. For this purpose they use a language consisting of the words 'block', 'pillar', 'slab', 'beam'. A calls them out; — B brings the stone which he has learned to bring at such-and-such a call. — Conceive this as a complete primitive language.[10]

Commenting on this Rush Rhees observes:

> But I feel there is something wrong here. The trouble is not to imagine a people with a language of such limited vocabulary. The trouble is to imagine that they spoke the language only to give these special orders on this job and otherwise never spoke at all. I do not think it would be speaking a language.

According to Rhees, what the builders are doing is more like playing a game with stones than using a language.[11] The implications should be clear. When presented with utterances like that of the builders in Wittgenstein's example we should hesitate to call them language. They need to be part of an institution involving such activities as questioning, asserting, commanding, commending and so forth. I am not, however, convinced that we should agree with Rhees's dismissal of Wittgenstein's classification of the language of the builders. His argument admits that it is *like* a language and I think we can add that it would perhaps be wrong or unjustified to say that it is definitely not a language. In *Zettel*, Wittgenstein also observes that in cases like that of the builders 'the life of those men must be like ours in many respects . . . the important thing is that their language, and their thinking too, may be rudimentary, that there is such a thing as "primitive thinking", which is to be described via primitive *behaviour*.'[12] So considering language like that of the builders we can remember that 'there is no clear break between these primitive games and more complicated ones: the more complicated ones can be built up from the primitive ones by the gradual addition of new forms.'[13] (5) is therefore not obviously a necessary condition of L being a language though (1)-(4) are. Now that we have some means of testing whether or not an utterance can be regarded as a use of language we can return to the idea of speaking in tongues and the claims made on its behalf.

Is Speaking in Tongues a Use of Language?

It seems that at least one of our conditions for an utterance being a use of language is satisfied when the utterance is speaking in tongues. For, as we have seen, it is claimed that there is regularity of sound present when someone speaks in tongues. If such regularity cannot be established then speaking in tongues cannot be regarded as using a language. But if it can then at least there is something common to speaking in tongues and using a language. Yet what about conditions (2)-(4)? Are there any rules for the correct application of the elements that comprise the utterances of speaking in tongues? Here there seems to be a more formidable block in the way of easily identifying speaking in tongues and using language. For where are the rules, syntax and public criteria? On the face of it there seem to be none and there are no charismatic grammar books that tell us otherwise. One cannot learn to speak in tongues as one can learn to speak German. Nor would this seem to matter, for if one spoke in tongues one could not make mistakes of misapplying words.

Advocates of speaking in tongues might at this point, however, urge the following considerations as relevant in response to these objections. First, they might observe that speaking in tongues, while not constituting speaking a known language from the point of view of the speakers, is nevertheless the utterance of a known language. Secondly it might be said that when a person speaks in tongues there is always the possibility that what he says may be interpreted by someone in such a way that there may be rendered a restatement in language known and understood by many of those present on the occasion of the speaking. As St Paul says: 'Therefore, he who speaks in a tongue should pray for the power to interpret' (1 Cor. 14:13). Let us consider each of these replies.

If it is true that speaking in tongues may, on a given occasion of its occurrence, be unambiguously identified with the utterance of a natural language then there is absolutely no reason why one cannot claim the instance as an example of a use of language. This is obviously true for it is tautologous that if X is a language X is a language. The question of interpretation is, however, more problematic.

Instinctively one is inclined to say that if a person can produce an interpretation of an utterance in intelligible form then what has been produced is a translation. I may not know what 'Le roi est mort' means but someone who understands French can listen to the sounds involved in the utterance of 'Le roi est mort' and say that it means 'The king is dead.' Here I would admit that 'Le roi est mort' is the use of a language which I do not understand. But the parallel between this situation and that which holds when an interpretation of tongues is offered does not seem to be exact. In the case of translating a language we do not simply accept a proffered translation as a genuine translation. It does not, so to speak, wear its credentials upon its chest. If A claims to translate L by offering Z it does not follow from A's claim that Z is a translation of L that Z really is such. Whether or not it is must be verified. Furthermore, the verification here is public. There must be agreed rules for translating. It must be agreed, for instance, that 'roi' means 'king' and not 'queen'. No matter what I say I cannot make 'queen' a translation of 'roi'. If you are to agree that my rendering of 'roi' is a translation you must therefore have access to agreed rules of translation. But where are the rules in the case of speaking in tongues? As far as I can see there appear to be none — at least where it is admitted that an utterance of speaking in tongues is not the utterance of a known language. Where an interpretation is offered one invariably has only the assertion of the interpreter that what he produces actually is a translation. But it has to be established that the interpretation is a translation. The principles of the language of which the instance of speaking in tongues is a usage must be displayed and the rules of translation established. Then the translation or interpretation offered must be checked against the rules and a verdict obtained. Otherwise there are no grounds at all for speaking of translation.

It seems then that we must say that on the question of intepretation the parallel between speaking in tongues and using a language can break down. Where the instance of speaking in tongues can be shown to be the use of a natural language this does not hold. But where one has only the translation of an interpreter to go on one is within one's rights in disallowing any claim that what one has here is the translation of a language utterance. But if this is so our fourth condition also remains unsatisfied in at least those instances where the translation offered of a particular occurrence of speaking in tongues is not identifiable as the use of a natural language. For where the principles of the language that is translated cannot be mapped and correlated with the principles of translation, the public rules governing the intelligible use of a term in the supposed language cannot be displayed either. So where T is an instance of speaking in tongues, T may only count as a language where it is identifiable as the use of a natural language. It follows from this that we may regard P (the person who utters T) as using a language only if T can be identified as natural language. But what about regarding T as spoken ultimately by God?

If T cannot be regarded as natural language then it cannot be regarded as language issuing from God. This follows from my previous argument. But if T can be identified as natural language this would not follow, nor does it seem clear to me that T in such an instance cannot be regarded as language ascribable to God. The case against such a conclusion would need to show *a priori* that the idea of ascribing language to God was absurd. And this would take a lot of argument. God cannot be thought to utter sound as a person does and T cannot be *uttered* by God. But it is possible for A to speak on behalf of B (for B may be inarticulate) and this could be held to provide helpful analogy to advocates of speaking in tongues. In *The Concept of Prayer*, D. Z. Phillips makes the point that any language user must have a background in a normal linguistic community. [14] But given that God exists and given that, as Christians believe, God is personal (issues which are clearly outside the range of the present discussion) it seems not impossible that an utterance may be viewed as a divine communication. Consider the following hypothetical situation which I borrow with modification from Terence Penelhum's book *Problems of Religious Knowledge*. [15] Two people disagree over the truth of the proposition 'God can work miracles.' Suppose that 'miracle' is defined in the Humean sense as a violation of a law of nature brought about by a god. The parties agree to test their respective positions by calling on God for a sign. They stipulate that if 'God can work miracles' is true the stars over London should spell out the words 'PRAISE THE LORD' every Sunday for three weeks. The stars behave in this way and this is verified by all reputable astronomers. If this were to happen I submit that 'God can work miracles' could be claimed by its proponent to be rationally established. He could claim that the proposition was endorsed by God. But if it is endorsed by God it may also be ascribed to God and since what is now ascribed to God is a use of language (i.e. the uttered proposition 'God can work miracles') one can just about see how it might be said that God somehow 'stands behind' a linguistic utterance, which is what is claimed in the case of speaking in tongues. [16] But whether or not such support can be given for particular instances of speaking in tongues is another matter and something for its defenders to tell us.

Notes

1 First published in *New Blackfriars*, vol. 57, March 1976.

2 cf. Peter Hocken, 'Pentecostals on Paper II', *The Clergy Review*, March 1975, p. 173.

3 cf. Henry Wansbrough, 'Speaking in Tongues', *The Way*, July 1974.

4 Kilian McDonnell, *Catholic Pentecostalism* (Ave Maria Press, Notre Dame, 1971).

5 *The Expository Times*, February 1973, p.137.

6. Simon Tugwell, *Did You Receive the Spirit?* (Darton, Longman and Todd, London 1972), pp. 67, 68, 69, 70, 72.

7 Kevin and Dorothy Ranaghan, *Catholic Pentecostals* (Paulist Press, New York, 1969), p. 192.

8 *Philosophical Investigations* (Blackwell, Oxford, 1968), para. 527.

9 Paul Edwards, 'Kierkegaard and the "Truth" of Christianity', *Philosophy*, April 1971, p. 102.

10 *Philosophical Investigations*, para. 2.

11 'Wittgenstein's Builders', *Proceedings of the Aristotelian Society*, vol. 60 (1959-60).

12 *Zettel*, para. 99.

13 A. Kenny, *Wittgenstein* (Penguin, Harmondsworth, 1975), p. 170.

14 D. Z. Phillips, *The Concept of Prayer* (Routledge & Kegan Paul, London, 1965).

15 T. Penelhum, *Problems of Religious Knowledge*; cf. Richard Swinburne, *The Concept of Miracle* (Macmillan, London, 1970), chapter 5.

16 Phillips would reject this argument on the grounds that it involves a misunderstanding of belief in God. The question is too large to discuss here but for a useful critique of Phillips along lines that I should largely follow see John Hick, 'Religion as Fact-asserting', in *God and the Universe of Faiths* (Macmillan, London, 1973). I have criticised details of Hick's remarks on related problems in my 'God and Language', *The Downside Review*, January 1975.

Epilogue:
Saved by a Miracle?

JOHN DRURY

Miracles are back.[1] At two clerical gatherings which I have attended recently clergymen have got up to bear witness to them: speaking with tongues, healings, sudden and drastic changes of personality (allegedly for the better) and exorcisms. On both occasions they spoke with a note of defiance, even exasperation, against the fairly rational and critical discussions which had preceded their utterances. But there was a note of hope, even triumph, too: the critical tradition of the last two hundred years has now come to the point where it so blatantly fails to produce the religious goods, where it so apparently undermines religion instead of supporting it, that it ought to be abandoned in favour of an enthusiastic surrender to older and gutsier truths.

I should not, really, have said that miracles are back. For this strong reactionary movement is made possible by miracles never having been out. In religion old positions are not abandoned as they are in, say, physics. Wherever the main army may be, you will probably find someone faithfully manning any backward position: like that Japanese soldier discovered sticking to his orders on a Pacific island thirty years after the war was over. But in religion there is a better chance that the war will come back into his theatre. After all, whatever the critics have said about the Bible with all its miracles, it is still read out in church, and they are not. Miracle has there a privileged and established position. So much was made clear by the myth fuss. A myth called a myth loses its miraculous character. A myth called history keeps it. So ecclesiastically those champions of miracle are not eccentric but have lines of communication with the centre. Their conservative friends who are embarrassed by their reactionary appeal can at least be glad that, with such people around, in such a setting, a muted and jovial fundamentalism about Bible or creeds looks positively mainstream and statesmanlike.

So there it is, and it is quite clear that rational criticism will make no impression on it after all. There are more things in heaven and earth, it says with some force, than form or redaction critics dream of. So the field of argument must be switched to the place where engagement is possible, the place where they are: the question of effective religious value. It can be put more sharply. Will this revival of miracle, in its fizzy or its still version, save us now? Will it result in a humanity clothed and restored to its right mind sitting at the feet of divinity? There could not be a more urgently practical religious question.

It only has to be posed for misgiving to arise strongly enough to demand a dental inspection of this gift horse. The inspection should not be negatively prejudiced. Modern man, sitting on his military stockpile, needs any help he can get, and just cannot afford to be aesthetically or intellectually dainty in his choice of helpers if he wants to survive. He needs religion, good and strong, and not just a clever debate about religion. That, at least, is in favour of hot gospelling. But why say that modern man needs religion? Because he needs to know goodness as something common and familiar and something extraordinary and rare. He needs both those things. Without the commonness he will neglect goodness in despair that it is beyond him, the top (but nastiest) ape who only dreams of the peaceable kingdom, cannot build it. Without the extraordinariness he will neglect goodness because he thinks it too common to need reverent cherishing. Religion is the alternative to muddling through and despair.

The trouble with the 'miracle' people is that they are, in these terms, seriously lopsided. Not only do they put all the emphasis on the rare and the extraordinary; they depend for their impact on doing so. In a definite sense they do not want goodness to be too common. Not yet anyway — and this is a situation which brooks no delay. It must travel at the speed of their juggernaut. They do not like explanations which connect wonders with the sociologically, psychologically, or medically common. When these are proffered, their faces cloud over. They like their goodness denominational. It is here, in their fervent exclusiveness, that they change from being supporters of imperfectible man's urgent search for a goodness which he can both worship and exercise, and become a drag on it — and even a threat to it.

Islam revived, Christianity in the miraculously triumphant style of the Acts of the Apostles revived: these can congratulate themselves on having become forces to be reckoned with. Other people can congratulate them on having demonstrated that man's need of religion is not dead. But those who want that need to be met by something which can save us from the death and everlasting damnation which is stored up and waiting, they will want something markedly different from this and something more. In particular they will want something more commonly available, however hard to practise; as well as being so wonderful as to command the allegiance of worship. It must be something that anyone can do — though it will take all his committed powers, summoned by fear and reverence for goodness, to do it. Anything less will not be good news, just sensational news with the promise of an appallingly nasty after-taste.

Notes

1 This piece first appeared in *Theology*, March 1981.

Index

234 *Index*

BR
1644
.S77
1984

Strange gifts? : a guide to charismatic renewal / edited by David Martin
and Peter Mullen. -- Oxford, UK ;
New York, NY, USA : B. Blackwell,
1984.
    xiv, 239 p. ; 23 cm.

    Includes bibliographies and index.
    ISBN 0-631-13357-7

    1. Pentecostalism--Addresses,
essays, lectures. I. Martin, David,
1929-   II. Mullen, Peter.

BR1644.S77 1984   270.8'28
                                84-8861
                           AACR2 MARC

Library of Congress
09515 *05 04249 794334   © THE BAKER & TAYLOR CO. 5313